SOUTH CAROLINA AND THE AMERICAN REVOLUTION

SOUTH CAROLINA AND THE AMERICAN REVOLUTION

A BATTLEFIELD HISTORY

JOHN W. GORDON

UNIVERSITY OF SOUTH CAROLINA PRESS

Published in Columbia, South Carolina, by the
University of South Carolina Press

Manufactured in the United States of America

07 06 05 04 03   5 4 3 2

Library of Congress Cataloging-in-Publication Data

Gordon, John W.
   South Carolina and the American Revolution : a battlefield history /
John W. Gordon.
      p. cm.
Includes bibliographical references and index.
   ISBN 1-57003-480-X (cloth : alk. paper)
   1. South Carolina—History—Revolution, 1775–1783—Campaigns.
   2. United States—History—Revolution, 1775–1783—Campaigns. I. Title.
   E230.5.S6 G67 2002
   973.3'3'09757—dc21   2002012311

For Claudia

CONTENTS

ILLUSTRATIONS

MAPS

FOREWORD

by John Keegan

I FIRST came to South Carolina in the summer of 1952 and at once fell under its spell. The spell remains, often as I have visited the state since. The beauty of Charleston is guaranteed to captivate the visitor, but there is also something about the landscape that holds the memory; the intermingling of land and water at the ocean's edge, the sense of remoteness in the sea islands, close as they are to shore, the denseness of vegetation along the estuaries and inlets, the intensity of cultivation in the rich lowcountry, the gently rising interior beyond the limit of the old plantations.

Geography is important to John Gordon. He understands how it shaped the military events of the War of the Revolution in the state, and he explains its importance to the reader of this fascinating study. He is well qualified to do so, both as a former professor of history at the Military College of South Carolina (the renowned Citadel) and as an officer of the United States Marine Corps—two institutions with which the military and social history of South Carolina intertwine.

South Carolina in the 1770s was far from the seat of the Revolution, and might have remained so but for the decision of the newly appointed British commander of operations against the colonies, General Sir Henry Clinton, to transfer his main force there. His object was to seize a region rich in supplies that were important to George Washington, to restore royal authority over a population he judged to be fundamentally loyalist, and to provoke a campaign he believed he could fight at an advantage over the enemy, after three years of frustration in the much more urbanized theater of the Middle Atlantic colonies.

The plan promised well in theory but was to fail in practice, for a variety of reasons. Clinton hoped to exploit divisions within the population, particularly between the "plantocracy" of the lowcountry, which

included some enthusiastic patriots, and the farmers of the back country, who were thought to prefer royal rule to that of coastal plutocrats.
Ill-advisedly, Clinton also sought help from the Cherokees, since Indian
allies had been so useful in helping to defeat the French in 1756–1763.
Cherokee participation guaranteed the disaffection of the backcountry
settlers and, all too soon, the British found they had on their hands a
guerrilla war in which their superiority in close-order tactics was negated
by the native skills of the locals, lacking training though they did.

What is astonishing about the war in South Carolina is how often the
two sides clashed in battle and, as a result, how many battles were fought
during the period 1779–1781. The territory of the state may contain as
many Revolutionary battlefields as Virginia does those of the Civil War.

The battles, of course, were tiny by comparison, though often very
hard-fought. The author knows the events, as well as the places, and
describes and analyzes them in penetrating detail. This is one of the
most exact accounts of fighting in a particular theater available for the
Revolutionary period. It is also an important contribution to the political and social history of the war. The author has written a fascinating
book that will be read with pleasure by the specialist and general reader
alike.

PREFACE

SOUTH CAROLINA—save for the period of the war 1776–1777, when British offensive efforts were thrusts into the middle colonies or down from Canada—proved a pivotal arena of the American Revolution. It was the crucial, issue-deciding battleground of the war in the South. The struggle there was a protracted one. Fighting in South Carolina commenced near the beginning and went on until the final days of the war in America, at a point when other sectors had long since grown quiet. It proved galling and wearisome to both sides—but far more so to the British one.

Because of what happened in South Carolina, the American cause prevailed; Great Britain's—and that country's American loyalists'—did not. The successful defense of the palmetto log-and-sand fort at the mouth of Charleston harbor in June 1776 thwarted British plans aimed at winning back South Carolina and perhaps much more of the South at an early stage of the war. So also did the smashing of a Cherokee offensive on the frontier and loyalist groups in the backcountry. Later, British efforts to raise and employ a substantial force of loyalists and to destroy a mixed force of American Continentals and militiamen were defeated at, respectively, King's Mountain and the Cowpens. These two were turning-point battles that unhinged British plans for overcoming the Americans and restoring South Carolina to Crown authority. Cowpens, indeed, stands as perhaps the most complete tactical victory of the war—and in truth the only time a force of Americans so effectively overcame a British force its approximate equal in size.

There were bitter defeats as well: Charleston, in May 1780, when the Americans lost that city and their only army in the South; and, three months later, Camden, when a second American army was routed and its fragments driven back to North Carolina. Finally, a vicious and brutal partisan war raged in the backcountry until almost the moment when British forces finally evacuated Charleston in December 1782.

This study examines those battles and South Carolina as an arena for them; South Carolina was the principal battleground of the Southern theater. An estimated one-third of all combat actions in the American Revolution took place in South Carolina. It was a contested zone, a place which forced the British to confront the difficult military problem of having to wage a conventional war against American regular forces, the Continentals, while at the same time having to wage a counterguerrilla war against hit-and-run American irregulars, the partisan bands of Marion, Pickens, and Sumter.

ACKNOWLEDGMENTS

I OWE A DEBT of gratitude to professors and mentors of years ago when this project was first discussed: John Richard Alden, I. B. Holley, and Theodore Ropp at Duke University, and James Logan Godfrey of the University of North Carolina at Chapel Hill. Later, Russell Weigley at Temple University and Henry Lumpkin of the University of South Carolina likewise offered helpful directions. So also, in the United Kingdom, did General Sir John Hackett, British Army, retired, Sir John Keegan, and Major General David Lanyon Lloyd Owen, British Army, retired. I am particularly indebted to Sir John Keegan for the remarks he so graciously prepared to introduce this book.

And then there were students of my own: cadets at The Citadel, cadets at West Point, students at Georgia State University, and American and international officers and representatives of government agencies attending the U.S. Marine Corps Command and Staff College, Quantico, Virginia. Their questions and comments in response to lectures shaped my own approach to the topic.

Colleagues at The Citadel have supported this project from the outset. In the Department of History, professors Larry H. Addington, Rod Andrew (now of Clemson University), Jane Bishop, Bo Moore, Jamie W. Moore, and David H. White have read portions of the manuscript or offered comments; Larry has been a mentor from the first efforts, and he will see his own scholarship reflected in this book. So also have colleagues in English: professors David Allen, James Hutchisson, James Rembert, and David Shields. Support as a Citadel Foundation Faculty Fellow enabled me to carry out the primary-source research in British archives upon which several portions of this work are based. I am indebted as well to my colleagues who recommended this project for the support of a sabbatical year's leave, particularly to Margaret Francel, chair of that committee. I especially appreciate the support as well of two presidents of The Citadel, Lieutenant General Claudius E. Watts III,

U.S. Air Force, retired, and Major General John Grinalds, U.S. Marine Corps, retired, who read the manuscript and offered comments.

Colonel Craig S. Huddleston, director, Command and Staff College, Marine Corps University, has over the years been a source of highly useful perspectives regarding command and leadership. At Quantico also, dean of academics C. Douglas McKenna and associate dean John B. Matthews gave of their time to read earlier drafts and offer comments regarding this manuscript. A longtime colleague at Quantico, Donald F. Bittner, will see his insights regarding a variety of topics in these pages.

Substantive assistance came also from colleagues at other institutions: professor emeritus Edward M. Coffman of the University of Wisconsin and professors Walter J. Fraser of Georgia Southern University, Don Higginbotham of the University of North Carolina–Chapel Hill, Allan R. Millett of Ohio State University, Dennis Showalter of Colorado College, and John Shy of the University of Michigan, who offered important ideas.

Three former students who currently serve as infantry officers or in special operational billets read the draft or provided comments: Colonel Daniel P. Bolger, U.S. Army, Colonel Benjamin Ravenel Clark, U.S. Army, and Colonel Kenneth F. McKenzie, U.S. Marine Corps. Attorneys at law Auley M. Crouch, C. Wilson DuBose, Vaiden P. Kendrick, and Julian L. Stoudemire read the draft, and, in Julian's case, also took me to key sites in areas of the old Cherokee territory. Dave M. Davis, M.D., reviewed the portions of the draft dealing with the Cherokees.

Important perspectives were also gained from active-duty officer colleagues at Quantico: Lieutenant Colonel Colin J. Beadon, Royal Marines, Commander David Austin Mee, U.S. Navy, and Lieutenant Commander Timothy Rogers, Royal Navy, as well as from Richard W. Hatcher III, Fort Sumter National Monument, National Park Service; and from Edwin C. Bearss, both experts on many aspects of Charleston's defenses.

I owe a long-standing debt of gratitude to a number of research facilities. In the United Kingdom, I particularly want to thank the staffs of the old British Army Staff College Library, Camberley; the National Army Museum, London; the John Rylands University Library, Manchester; the National Maritime Museum, Greenwich; and the Public Record Office, Kew. In the United States I wish to thank the staffs of the U.S. Army Military History Institute, the South Carolina Department of Archives and History, the South Carolina Historical Society, and the South

Caroliniana Library of the University of South Carolina. I am indebted to the superb reference librarians, most particularly Herbert Nath and David Heisser, at the Daniel Library, The Citadel, and to its director Anne Whaley LeClercq, for her excellent ideas and directions. Her predecessor, the late Zelma Palestrant, likewise was of great assistance.

At the Gray Research Center, Marine Corps University, Carol Ramkey, head of the library, and Theresa Anthony and Pat Lane, reference librarians, continue to provide superb support.

I also appreciate the support and assistance of my editors at the University of South Carolina Press, Alexander Moore and Barbara A. Brannon, and Catherine Fry, former director. John Breitmeyer copyedited the volume.

Judy Burress, cartographer, of Columbia prepared the maps that appear in the text of this work. Beverly Singleton of Atlanta typed the entire manuscript. Carol-Anne Parker typed all endnotes and a substantial amount of the bibliography. To each of these women I am very greatly indebted indeed.

In childhood my first awareness of hearing about the events and issues of the American Revolution came from my late parents, Lieutenant Colonel John William Gordon, U.S. Air Force, and Doris Vivian Gleason Gordon, and I express my debt to their memory.

SOUTH CAROLINA AND THE
AMERICAN REVOLUTION

INTRODUCTION

Left mainly to her own resources, it was through the depths of
wretchedness that her sons were to bring her back to her place in the
republic . . . having suffered more, and dared more, and achieved
more than the men of any other state.

—George Bancroft, *History of the United States* (1857)

THE GENERATION of South Carolinians who fought the War for
American Independence, 1775–1783, would wholeheartedly have agreed
with this statement by the nineteenth-century historian George Bancroft concerning South Carolina. Particularly during the time of British
occupation after 1780, with the South as the principal theater of the
war and South Carolina its main battleground, the men and women of
that generation confronted both the actions of an invading army and a
vicious cycle of rebel and loyalist partisan raids and reprisals that devastated the country. The war continued to rage on in full cry in South
Carolina when it had departed from other sectors.

In its last two years, more than a thousand Americans died on battlefields in that state. This amounts to nearly twenty percent of all the
Americans who perished in combat in the entire war. The figure counts
neither loyalist deaths nor those who died from sickness in camp, numbers that, if known to certainty, would drive the figure higher.[1]

South Carolina played a decisive role in the winning of the American
Revolution. The struggle in that state spanned the war from its opening
stages to the very end of the fighting, and saw the involvement of the
full range of eighteenth-century forces for sea and land warfare. More
pitched battles, clashes, and actions involving guerrilla forces were
fought in South Carolina than in any other state of the original thirteen
during the war. In many respects, the war itself marked a kind of evolu-
tionary step between the era of warfare sometimes described as "dynastic"

or "neoclassical"—an affair of kings, princes, or their ministers, fought with small professional armies—and the beginnings of mass-national conflict. This second type aroused the full passions and violence of the whole embattled population, as opposed to a struggle limited to clashes between relatively small regular forces exclusively.[2]

South Carolina experienced features of both, serving as the scene for a variety and intensity of conflict not equaled in any other state. Powerful British naval and land forces twice, and land forces once, moved to attack Charles Town—the capital of the state, one of only five "census definition" cities (that is, ones with populations of ten thousand or more persons) in the thirteen colonies and the only such city in the South—the second time successfully. The loss of Charleston (the official name after the war and already in use by some during it) in 1780 was Britain's biggest gain of the war, costing the Americans not just a critical port but their only army south of Washington's (a loss of American troops equal in number to the British captured at Saratoga, usually regarded as the point where the war turned in favor of the Americans, three years before), and an event that laid all of South Carolina open to invasion.

Thereafter, inland from their fallen capital, the people of the state either engaged in or were the victims of a campaign of guerrilla warfare that fought its way from lowcountry to midlands to upcountry and back again. In a very real sense, the war in the backcountry turned into a civil war between loyalist and patriot neighbors—more truly a civil war than the War Between the States one eighty years later. Black South Carolinians fought as members of Marion's band and at King's Mountain and Cowpens—or on the British side. South Carolina's large and substantial Cherokee population participated in a struggle that flamed up and down the American frontier, and for which involvement that Indian nation paid a price in lands lost and warriors and noncombatants killed that helped to break its power.[3]

The conflict not only continued as a guerrilla war but also phased into a struggle involving conventional forces as well when the Americans dispatched a new army under Nathanael Greene into the Carolinas. Winning backcountry outposts one by one, the efforts of the mix of American regular and the irregular forces of the South Carolina partisans pushed the British back into Charleston and also helped Major General the Earl Cornwallis to make decisions that resulted in British disaster at Yorktown in Virginia. British forces did not finally depart the state until the end of 1782, when, with Nathanael Greene's American troops marching down King Street into Charleston, they departed on their ships, never to return.

More Americans died in the Civil War, fought eight decades later, than in all of the nation's other wars combined—in South Carolina, something on the order of fully one of every fourteen or fifteen white male or female South Carolinians. And yet South Carolina's losses in the Revolution, counting those from disease, dislocation, the major combats, and the viciousness of the partisan war and the war on the frontier, must have come, as a percentage of the whole, very close to the Civil War levels. And descriptions of the physical devastation that occurred—public buildings, churches, plantation houses and farms plundered and destroyed—sound almost as if they were taken from descriptions of the aftermath of Sherman's march of 1865, an event usually regarded as one of the most horrendous in South Carolina's history.

In the Revolution, South Carolina played no lost-cause role but the winning one of fighting the war that won the independence of the United States of America. South Carolina was never abandoned by its friends. In the state's hour of need, men from North Carolina, Georgia, Virginia and Tennessee, not yet a state, and men from other states came to South Carolina to fight for the Revolutionary cause. Battles fought in South Carolina both preserved the political revolution that had been made and acted to secure its continuation after the return of British forces in strength to try to win back the South. In the end, they helped gain the final American victory by being a factor in inducing Cornwallis to march northward to Virginia and defeat at Yorktown.

Various military concepts, weapons, and practices of that age—or main terms and organizational approaches—are dealt with briefly in the sections below.

Strategy, Tactics, and Campaigns

War, an open armed conflict, is a political act in which one state or side applies force against another in order to achieve the ends it wants.

"Strategy" is the overall plan by which the war is fought, the way by which violence is applied in order to achieve the desired ends. It is the game plan, the grand concept for assembling and then employing forces in space and time to gain the stated goals of national policy. The formulation of strategy involves issues of *ends, ways,* and *means:* What are the desired outcomes to be achieved? How are they to be reached? What resources are necessary for the task?

"Tactics" is the employment of forces in a single battle or engagement, and involves the practices, methodologies, and formations by which the forces are so employed. The purpose of a battle is to secure defeat of the enemy's armed forces. A series of battles leading to the accomplishment of a larger strategic step or goal is sometimes spoken of as a campaign. The process of planning and sequencing the battles that comprise the campaign that achieves the larger strategic goal is called the "operational level of war" and is regarded as a sort of bridge between tactics and strategy.

"Logistics" is the process of organizing and moving quantities of ammunition, food, and other essential supplies so that they reach the troops doing the fighting.[4]

Land Warfare in the Eighteenth Century

The land battles of eighteenth-century warfare were fought by armies made up chiefly of infantry and employing the dominant weapons system in use for that era, the smoothbore, muzzle-loading, flintlock-ignition musket. Long lines of infantry, deployed by battalions as the basic unit for fire and maneuver, operated in three-rank firing lines that maximized firepower and command and control. Equally important, the musket was a firearm that also carried cold steel for shock action: the socket bayonet that could remain fixed even while the weapon was being loaded and fired. Horse-drawn, smoothbore field artillery pieces of relatively (as compared to the much heavier guns mounted on warships) small size and number (as compared to the massed artillery of the French Revolutionary and Napoleonic era that followed) supported the infantry by firing roundshot (solid iron balls of four to six or more pounds) and grapeshot (much smaller balls, fired in a cluster) into the enemy line a football field or so away. The mounted arm, cavalry carrying sabers, pistols, and carbines, was used to reconnoiter, charge the enemy, or ride down the enemy's retreating forces. Engineers specialized in preparing fortifications and attacking or defending fixed positions, in demolition work, in building bridges, and making maps.[5]

Infantry units practiced speed of loading and firing by volleys. The musket had an effective range of just over fifty yards (or half the length of a modern football field), although practice with it—even though it came without a rear sight—could increase its accuracy. The British Army musket, known as the Brown Bess, was .75 caliber and fired a four-ounce lead ball and sometimes a load of buckshot as well. The French musket, the Charleville, was slightly smaller in caliber but generally similar in appearance and performance characteristics. American troops fighting in South Carolina used both types of weapons. Ammunition (powder and ball) came prepackaged in paper cartridges. In combat, well-trained troops were expected to get off three shots per minute. In addition to loading and firing drills, training emphasized maneuvering on the battlefield without loss of formation—and fighting with the bayonet. Officers carried swords and sometimes short spears called spontoons.[6]

Infantry was the dominant arm because it offered the best mix of firepower, shock action—the bayonet charge—and capacity to maneuver. It was also less expensive to equip and train than the other two branches. Dragoons were a kind of all-purpose cavalry unit, capable of conducting reconnaissance, deep strikes, or charges against enemy infantry perhaps already demoralized by artillery or musket fire. Especially in the Southern theater of the American Revolution or War of American Independence, with much of the campaigning being characterized by relatively small forces operating over large distances, both sides, British and American, employed a kind of mixed cavalry-and-infantry force called the legion. In this type of unit the foot soldiers were ready to operate as mounted infantry as horses became available, or perhaps to ride double behind the troopers.[7]

The basic approach of the British Army—and of the Americans' Continental Army in the Revolution—was to fire by platoons and operate as companies of which a multiple made up an infantry battalion. The British battalion comprised five hundred men and was commanded by a lieutenant colonel. Two battalions made up a regiment, commanded by a colonel. Most companies in the battalion comprised what was called line or regular infantry. Special "flank companies," grenadiers and light infantry, were considered elite because they were made up of picked men: taller men reckoned better able to throw the lighted-fuse hand grenades of the day in the case of the grenadiers; and men trained to operate in open, more flexible formations in the case of the light infantry.[8]

Although in the American Revolution some of the fighting—as around Saratoga in 1777 or in portions of the Southern campaigns of

1780–1781—was fought in wooded terrain or outright forest, the largest part took place in farmland or in the settled regions around cities. It was not, therefore, significantly different from the style or manner of combat that had characterized the Seven Years' War in Europe a decade and a half before. This had placed a premium on maneuver and battles fought using linear tactics for volley firing and bayonet fighting at close range, the kind of tactics of which King Frederick II—Frederick the Great—of Prussia was regarded as master. To handle both types of warfare—the fighting in wooded areas on the one hand, that associated with the European manner and Frederick on the other—the British Army proved in the Revolution a good deal more flexible and innovative as to tactics than long-held stereotypes might suggest. And the Americans, for their part, had to operate a good deal more like the British than those same stereotypes will admit. Both sides were increasingly willing to experiment with light infantry forces. George Washington, the Americans' commander in chief but perhaps speaking for his opponents as well, had in mind forces made up of young, physically active men selected for their skill in marksmanship. British light infantrymen carried a lighter version of the musket called a fusee, and were trained in "immediate-action" drills to deploy and flush out American riflemen.[9]

Some kinds of American troops, especially in the South, carried the long-barreled rifle of the frontier, called variously the Pennsylvania rifle, the Kentucky rifle, or simply, from its length, the long rifle. Like the musket it was muzzle-loading and flintlock-ignited. Unlike the musket, however, it was not smoothbore but was cut inside the barrel with the spiral grooves or rifling that gave the bullet its spin and greater range when fired. It was accurate to two hundred yards or roughly four times the range of the musket. Its disadvantage was that it was slower to load than the musket. The process of loading the two was essentially identical except that, in the case of the rifle, it was necessary to "patch" each ball—that is, to insert the bullet in a lubricated disk of cloth or buckskin before ramming it down the spiral-grooved barrel. This step took additional time and reduced the number of shots that could be discharged per minute. Also, the rifle in reality was a personally owned weapon used primarily for hunting. It came in no one standard caliber (most were from approximately .40 to .50 caliber) and was not fitted to mount a bayonet—even had the riflemen themselves regarded the bayonet as a useful thing to put on a rifle in the first place. The Americans had no monopoly on the use of these weapons. American loyalists used them on the British sides, and British officers bought their own or experimented with issuing rifles to their picked marksmen. As military weapons, rifles were effective for deep-woods and frontier fighting, or under certain circumstances could be used in combination with troops armed with muskets.[10]

The American army, the Continental Line, comprised units of regulars supplied by each state—the First South Carolina Regiment, for example. In trying to build the Continentals into an effective force, Washington modeled its training, organization, and discipline on the only army he had ever seen or served with: the British Army, in the French and Indian War. A British army in the field was commanded by a general officer (i.e., an officer exercising general, overall command of all arms and services) and used a system of brigades, divisions, and corps that was ad hoc rather than drawn up according to a precise table of organization. In the eighteenth century Britain was a nation with a big navy and a small army. The redcoats on the eve of the American Revolution comprised only some 48,000 men, spread out from America and the Caribbean to the Old World, while the armies of Continental European rivals, such as France, were much larger.[11]

Warfare in that century is sometimes spoken of as dynastic warfare, rather than nationalistic struggles between whole peoples as would be the case in the French Revolutionary era that followed. It was also an age of limited warfare, warfare limited in its goals and the means of attaining those goals. Reaction to the Thirty Years' War (1618–1648) had by the eighteenth century led to the adoption of rules and conventions that (in theory) acted to clean up warfare to some degree. The battles remained bloody, but now there were rules and prohibitions against applying violence to the civilian population.

As were other armies in this period, the British Army's officer corps tended to be drawn from the aristocracy and the gentry, or those with pretensions to the style and status of these classes. The enlisted soldiers or "other ranks" came from the opposite tier of society, farm laborers or the urban poor. Discipline was strict—but no more so than what Washington and other American commanders tried to impose on the Continentals. British troops were long-service professionals who fought from a sense of pride in their units and the leadership of their officers.

American officers also tended to come from the upper tiers of society, but colonial society reflected a substantial dynamic of upward social mobility. Some elements of the Continental Army gradually acquired unit pride and the same depth of officer leadership and skill on the part of sergeants characteristic of their British opponents. In the meantime, some fundamental sense of nationalism or faith in the cause had to keep its men in the ranks—or to bring them back again, since many deserted only to return to fight again another day.

Sea Warfare in the Age of Sail

Large sea battles in the Age of Sail were fought by fleets (the British usually organizing theirs into van, center, and rear squadrons) made up of the dominant warship of the time, the ship of the line. That vessel was three-masted and full-rigged—that is, it had full suits of both square and fore and aft-rigged sails—and was approximately 150 to 190 feet long at the waterline. Below the waterline, its oak-timbered hull was covered with a sheathing of copper plates to protect against damage from the worm infestation that was a particular danger in warmer tropical waters. It had two full gun decks, where were mounted the sixty to ninety or more guns it carried. The guns, each operated by a crew of half-a-dozen men or more, were fired in broadsides through open gun ports.[12]

The ship-of-the-line or line-of-battle ship was so called because it fought in a tactical formation called the line-ahead. This both facilitated signaling (by a complex system of flags), and therefore command and control by the admiral, and massed firepower out to the side. Only ships of a certain power or "rate" as the British navy called it—a function of size and the number of guns carried—could "lie in the line." The heaviest guns fired solid iron balls of thirty-two and twenty-four pounds. A special kind of lighter-weight gun, called the carronade or "smasher" and throwing an even heavier ball but at lower velocity, was introduced in the British navy in the first year of the American Revolution. It increased firepower but had the disadvantage of a shorter range than the long guns.

By that time also the Royal Navy—Britain's navy and the dominant fleet in the world—had set sixty guns as the minimum number to qualify for ship-of-the-line status. Smaller, less well-armed but faster ships were the ships below the line. These were frigates, in the British navy usually carrying some thirty to forty guns, and sloops of war (called corvettes by the French), carrying twenty or fewer guns. These differed also from the ship-of-the-line in that their guns were carried on a single gun deck in the case of the frigates, or on the top or "weather" deck in the case of the sloops. Too small to lie in the line, vessels of these two classes were usually employed in cruising, scouting, commerce-raiding, or other specialized tasks. A detached cruising squadron, comprising a large ship or two and a number of these smaller ones, might operate under the command of a commodore.[13]

The largest British ships-of-the-line were called first-rates. More numerous and more economical to build and operate were the third-rates, of sixty-four or perhaps seventy-four guns. Only the top three classes rated as ships-of-the-line. Ships of this type carried crews of five hundred to eight hundred sailors and marines. The marines, special sea soldiers, fought from the fighting tops of the masts as sharpshooters or formed the nucleus of boarding or landing parties.

The formalist tactics in use dictated the line-ahead formation, and also dictated that fleets would typically engage each other in conterminous line. The Royal Navy preferred to fight from the weather gage, or offensive, windward position. Its gunners were trained to shoot on the downward roll of the ship and aim for enemy hulls and decks. French gunners, by contrast, were trained to shoot on the upward roll and aim for British sails, masts, and rigging—a reasonable practice, since the French usually fought from the lee gage or defensive, downwind position. British admirals could release their captains to maneuver independently of the line by raising the signal "general chase."

Three approaches to navy strategy dictated how these varieties of ships would be employed. The kind of overall naval plan or strategy which aimed at winning command of the sea—that is, the ability to use the sea for one's purposes and to deny its use to one's enemy—was called grand war. The usual British approach was to win and maintain command of the sea. This was accomplished by defeating the enemy fleet in battle or else keeping it blockaded in its ports. An approach in which one nation had a fleet inferior in size to its enemy's but which still threatened the larger fleet's command of the sea, and might yet fight at an advantage, was called the strategy of the fleet-in-being. This was the French approach in much of the Age of Sail. A final kind of strategy—one of the indirect approach, aimed not at the enemy's battle fleet but at the enemy's commercial shipping, and intended to make the war prohibitively costly—was guerre-de-course. It represented in effect a form of guerrilla warfare at sea, and was the resort of nations that lacked a battle fleet—the Americans in the Revolution, for example. It was conducted by government-owned warships or by armed civilian ones called privateers, operating under sanction of a document called a letter of marque.

A number of factors contributed to Britain's rise to naval dominance in the Age of Sail: the nation's basic insular situation—along with what the American naval officer Alfred Thayer Mahan called "geographical position," a location that enabled the British to blockade the European coast; favorable attitudes towards sea power on the part of government and of the private sector; and a strategic imperative—the thing a nation must do to defend its people, homeland, and interests—that naturally inclined towards operations over a 360-degree salt-water frontier. The benefits of this naval dominance were enormous. Not only did Britain's dominance assure the nation access to trade and to colonies, it permitted it to "punch above its weight" in European balance-of-power struggles. With their own coasts secure, the British could intervene with their small army as a part of coalitions that kept the balance of power adjusted in their favor.

England's sea officers in particular early developed highly specialized levels of skill and a professional ethos. While by no means all Royal Navy officers came from the upper reaches of society, many of them did. The practice of requiring aspiring officers to serve at sea as midshipmen, frequently from boyhood through teenage years, provided a solid grounding in seamanship, navigation, and gunnery. And gunnery in particular —both accuracy and rate of fire—was the British navy's strong suit, consistently developed through drills and practices. The system withal yielded Britain a large pool of talent from which to select officers for key commands. Other men, warrant rather than commissioned officers, worked their way up from the ranks and likewise possessed very high levels of expertise. The enlisted sailors or ratings were sometimes brought in through the practice of forced service or impressment. Others came as volunteers, particularly for the appeal of prize money—their officially adjudicated share of money to be awarded from the sale of enemy vessels captured at sea. This was especially an incentive for joining the crew of a frigate or a sloop, the types of men-of-war most likely to be engaged in preying upon enemy commerce.[14]

The French navy, often defeated in the Seven Years' War, had gone through a program of expansion and reformation in tactics that enabled it to challenge the Royal Navy by the period of the American Revolution (or War of American Independence). It was to this navy that George Washington looked for help to break Britain's control of the sea long enough for the Americans to win a victory. The Royal Navy, for its part, was beginning to experiment with new and innovative tactics. It was a service whose own traditions and the expectations of the British nation as a whole demanded very high standards of performance. British naval officers had also developed expertise in working with their British Army colleagues to conduct amphibious operations, and they would put this skill to the test in operations along the South Carolina coast.

The Americans formed a Continental Navy and Corps of Continental Marines in fall 1775. Individual states—including South Carolina—operated their own navies, and privateering also took a substantial toll of England's merchant fleet. Ships being constructed for the Continental Navy at Philadelphia had to be destroyed before the British captured the city in 1777, and later construction was signed over to France to help pay America's war debt to her ally.[15]

The Colonial Militia

The system of militia service employed in South Carolina and other royal colonies on the eve of the American Revolution was essentially a system developed in England in Elizabethan times and thereafter transported to America. The fundamental concept was that defense of the colony was essential and that every able-bodied white male citizen owed military service to that end. The manner and practice of organizing such men into "trainband" units or companies (the basic unit) and training them varied over time. At a minimum, all were subject to be called up and appear at stated muster times. The number of muster days per year varied (four seems to have been the minimum number), as did the quality of training conducted and level of efficiency expected.[16]

To be a male citizen of the colony was to be a citizen-soldier of the militia. Each member was expected to provide his own weapon and equipment. The Crown furnished muskets to those who could not afford them and also stockpiled additional weapons, equipment and ammunition in case of emergency.

In South Carolina as in other colonies, the same impetus that led the lower house—the Commons House—of the assembly to gain power at the expense of the council and of the royal governor also led that same body to exert civilian control over the military forces of the colony. That is, the governor himself might possess the theoretical right to control the militia through the appointment of officers, but the lower house would control what the militia would actually *do*, through its power of the purse: the power to vote—or not vote—for funds for military or other purposes. This form of military service via a citizen-soldier militia, the whole controlled by the legislature, was regarded as adequate and vastly superior to (and certainly less costly than) a standing army, regarding which, from the English past, there was great suspicion.[17]

The militia system remained active and reasonably effective where a threat existed to keep it so. Where no threat existed, the militia fell into disuse and inactivity. In South Carolina, two external threats and one internal one existed all through the eighteenth century to keep the militia at relatively high levels of effectiveness: the threat of French and Spanish attack (particularly in the early portion of the century, Queen Anne's War, 1702–1713); the threat of Indian attack (at a variety of times, but especially during the Cherokee War, 1759–1761); and the threat of internal slave revolt (a thing feared throughout the entirety of the period and beyond it).[18]

South Carolina's militia system served also as a feeder program for organizing expeditionary forces, for creating full-time units to man forts or to patrol the Indian frontier, for raising provincial units, and for mobilizing units that could operate with British regulars. It was also an important training ground for members of the planter elite who rose to positions of political leadership in the colony, and for a number of men about to provide military leadership to the Revolutionary cause in South Carolina after 1775, including Francis Marion, William Moultrie, Andrew Pickens, and Thomas Sumter. All had gained combat experience in the Cherokee War (although Sumter's was gained as a member, at that point, of the Virginia forces), which served also as a vehicle for lowcountry-backcountry contacts and networking.

Using the common militia to garrison frontier forts on a long-term basis proved a poor solution, so special full-time men were instead recruited from the militia for that purpose. Equally, forts situated astride main trails could by themselves hardly be expected to stop (or even detect) the movement of hostile Indians, so special units were likewise recruited from the militia. These men, organized as rangers, were militiamen on full-time pay from the colony and were used to patrol the trails and to keep an eye on the Indians generally. Rather than sending the whole force of the militia off on an expedition or against the Indians, units were usually formed by asking for volunteers or drafting men on a quota basis from the militia. The periods of such service were carefully specified and were treated as forming part of a contract. Provincial units raised in this manner acted with British troops—usually of the Independent Company (that is, one stationed in the province and not affiliated with a regiment) type—and were regarded as adequate for dealing with the menace posted by the Indians.[19]

By the coming of the Revolution, South Carolina had a viable militia force and a tradition of service in it, a cadre of trained militia officers and men, and substantial stockpiles of weapons and ammunition. The campaigns against the Cherokees, it has been argued, not only provided experience of frontier warfare but also somewhat brutalized some of its practitioners, since warfare on the frontier was fought without resort to the rules that pertained to "civilized" warfare of the European pattern—rules which governed who could be a target, under what circumstances, etc. This supposedly proved a factor in helping to brutalize the civil war eventually fought during the Revolution in the backcountry, 1780–1781. With the outbreak of that war in 1775, both sides, Whig/rebel and Tory/loyalist, understood very clearly that it was very important to appoint officers of one's own political persuasion so as to gain control of the militia, and to seize all stockpiles of arms and munitions before they fell into the hands of the other side. Although British regular officers had little faith in the military capacities of the militia—a feeling shared by not a few American officers of the Continentals once the Revolution began—the fact remained that the militia could effectively supplement the efforts of regular troops. Perhaps as important, the militia could also, when the Revolution came, gain control of a particular area and intimidate the opposition into immobility or silence. And it was the Whig side which at the start gained control of the militia, thus controlling much of the coastal region and much of the interior of South Carolina.[20]

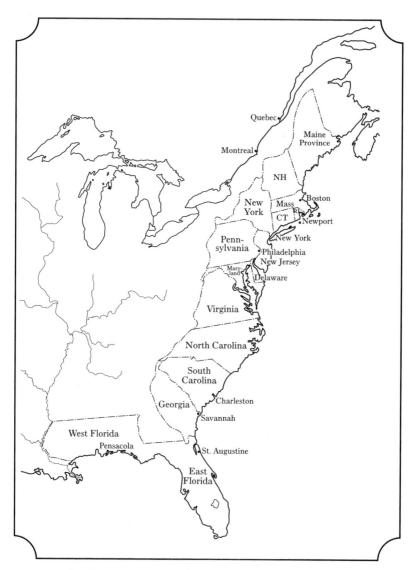

1. REVOLUTIONARY AMERICA AND CANADA, 1775

CHAPTER 1

SOUTH CAROLINA MAKES A REVOLUTION

1775

The maternal eye of Britannia, which with the same care watched over all her children in America . . . seemed especially watchful over . . . South Carolina. . . . The greater part of the rural population . . . are, I believe, favorably inclined towards peace, for they gain nothing by this war. . . . [O]n the side of the enemy are a few enthusiasts and some pseudophilosophical-political dreamers.

—Hessian jaeger captain Johann Hinrichs

Wars are not tactical exercises writ large. They are . . . conflicts of societies.

—Sir Michael Howard

ON THE EVE of the American Revolution, the royal colony of South Carolina seemed an unlikely candidate for revolt against Great Britain. Of all the Thirteen Colonies, and perhaps to the envy of some, South Carolina was conspicuously a bright jewel in the crown of empire. The colony benefited enormously from its British connection. The big-money crops of rice and indigo that the planters grew and the merchants shipped from Charleston flowed over sea lanes protected by the Royal Navy, the most powerful fleet in the world. London was the financial and governmental hub of an empire that provided markets and profits for these products so valuable to the British economic system. In 1775, in terms of per capita wealth, the richest man in America, Peter Manigault, was a South Carolinian as were fully eight of the next top ten. Withal, the slave-holding lowcountry elite whose crops and mercantile efforts brought such wealth and who dominated the political affairs of the colony appeared to have almost everything to lose by creating trouble with the mother country.[1]

And yet the trouble was there, had been brewing for years, and was about to boil over into armed conflict. It is a familiar story, a major theme in any American history text. More importantly, its main arguments were on the lips of many South Carolinians and other colonial Americans at the time. It was much more than a piddling dispute about taxes on this or that item; it had to do with self-government. The basic issue was one which increasingly bound them together in common cause: the assertiveness of Parliament in the imposition of new British policies for heightened control. These were seen as injurious to American interests and practices of self-government that had evolved since settlement. In the eyes of many, they amounted to tyranny, pure and simple; to others they were, at the least, a heavy-handed way to bring the colonies to heel.

The new policies dated from the end of the Seven Years' War (1756–1763)—called in its American theater, beginning in 1755, the French and Indian War—and they seemed rational and appropriate in British eyes. That war had left Britain the dominant power in the world —with a debt to match. The Americans, as the British had begun calling the people of their North American colonies by 1730 or so, needed to pay their fair share of that debt and of the overall burden for imperial defense. In addition to their no-taxation-without-representation argument, the Americans responded that they had contributed men, money, and supplies to the effort against France. As to defense, they could take care of any local troubles themselves.

In London, the response of Whitehall—that is, the executive departments of the British government—was to reassert and continue with the new measures. The effect of that response was to set the British on a collision course with American institutions of government and the Americans' growing sense of autonomy. There was then no concept of self-governing dominions within a British Empire/Commonwealth as would evolve in Canada, Australia, and New Zealand a century later. Parliament argued that it had the right to make laws for all the empire; the Americans claimed that the colonial assemblies, and only these, could legislate for the colonies. Said another way, the very fact that the colonial assemblies had modeled themselves on the Mother of Parliaments now compelled them to oppose measures voted by that same body. Rather than acting to strengthen ties to the mother country, the new measures had the opposite effect. They helped instead to stoke a sense of grievance, encouraging an identity distinctly American, not British.[2]

In South Carolina, a focal point of resistance was the lower house of the colonial assembly. Officially known as the Commons House, its members were elected to office and drawn heavily from the "plantocracy" and the wealthy merchants. Women might do a better job of managing plantation affairs than men, but they could not vote; nor, of course, could blacks. But the lower house represented a political elite, an oligarchy that had won power and tended, consciously and subconsciously, to take as its model the House of Commons in Britain. Certainly its members were cognizant of the historic struggle for supremacy between Crown and Parliament that had taken place the previous century. The lower house was the dominant branch of government and had acquired its power at the expense of the upper house (the Royal Council), made up of "placemen" or favorites appointed by the royal governor. This last-named official was sometimes a British ex-soldier or sailor of aristocratic birth, and the appointed, personal representative of the king.

That king was George III, long to rule, by choice an active participant rather than a figurehead in government, and popular enough among England's gentry to be called the "Patriot King." He came to the throne in 1760. The new imperial measures he favored towards the colonies were implemented by successive ministries of "King's Friends," men much inclined towards strong support of the monarchy. From 1770 on, it was the ministry (or administration) of Frederick, Lord North, that was most associated with the new initiatives coming from the imperial capital. These—whether taxes, forced billeting of troops on communities, or efforts to prevent settlement of western lands claimed by Indian tribes—caused mounting resentment.

Yet converting that resentment into outright opposition was not a matter to be taken lightly. The population of the British Isles, eleven million, was more than four times that of the American colonies' 2.5 million. And South Carolina, while wealthy, was hardly reckoned a populous colony. At 174,550 (of which 59 percent, or 104,000, was black; indeed, of the six hundred thousand people of African descent then living in America, a sixth of them lived in South Carolina), its population was a fraction of that of the three most heavily populated colonies: Virginia (538,000), Pennsylvania (327,305), and Massachusetts (then including Maine, 317,760). Moreover, the ratio of the militia to the whole population was approximately 1 to 4 or 5 in these more northerly colonies but only 1 to 7 in South Carolina—meaning that the number of fighting men available was relatively small. Yet these small numbers did not deter South Carolina from consistently choosing to stand firm with the other colonies. This was the case during the Stamp Act Crisis of 1765 and, nine years later, the calling of delegates to meet in the First Continental Congress. That body met in fall 1774 under emergency conditions to consider what to do about the harsh measures being visited upon sister colony Massachusetts in retribution for the Boston Tea Party.[3]

To punish Boston for the destruction of a large and highly valuable cargo of tea, the British moved in troops and closed the harbor by blockade. They also suspended civil government in a colony judged to be in a state of rebellion. The other colonies regarded these measures as extreme and threatening to all. If Britain could do this to Massachusetts, then why not to any of the others, should they so choose?

As tensions mounted, South Carolina called into being a Provincial Congress. This congress had essentially the same representation as the previous Commons House: it now became the de facto government of the colony. A significant feature was that its membership included representatives—but only the merest handful—elected from backcountry districts. For the colony of South Carolina was, at the midpoint of the 1770s and until much later, in many respects two separate and distinct entities: the seaboard lowcountry, with its plantations, dominant French-Huguenot but mostly English planter-merchant oligarchy, and control of courts, commerce, and government; and the backcountry—at that juncture simply everything that was inland and not lowcountry. Settlement reached in along rivers and spread into the best lands. The backcountry included out-and-out frontier, that area closest to the mountains in the northwestern foothills territory belonging to the Cherokees, as well as the more settled areas in the interior. These last, a kind of not frontier–not lowcountry middle zone, supplied tobacco and other products to the slave-worked plantations of the lowcountry.[4]

Communication by road or trail between the two was difficult. The backcountry was almost a separate province, a hodgepodge of English, Welsh, German, and other groups. Many of its people were Scotch-Irish. These groups had, over the previous two decades or so, moved south from Pennsylvania and Virginia. Some were frontier people, others small farmers with few slaves who resented the control the lowcountry exerted over prices and government. They also resented the fact that their tax money—many were Baptists or Presbyterians or, in the case of the German settlers, Lutherans—went to support the established, but minority, Anglican Church. They particularly resented the absence of law and order in their region. In outlook, background, and economic interest, the Scotch-Irish had more in common with their counterparts across the line in North Carolina or on the far bank of the Savannah River than they did with their fellow citizens living on the South Carolina coast.

Those living nearest the frontier were ever cognizant of the threat of Indians, chiefly the large and powerful Cherokee nation. The number of warriors actually living in South Carolina was small, not more than 350 men. But these Cherokees were tied to a nation that ran from Virginia to Georgia and west to what became Tennessee, and they could call upon their kinsmen for help. Ten years before the Revolution, the grievances of backcountry people had flared into the vigilante action and clashes with colonial authorities called the Regulator movement. Eventually, people in the backcountry were somewhat mollified by the establishment of courts and jails in their districts and token representation in the lower house. Their prevailing interests remained: that the frontier be kept quiet, the Indians kept in check, and law and order maintained. With no love of the merchants and planters centered on Charleston, not a few of them looked to the Crown to keep the frontier safe and to counter the lowcountry—which was, in their eyes, more interested in aggrandizing its own power than in looking after the people on the frontier. It was by no means certain that these people, some of them substantial planters of emerging prosperity, had any inclination other than to remain true and loyal subjects of their British king.[5]

Opening Moves
APRIL 17–JULY 27, 1775

Yet affairs were soon out of the loyalists' hands. Almost overnight, protest and debate would turn into overt acts of hostility against British authority—specifically, the seizure of arms and ammunition—in Charleston and along the coast, commencing in spring 1775.

On April 17, a special, lowcountry Whig-dominated five-man "secret committee" of the Provincial Congress of South Carolina took the step of seizing official mail brought from England on the packet *Swallow.* The seized dispatches made it clear that British authorities would not hesitate to use force to restore order in the colonies. Two days after the clashes at Lexington and Concord between militiamen and British regulars had started the war a thousand miles to the north—although the actual news would not come down the coast until the following month—the secret committee moved to seize arms and ammunitions stored in the colony's various arsenals and magazines in and around Charleston. On the night of April 21 a party took muskets and other arms stored in the statehouse, a building located at the northwest corner of Broad and Meeting Streets. On that same night also, with all moves carefully coordinated, other parties removed gunpowder stored in magazines on Cumberland Street, near Shipyard Creek further up the peninsula, and across the Cooper River at Hobcaw Point.[6]

When the news of Lexington and Concord finally "flew over the continent" as Colonel William Moultrie, soon to be the defender of the palmetto-log fort on Sullivan's Island, put it, the Americans were enflamed to action. In South Carolina the Provincial Congress moved to name a Council of Safety, which was given executive powers of an emergency nature. Three "standing"—that is, full-time and volunteer as opposed to militia—regiments of troops (one of them mounted rangers) were also voted into being, care being taken to appoint officers whose politics were in concert with those doing the voting. Soon the council dispatched, under two militia captains from Beaufort, a forty-man detachment of volunteers to take station at the southern end of Daufuskie Island. This particular point was sheltered by Hilton Head (then also referred to as Trench or Trench's) Island, and it was advantageous because it offered an unobstructed view of Tybee Roads, the route by which British ships would have to proceed to reach Savannah. It was believed that Savannah, the capital of the royal colony of Georgia, would soon receive a substantial cargo of gunpowder. The South Carolinians linked up with like-minded Georgians. Conspicuously aided by the fact that the Georgians possessed an armed vessel, the combined party used this vessel to intercept the expected cargo, carried in the *Philippa* merchantman. The effect of this action was that, rather than going to the Cherokees and the Creeks, its intended recipients, the gunpowder ended up being divided up between South Carolina and Georgia militia units now clearly acting against British authority.[7]

Other efforts by the council included plans to raid British magazines and arsenals as far away as the Bahamas. One South Carolina vessel,

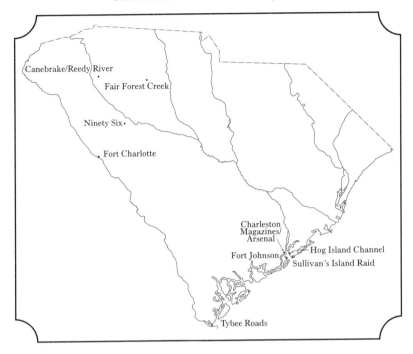

Canebrake/Reedy River
Fair Forest Creek
Ninety Six
Fort Charlotte
Charleston Magazines/Arsenal
Fort Johnson
Hog Island Channel
Sullivan's Island Raid
Tybee Roads

2. ACTIONS IN 1775

captained by an experienced, ex-privateering skipper, was diverted to St. Augustine in East Florida when it was learned that a large shipment of arms, munitions, and military supplies was headed for the British fort (the old Spanish-built San Marcos) there. This vessel at length managed to catch up with the British one as it rode at anchor outside the bar, awaiting a favorable tide. In a broad-daylight capture, the South Carolinians made off with six tons of gunpowder. They were pursued up the coast, but their vessel came safely through Tybee Roads and, using inland routes, eventually arrived at Port Royal.

By early summer 1775, particularly in Charleston, along the coast and in the Pee Dee region, anti-British feeling and talk of war predominated. Intimidation cowed into silence many of those inclined towards loyalty to the Crown. A particular target was the harbor pilot Thomas Jeremiah. A free black who was himself a slaveowner, Jeremiah had supposedly threatened to lead a slave revolt, aid the British, or both. He was hanged for the suspicion he aroused and on charges the British decried as being without foundation. The backcountry, and indeed much of the rest of the colony, then watched and waited.[8]

Such was the climate on June 18 when the new royal governor (as it happened, the last) of South Carolina arrived in Charleston by ship to take up his post. Lord William Campbell, a younger son of the Duke of Argyll, was an able individual with well-established credentials as a colonial administrator. His reception in the warm June weather was, however, unseasonably chilly and was not to improve with time.[9] Neither his considerable experience of the area (a career Royal Navy officer, he had earlier commanded a ship based in Charleston) nor his marriage to a daughter of a prominent local family could help him. He almost instantly erred by intriguing to gain the armed support of loyalist factions in the backcountry—only to be found out before his plans could reach fruition. This exposure destroyed whatever credibility he may have had and gave powerful ammunition to the anti-British elements in the colony. These elements meanwhile continued to acquire plenty of real ammunition of their own.

Seizure of Fort Charlotte
JULY 12, 1775

Fort Charlotte, a frontier outpost left over from the last round of Indian troubles, contained fully a ton or more of gunpowder, plus artillery pieces and ammunition. Its other appeal was that it was guarded only by a single captain of the province's handful of full-time military personnel and his family—more caretakers than garrison.

The fort itself was situated on the upper Savannah River and located so as to guard a ford (now under the waters of Clark's Hill Reservoir) frequented by Creek warriors given to crossing over from Georgia and raiding into the frontier settlements just beyond. The principal one of these, the village of Ninety Six, was distant some thirty miles to the north and east. Constructed of stone, the fort was initially occupied by British regulars, now long since withdrawn.[10]

Late in June, the Council of Safety ordered Major James Mayson, a resident of the Ninety Six area, to seize the fort and its munitions. Mayson was given two companies of the mounted rangers recently raised. The colony had a long history of using troops of this sort, and indeed a substantial number of Mayson's men apparently were veterans of ranger service. The two companies were themselves respectively commanded by captains James Caldwell and Moses Kirkland. Kirkland had been prominent in the Regulator movement of eight years before and was a

leader in his community. He now supposedly harbored a grudge, however, since Mayson, rather than himself, had been the choice for this new
field-officer's command.

Kirkland's supposed grudge did not, however, prevent the column's
marching, with Mayson in the lead, unhindered into the fort. Mayson
seized it in the name of the Provincial Congress and, leaving Caldwell
and his rangers in charge, decided to proceed for Ninety Six with some
of the gunpowder. Mayson was accompanied by Kirkland and his company as escort. By then, news of the fort's seizure had had time to reach
those elements in the backcountry inclined towards loyalty to the British
Crown—or outright animosity towards the lowcountry Whigs controlling the Council of Safety. This sudden move—taking the fort and its
powder—was in their eyes provocative to the point of outrage.[11]

It was at this juncture that Kirkland formally decided to change sides.
He took the step of urging his neighbors who were loyalists to seize
the gunpowder taken by Mayson and now stored in the courthouse at
Ninety Six. When the loyalists arrived there, they gained both the gunpowder and Mayson, most of whose troops were members of Kirkland's
company and had already decided to leave before a fight could develop.
Mayson was arrested by the loyalists, charged by his fellow Americans
with stealing Crown property, and locked up—only to gain release a few
days later. For the moment the various elements of the backcountry—
those pro-Whig in outlook, those who were out-and-out loyalists, and
those just plain neutral—continued either to press their case or to sit
back and see what happened next. But a point of departure had been
reached. In fact, this seizure of the fort marked the first expansion of
the war into the backcountry region—as opposed to Charleston and the
coast—of South Carolina, and it revealed clearly the fault lines of a
divided populace.

Meanwhile, representatives of South Carolina's political elite—and,
indeed, precisely those most inclined to oppose the new British policies
—were taking steps in concert with those of the other colonies to help
shape both a system of government and an overall military response. In
the wake of Lexington and Concord, and as New England militia gathered against the British in Boston, the Second Continental Congress met
in Philadelphia. It assumed general direction of what was becoming a war
effort and would be the means of government until adoption of the Articles of Confederation some five and a half years later.

South Carolina's representatives were Christopher Gadsden, Thomas Lynch, Arthur Middleton, and Edward and John Rutledge. Few among this or any other colony's delegation were ready as yet to take the plunge of declaring independence from Britain. For the moment, their cause remained that of restoration of historic rights within the imperial context. They made it clear that even though all the colonies, including South Carolina, stood to forfeit lucrative economic benefits as a result of trouble with Britain, they would stand by New England. Their support took specific military form. They voted to support the militia units investing Boston and to create a force of regular troops eventually to be termed the Continental Army, whose "Continental Line" would be made up of regiments provided from each colony. As important as these measures were, however, they were not more important that the naming of George Washington to be commander in chief of that army. Washington was a Virginia planter schooled by service in the House of Burgesses, his colony's lower house and the oldest such representative body in North America, and by active campaigning in the war just past. Finally, he represented the South. He thus helped tie that region's fortunes irrevocably to those of Massachusetts and New England. The South Carolina representatives played a crucial role in his appointment and they could not have been, in the words of the historian John Richard Alden, displeased to see a man of "their kind and country" appointed to command a military effort to be made by all the colonies.[12]

In South Carolina, though, only gradually did the war turn from arms and ammunition seizures into a shooting one. Rather, a sort of slow dance prevailed as the two groups—those acting in the name of colonial rights on the one hand, Britain's loyalist adherents on the other—maneuvered for position. The loyalists were called by their opponents Tories because that name denoted in their minds the party of support for the king and the policies of control from Whitehall. The other side called themselves the Whigs after the king's opposition in Parliament. A particular favorite of the Americans was William Pitt, the "Great Commoner" now raised to the peerage as the Earl of Chatham. The British already spoke of the Whig group as rebels but the rebels saw themselves as patriots, a term thereafter to be enshrined in triumphalist, nationalistic accounts of the struggle. This present discussion will use, simply, *Americans* to denote those who ultimately prevailed in that struggle, and *loyalists* for those who fought to maintain the American connection to Britain's empire.

The side acting against the British was better off than might have been supposed. The Royal Navy had been allowed to decline in strength since the Seven Years' War. Also, the North ministry remained more interested in paying off the costs of the previous war than in incurring costs in some new struggle. The reality was that, other than a warship or two in Charleston harbor, available British forces were concentrated in Boston and far from South Carolina. For the moment, British arms could do little in the colonies until reinforcements arrived. Their opponents thus had time to seize the initiative.

Seizure of Fort Johnson
SEPTEMBER 15, 1775

In Charleston, Lord William Campbell's fortunes had not improved since his arrival. If anything, feelings ran even higher against him. But he was still the royal governor and the symbol of Crown authority. He was suspected of trying to bring in reinforcements, of actively plotting to stir up the backcountry loyalists, of rousing the Indians, or all three. It was this latter perception that led the Whig side to want to seize Fort Johnson, the key fortification that guarded the colony's principal harbor.

In fact, though, it ended up being Campbell who moved first. His goal was to neutralize the fort by dismantling its guns. Until the construction of works on Sullivan's Island in spring of the next year, Fort Johnson on James Island remained Charleston's primary outer-harbor defense work. It had been built in 1708 during the War of the Spanish Succession (or "Queen Anne's War," 1702–1713), near a point where provincial troops of the colony had previously repulsed a joint French-Spanish attack. Campbell apparently believed he could now gain an advantage by destroying or at least neutralizing the fort's lower battery of some twenty-one cannons. To that end, he dispatched a landing party on the night of September 14.[13]

The party was landed from the *Tamar*, a sixteen-gun Royal Navy sloop stationed in Charleston; they arrived just after dark. For the rest of the night the party worked on the guns, removing the cannons (the heavy tubes of brass, bronze, or iron) from their carriages. Both carriages and cannons were then heaved to the ground from their firing positions. Thereafter the party, the fort's gunpowder in hand, boarded its boats and rowed away.

Soon, however, a contingent of South Carolina troops arrived—grenadiers and light infantrymen drawn from the elite or "flank companies" (one of them commanded by Captain Francis Marion) of the First and Second regiments. Moving into the fort, the Americans were pleased to find that the guns were not destroyed at all, but could actually be reassembled to function again. The *Tamar's* landing party had not taken the step—undoubtedly because Campbell intended to make use of them later—of "spiking" the guns (to render them inoperable by pounding metal spikes into the touchholes).

The troops apparently also had raised a new flag at Fort Johnson. This one had a crescent moon, situated in the upper corner of an indigo-blue field. That particular flag may also have included—stitched in large white letters across the bottom—the word "Liberty." Other accounts suggest that the flag itself, with or without the word Liberty on it, was referred to as "Liberty."[14]

It had been Colonel William Moultrie, acting on behalf of Henry Laurens, president of the Council of Safety, who had made the decision to send troops to seize the fort. This was an overt act of war and done practically under Campbell's nose; it was too much for him to tolerate. His reaction was swift—and ineffectual. He first took the step of formally dissolving the Royal Assembly of South Carolina. He next closed Crown offices in Charleston and, taking with him the great seal of the colony, fled from his house on Meeting Street to the *Tamar*, anchored out in the harbor. From the safety of this floating governor's mansion, isolated and daily in full view of Charleston, he spent the next two months trying to keep the colony under British control. Of course that authority was not, and had not been since the spring, in effect nor was it likely to be made so by the mere presence of a pair of warships, the *Tamar* and the smaller *Cherokee*. In reality, Campbell's flight to the harbor was a bad decision on his part; it handed a victory to the very people he sought to defeat. It removed him further from those who looked to him for leadership and outside support, the loyalists, and with Campbell's departure, the Provincial Congress was left with a free hand.[15]

The Hog Island Channel Fight
NOVEMBER 11–12, 1775

Campbell and his entourage were aboard two "station ships"—that is, warships stationed by the British navy in Charleston to deal with piracy, enforce laws, or in general show the flag in regional waters. Campbell himself, during his own Royal Navy career, had commanded just such a ship operating out of this same harbor and knew well both the harbor and the rivers leading into it. His objective, by November, was to be able to pass from the harbor and up these rivers, since both the Cooper River and the Wando represented routes by which he might hope to link up with the loyalists inland. Also in this same period, he permitted his ships to begin making amphibious forays against local plantations. African Americans held in slavery were a particular, and profitable, target of these raids. Some were carried off; others proved happy enough to accompany the British to what they hoped would be freedom.

In anticipation of Campbell's probable move up the Cooper River, the Council of Safety decided to block a secondary channel that reached it from the inner harbor. The method of blocking would be by sinking ships at its mouth. The channel was narrow and relatively shallow. It lay between Shute's Folly Island and an exposed sandbank on one side and the east bank of the Cooper River on the other. The advantage of blocking the Hog Island Channel was that it would force Campbell's two vessels to use the main channel. This would bring them effectively under the fire of several batteries on the Charleston peninsula, most particularly the heavy guns of Granville's and the Half-moon batteries. In addition, though the range was great, a lucky shot from Fort Johnson might just hit one of Campbell's warships—particularly if it had to tack in that direction. Either way, the possibility of hitting Campbell's ships was far greater if the British could be kept from using the Hog Island Channel and forced into the main one.[16]

To that end, on the afternoon of November 11, the Council of Safety dispatched four hulks—formerly coastal or inland trading vessels of various sizes—into the appointed place in the channel. There they would be anchored and, once scuttled and sunk, would form a physical barrier across the channel. The effort was covered by the armed merchant schooner *Defence*, carrying nineteen guns of various sizes as well as the president of the Provincial Congress, William Henry Drayton. Drayton was altogether unfamiliar with shiphandling or naval affairs; he was, however, determined to get the channel obstructed—even at the cost of a clash with the British.

The *Tamar* meanwhile, observing these movements and her captain spurred on by Campbell, promptly sailed into position and opened fire.

Just as quickly her fire was returned by the *Defence*. The *Cherokee* also soon moved to join in on the firing. It was already afternoon. With darkness the Americans resumed the process of scuttling their hulks. At dawn next morning, the two British ships took advantage of a rising tide to move in closer and resume firing. This continued until a British boat party successfully towed one of the hulks into shallow water, setting it afire. But by then the other three hulks had been sunk in position. Irrespective of the casualties on both sides—either light or nonexistent—the fact remained that the first actual shots of the war in South Carolina had been fired.[17] In addition the Hog Island Channel was blocked, and Lord William Campbell was nowhere nearer his goal of linking up with the loyalists.

Campbell's opponents, meanwhile, continued to do everything possible to limit his power to mobilize that element. In terms of the Indians, a key target was an important Crown official located in Charleston, the superintendent for Indian affairs in the Southern colonies. That officer, Major John Stuart, long in office and highly experienced, enjoyed a considerable standing not just with the Cherokee but with the Creek and other Southern tribes as well. The Americans saw him as a threat. Before he could influence the Indians, particularly the Cherokees, to take up the hatchet for the king (in fact, Stuart was against such a move at this point), the Council of Safety was able in June 1775 to force him to leave town.

Stuart ended up in St. Augustine—in the council's eyes, safely out of the way and too far from the action to do any mischief. Also, his wife remained in Charleston, held under virtual house arrest. By such steps, the royal governor was deprived of cards he might have played to British advantage.[18]

Depriving him of the loyalists was a step less easily accomplished. Sent by the Council of Safety, a handpicked delegation in July and August had traveled to the backcountry to see if some of those neutral— or even conspicuously loyalist in outlook—could not be won over to the Whig side. The delegation was careful to include in its ranks both a Presbyterian and a Baptist minister, as well as Drayton, president of the Provincial Congress. Even so, its members met sufficient hostility to make it abundantly clear that their cause had less than universal support. Not only that, it was deeply opposed in much of the region.[19]

Efforts at reconciliation went forward, supported by at least some on both sides. But the issue of gunpowder—and its potential passage into the hands of the Indians—was so powerful as to overcome these efforts and lead to the first actual encounter on land to be fought in the Southern colonies.

The Siege at Ninety Six / Savage's Old Fields
NOVEMBER 19–21, 1775

The next major encounter would occur at "Old Ninety Six," a frontier village of a hundred or more souls where three roads intersected (one of them an ancient trail known as the Cherokee Path), some two miles south of the present-day community of that name. The village, a point on the road used for bringing goods to the Indians from Charleston, was reckoned by traders to be ninety-six miles from the major Cherokee town of Keowee—hence the name. A trading post had been established at this location and, prospering, had helped to build up the town as a hub of the backcountry. During the Cherokee War (1759–1761) a barn had been expanded into a palisaded wooden fort or stockade, this fortification subsequently successfully withstanding two attacks. Daniel Boone, on the eve of his treks into the Kentucky wilderness over the mountains, visited the trading post. A courthouse and a jail—two items high on the law-and-order agenda of the Regulator movement—were added in the early 1770s.[20]

With the start of the new trouble, the Council of Safety decided to send a shipment of a thousand pounds of gunpowder, and twice that weight in lead for bullets, up to the Cherokee towns located in the foothills of the Blue Ridge. This, obviously, was a move intended to win the good graces of these Indians. What happened instead was that on November 3, the wagon train and escort hauling the munitions were intercepted by a party of loyalists led by Patrick Cunningham. A staunch leader of that faction in the region, and irritated by the seizure of Fort Charlotte in July, Cunningham was not about to permit the Indians to gain this gift from the Whigs. He and his men made off with the powder, soon dispersing back to their farms and plantations.

News of the interception prompted the council to immediate action. A force intended both to regain the powder as well as to intimidate the loyalists was dispatched under Major Andrew Williamson. Williamson was assisted by the same Major Mayson who had seized Fort Charlotte, and by Captain Andrew Pickens. These officers assembled a body of militiamen drawn from the region around Ninety Six. It numbered 594 men; arriving at the village itself, they quickly set to work to erect a new stockade, improvised from a barn and other buildings. Using hides, fence rails, and any other available material, it was located just west of the town itself at a point known as Savage's Old Fields. Hearing the news, Cunningham and fellow loyalist Joseph Robinson quickly rounded up their own men. Ultimately some 1,900 loyalist militiamen converged on the makeshift fort held by Williamson.

The battle itself erupted on a Sunday morning in the midst of negotiations between the leaders of the two groups.[21] The firing began when loyalists happened to grab a pair of Williamson's men outside the walls of the stockade, and it went on for the next two days. A substantial number on both sides carried the long-barreled rifle of the frontier, generally regarded as accurate to two hundred or more paces and just the weapon for aimed, deliberate shots from behind cover. Also, the Whig side had at least one swivel gun, a sort of light artillery piece. Yet the casualties proved surprisingly light, Williamson reporting only one man killed and a dozen wounded. Losses on the other side were higher, with four killed and twenty wounded. There occurred no general assault by the loyalists, who enjoyed the three-to-one attack ratio advocated by tacticians. The loyalists tried to set the stockade afire but were diverted when other bands of Whig riflemen began shooting at them from behind.[22]

Perhaps another factor was that, at this stage of the war, with the bloodiness of the backcountry conflict yet to rage into its full development, the zeal of the riflemen to kill their neighbors was limited. No trained British regulars were present to force the issue. This had been the case in the clashes near Boston in April. The effect of these hard and professional troops—far more reliable as an instrument for combat than the farmers-turned-soldiers of the militia—in these early stages of the war is clear. Where they were present, they had an effect both polarizing and catalyzing: the potential for fighting—and for casualties—went up. There were no redcoats in this fight, just two groups of neighbors. At Ninety Six there were shouts back and forth, several main fusillades, and then the occasional rifle shot. Williamson's side was running low on water. The Cunningham-Robinson group feared possible attack from the rear by a second group of Whigs. Ultimately the siege turned into a stalemate, with the two sides finally agreeing to recover their dead and wounded and go home.

Both sides withdrew as agreed. The loyalists moved above the Saluda River, and Williamson, gathering up his men, likewise fell back. But

Ninety Six was a turning point. It was a district now conspicuously marked in Whig eyes as a stronghold of the Cunninghams and other loyalists. More, the debate over the constitutional and political issues might continue, but the conflict in South Carolina had turned into one to which the words spoken in debate had been joined by shots fired in anger. Blood had been spilled, and things would not be the same again.

It was a conflict in which the Whig side soon gained the advantage. In late November, a sizeable column of militia was dispatched into the backcountry to bring the loyalists under control. Called the "Snow Campaign" because of its harsh weather and remarkable snowfall, the effort would force the disbandment of loyalist militia units and capture of key leaders. One loyalist unit offered serious resistance but was put to flight after a sharp fight three days before Christmas, on the Reedy River in the northwest corner of the colony and in what is now Greenville County.

The Canebrake/Reedy River Fight
DECEMBER 22, 1775

Following Williamson's withdrawal from Ninety Six, a second force sent by the Council of Safety pushed into the backcountry. It was commanded by seventy-one-year-old militia colonel Richard Richardson.

The force initially numbered some 2,500 men and was drawn from militia units, the regiment of mounted rangers voted on the previous spring, and troops sent by North Carolina. It was also the largest force ever seen in that region; it daily grew even larger. Many loyalists came into Richardson's camp as he advanced, offering to hand over weapons if he would promise to leave their families and farms unmolested. Others, though, occasionally traded rifle shots with the column as it moved into the foothills. The loyalist leader Thomas Fletchall, prominent for his opposition to the lowcountry Whigs, was captured after one of these skirmishes; he was found by Richardson's men, hiding in a hollow tree on Fairforest Creek.

This left only Cunningham and a few others who continued to resist, and these fell back into the Cherokees' territory (to the west of the present-day Greenville-Spartanburg county line). Word soon reached Richardson that their camp was in a canebrake in the bottomlands of the Reedy River. Keen to run Cunningham down, he sent forward a third of his force under Lieutenant Colonel William Thomson of Orangeburg. Thomson was an Indian wars veteran born in Pennsylvania, reared in the South Carolina backcountry, and now in command of the mounted rangers of the Third South Carolina Regiment. The rangers used the darkness to reach the vicinity of Cunningham's camp; Thomson planned to attack at dawn. With his men at the point of surrounding Cunningham, however, the loyalists spotted their attackers. An exchange of shots followed in which six loyalists were struck down instantly. The rangers took a further 130 men prisoner. Cunningham, however, was able to get away, along with a few others.[23]

Crushed and overawed by this loss, at the end of 1775 the loyalists either laid low—or, as did Cunningham's hardcore handful, fled to the Cherokee villages to the west. Some also fled south to the British territory of East Florida. Richardson's Snow Campaign had demonstrated the power of the Provincial Congress to subdue, with numbers and force, the loyalists in the backcountry. Fear of the Cherokees had initially led some in that region to look to the Crown for protection, but opposition to the Whigs led them now to make common cause with these same Indians. Their sense of loyalty to the Crown was only strengthened by this new turn of events.

The Cherokee nation had paid dearly for its support of the losing side in the French and Indian War, and they now saw every reason to support the British against the land-hungry Americans in this latest of the white man's wars.[24] Yet any British plans for unleashing the Cherokees against the Southern frontier had for the moment to be set aside: both the ship earlier seized in Tybee Roads and others like it had been carrying gunpowder intended for the Indians. Without gunpowder, no offensive could be made. Thus, by these early actions—and far more than their handful of casualties might suggest—the side arrayed against the British had won a considerable prize: the control, however tenuous, of the South Carolina backcountry, and quiet along the frontier.

There remained as a visible symbol of Crown authority only the royal governor, Lord William Campbell, still ensconced in his ships in Charleston harbor, considering this plan or that to reestablish control. He was soon joined by another British warship and another royal governor, Josiah Martin of North Carolina, likewise currently unwanted by his constituents and out of a job. Both were running out of options.

While the standoff continued—the royal governors lingering in the harbor, the same Charleston merchants continuing to sell provisions to the British ships as before the troubles—landing parties continued to raid plantations they could reach by water. The Council of Safety repeatedly demanded that any slaves taken—or electing to leave with the British voluntarily—be returned to their owners as runaways. Campbell refused to comply; indeed he soon sent a sloop carrying forty such slaves sailing away. This struck the South Carolinians as an affront against not merely the Council of Safety but against the established order of things.[25]

The council resolved to strike back by finally cutting off the supplies and by sending out rangers. The objective of the rangers was the place on Sullivan's Island which the British used as a watering station for their ships. It was the place as well where the fugitive slaves reportedly were concentrated. This was probably just inland from "the Cove" on Sullivan's Island and at the location of the present-day water tower. The ranger unit selected, styling itself the Raccoon Company, was one given to wearing leggings and breech clouts, and conducting operations in the Indian manner; also, they had experience in dealing with runaway slaves.

A party from this company was landed by boat, in the third week of December and under cover of darkness, at the north end of Sullivan's Island. Attacking at dawn, the rangers exchanged fire with British sailors who were by now trying to get away in boats. The rangers then killed some of the slaves either out of hand or because they resisted—exactly how many or under what circumstances is not clear—and ended up taking a dozen more, as well as some loyalists, prisoner. After burning huts and water casks left behind by the sailors of the *Tamar* and *Cherokee*, they loaded up their captives and departed. Soon, so did Campbell. Early in 1776 he and his warships (Martin had already left) had no choice but to sail across the bar and out to sea.[26]

At the end of the first nine months of war, the South Carolinians— or that element of them ready to oppose British rule through legislative means or action in the field—had won their other great prize. The city of Charleston was theirs. Charleston was the seat of government and trade in their colony, a vital seaport, and the only actual city (that is, one numbering 10,000 or more inhabitants) of that period south of Philadelphia (the largest American city, with 29,000 people). It was one of only five such in all the Thirteen Colonies. British authority had departed South Carolina. The whole colony, from the mountains to the sea, was under the hand and authority of the Provincial Congress.

CHAPTER 2

COUNTERATTACK

1776–1777

On the 4th [of June, we] anchored off Charleston bar. The 5th sounded the bar and laid down buoys preparatory to the intended entrance of the harbor. The 7th all the frigates and most of the transports got over the bar into Five Fathom Hole. The 9th General Clinton landed on Long Island. . . . The 10th the *Bristol* got over the bar with some difficulty. The 15th gave the Captains of the squadron my arrangement for the attack of the batteries on Sullivan's Island, and the next day acquainted General Clinton that the ships were ready. . . . [After being held up by adverse winds, on the] 28th, at half an hour after nine in the morning, informed General Clinton by signal that I should . . . attack.

—Commodore Sir Peter Parker

Aaron Smith's family on Little River, consisting of fifteen souls, male and female, white and black, had all been massacred, except two sons: one of these had escaped to Whitehall, to alarm that settlement whilst the other, hard-pressed by . . . [the Cherokees,] had succeeded in reaching . . . Coranaca Creek [in the vicinity of Ninety Six], and there holding up . . . his mutilated hands, told the fearful tale of the slaughter.

—Address of Samuel McGowen at Erskine College,
August 8, 1855, in John H. Logan manuscript,
A History of the Upper Country of South Carolina,
Historical Collections of the Joseph Habersham
Chapter, DAR (1910)

THE AMERICANS at this point appeared successful almost everywhere—surprisingly so. Far from being on the defensive, they were the ones currently enjoying the capacity to attack at times and places of their own choosing. As in the case of South Carolina, they had successfully thrown

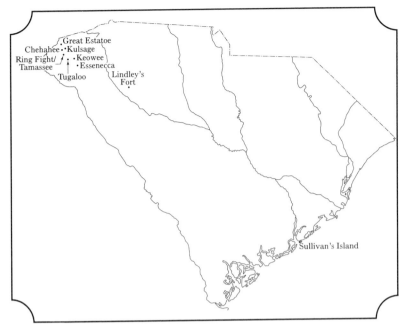

3. ACTIONS IN 1776

out the royal governors and established their own institutions of government. In the north they continued to lay siege to Boston (which the British were to evacuate in March 1776) and had also sent a two-pronged invasion into Canada against Quebec. Yet how long might this string of successes be kept going against the world's paramount power?[1]

Britain was the richest nation in Europe. Long dominant on the seas, the country possessed a navy renowned for its strength and quality. Its army likewise was of high quality, although at 48,000 men only a fraction the size of the Prussian (160,000), the French (180,000), or the Russian (200,000) armies on the European continent. British soldiers were, moreover, responsible for garrisoning an empire that stretched from the New World back to the Old and out to India. Yet it must be only a matter of time before they would choose to return in strength and strike down this rebellion and the rebels who made it. Lord North, the king's leading minister, already favored an approach that he believed would smash resistance wherever offered. Such a strategy found agreement with the king and promised to restore British authority as quickly as possible. At the same time North held out hope that accommodation might somehow be possible. Thus it was that the two new British commanders (brothers, as it happened) appointed to run the war in America—Major General Sir William Howe, commander in chief for the land war and Admiral Richard Viscount Howe, commander in chief for the naval one—were also empowered to negotiate with the rebels. This dual mission to wage war and yet talk peace was consistent with North's hopes for reconciliation, but on British terms. It was, however, hardly in agreement with accepted principles of military command, a point that members in opposition to the policy were quick to make.[2]

Such concern notwithstanding, Whitehall in 1776 set in motion this plan for defeating the Americans. A primary objective was to cut off and isolate New England, regarded as the main source of trouble. The task of cordoning off that region would begin with an attack on New York City. With the mouth of the Hudson River in their hands, a second force would drive the rebels out of Canada and move down via Lake Champlain. The two British forces could then join somewhere in the valley of the Hudson. With that river under British control, the New England colonies would then be cut off, any "rebels in arms" met with dispatched, and the war won.[3]

The offensive required a massive effort: upwards of 30,000 troops (including German units, leased from the Hessian elector because they were cheaper than wholesale expansion of the British Army), substantial naval reinforcements—nearly half the Royal Navy—for operations in North American waters, and all the supplies and munitions necessary to support these forces. In the planning for this offensive, neither the southern colonies nor South Carolina had figured in any large way. And yet they soon did. Time and circumstances provided the opportunity. The first big moves of the 1776 offensive, the attacks against New York and down from Canada, were intended for the summer. But this left plenty of time in the interim. Also, some of the forces being assembled in Britain and elsewhere could be made available sooner than others and could thus be used for earlier operations. North's ministers gave thought to trying something in the south. An effort there would make good use of time and might also yield productive results. To mobilize the loyalists was the goal, but a base was needed by which to rally, organize, and supply them with arms. The ex-royal governors had lobbied both the Howes and North's ministers to the effect that the South was full of loyalists, and that these merely awaited the raising of the king's standard to take up arms against the rebels.

It was the hope of gaining this kind of support that led to the first British venture of the war in the South—and to the first venture against Charleston. The possibilities seemed good. Forces intended for New York could first win a base in the South and then, that task completed and still in good time, sail up the coast for the big attack. Yet the first place intended for this effort was not Charleston but the Cape Fear River region in North Carolina. That situation changed, however, when the loyalists who were to be met were ambushed by Whig militiamen before the promised support could arrive. The British therefore had to look for another objective. Still keen to raise loyalists, they chose Charleston—or more precisely, Sullivan's Island lying at the mouth of its harbor.[4]

The British force comprised a squadron of warships (two 50-gun two-decker "fourth rates," four 28-gun frigates and a half dozen other vessels of substantial potency) plus transports under Sir Peter Parker— fifty sail in all. Parker's two largest ships, *Bristol* and *Experiment*, were ships one class below the dominant warship class of the era, the 60- or- more-gun ship-of-the-line. Four more of his ships, *Soleby, Actaeon, Syren,* and *Sphinx*, were 28-gun frigates, and a fifth was a sloop of war mount- ing twenty guns. In addition to other armed vessels, Parker's squadron also numbered a bomb ketch—a vessel mounting a large mortar and useful for pounding shore fortifications with exploding shells.[5]

A landing force of some 2,500 redcoat soldiers and marines (to be designated Royal Marines in 1802) was available to Major General (later Lieutenant General Sir) Henry Clinton and Lord Charles Cornwallis, his second in command, and sailed in the transports or in detachments (the marines) aboard the men-of-war. The warships were technically not the British "fleet" (Parker was a commodore rather than an admiral, commodores commanding squadrons rather than fleets; and there were no ships-of-the-line) that the Americans later claimed to have repulsed. Yet nothing like its power had ever been seen near Charleston before. Moreover, by that point in eighteenth-century warfare, the Royal Navy and British Army were without peer in their capacity to mount the kind of effort that the situation appeared to call for: a joint operation, amphibious in nature, with the army and navy acting together. In the previous war, for example, the British had been sufficiently good at this sort of endeavor to take such redoubtable points as Louisbourg (1758), Quebec (1759), and Havana (1762). Parker was a seasoned ship-handler, later to be highly regarded in the navy for his role as mentor to the young Horatio Nelson, and a future admiral of the fleet. The expedition against Charleston appeared to offer every prospect for just such another triumph.[6]

And yet Charleston would prove no Louisbourg, no Quebec. Rather, bad luck and fumbles in execution would be the fate of the expedition. Parker's ships arrived off the bar early in June. By then, they had been warned by a reconnaissance party that the American defenses had been improved by the addition of a fort on Sullivan's Island, but that the works on two of the fort's sides were not yet complete. The fortification was made of parallel walls of palmetto trunks raised sixteen feet apart, constructed with embrasures, or firing positions for artillery, and filled in with sand between the logs. The walls were ten feet high. The fort's guns were positioned such that they could sweep the channel leading into the harbor, and bastions were situated at either end of the rampart that paralleled the water.

Unbeknownst to the British, in the American camp there had been division over the wisdom of trying to hold this fort at all. John Rutledge, newly elected president of the Provincial Congress, had pushed forward the work of fortification. In addition to artisans and workers—nearly all of whom were black—he had stationed on Sullivan's Island the gunners of the colony's Fourth Artillery and its Second Regiment of the Continental Line, commanded by the highly regarded William Moultrie. But the American commander in the south, Major General Charles Lee, an experienced ex-British Army officer, had pronounced the place a trap, a slaughter pen. It seemed to him that the British could with ease cut off the fort and destroy it or compel its surrender. Lee told the fort's commander, Moultrie, not to try to hold it, but Moultrie—with Rutledge's backing—was determined. He and his South Carolinians stayed.

Rutledge soon came up with a concession to Lee who, appointed by the Continental Congress, was after all the senior Continental officer present. Certainly Lee, intrigued by theories about partisan or irregular warfare, was regarded by some as bright to the point of brilliance, and indeed had been considered, against Washington, for command of the entire Continental Army. Some, though, found him eccentric and difficult to get along with. Rutledge's compromise gave Lee a role—and also ensured that the fort would be defended by South Carolinians. Lee was placed in overall command of the defenses of Charleston—and Moultrie in charge of the defenses of Sullivan's Island per se. A force of some three thousand men (South Carolinians, North Carolinians, and Virginians), placed at Haddrell's Point in Mount Pleasant, gave Lee a reserve should Moultrie's command on the island be overcome. A bridge of pontoon boats that Lee insisted upon, running over to the island from the mainland, likewise in theory gave Moultrie's men a way out should events go against them.[7]

On the British side, Clinton from the start was more interested in taking Sullivan's Island as a base for loyalists than the larger prize of Charleston itself. Such a step would give the British the base they needed and could be useful also for cutting off Charleston's considerable sea commerce. The city itself could be picked off in due course; further operations could thereafter restore the Southern colonies to British authority. The force of troops available seemed to him too few to take the city either by siege or direct assault. But an island would be far easier to take and, once taken, could be defended and kept supported from the sea. Aggressive promoting by Lord William Campbell helped to convince Clinton that Sullivan's Island was indeed his island.

His naval counterpart, Parker, harbored not a doubt that his ships alone (they carried 270 guns), never mind the soldiers, would be sufficient to batter the South Carolinians into submission. Certainly the British, in the previous war, had taken places whose stone fortifications looked rather more formidable than this log-and-sand fort situated on a low island. The two commanders proceeded in their preparations for attack. Their plan was for the warships to sail in, reach and anchor in firing positions, and then open up in full force on the fort's walls. While the ships so engaged the fort, the troops under Clinton and Cornwallis were to cross over Breach Inlet to Sullivan's Island from the Isle of Palms (then called Long Island, and upon which they would previously be landed) and hit the Americans from the rear—the classic one-two punch. From some source Clinton had convinced himself that the inlet could be forded at low tide. He was sure that, once over the inlet, his men would have no trouble in pushing over the length of Sullivan's Island to reach the fort.[8]

Parker soon had most of his warships and the transport vessels safely over the Charleston bar. The naval force, riding at anchor in an area called Five Fathom Hole, was thus in a position to attack any time wind and tide would permit. The bar itself amounted to a shoal at the mouth of the harbor and was cut by a number of narrow channels. Once across the bar, a vessel could, keeping Morris Island on the left, sail towards the mouth and then pass into the harbor itself. Ships-of-the-line (of which Parker had none) drew too much water to negotiate the bar; merely moving over his two largest ships, *Bristol* and *Experiment*, required a difficult lightening of the ships. Heavy guns had to be lifted out and into support vessels waiting alongside. Then, once the big ships rode high enough, they could be sailed over the bar and the guns recovered. These were tricky steps but accomplished without flaw. The combined naval and military might of the British appeared unstoppable. A proclamation was sent ashore to the rebels, enjoining them to return to their lawful sovereign or face the consequences.

By this point, Clinton had been put ashore on Long Island, searching Breach Inlet for the route by which it could be forded at low tide. He found, rather than the eighteen inches reported, that the inlet was in fact seven feet deep and thus quite impossible to ford. But his attention to the inlet had also drawn the attention of Moultrie, who soon shifted forces to guard against attack from that direction. Placed in charge of these forces was the same William Thomson who had made the attack on Cunningham's camp on the Reedy River the previous December. With Thomson was his Third South Carolina Regiment, as well as North Carolina Continentals, South Carolinians of the militia, and a special unit of backcountry rangers—part of the Third Regiment—that included in its ranks Catawba Indians. Two pieces of artillery were brought up and Thomson's men set to work building entrenchments and a redoubt of bricks and palmetto logs.[9] By now, across from the Americans and on the other side of the inlet, the British were in bivouac among thick oaks and palmettos. Their troops and artillery, landed at the Dewees Inlet some five miles away, had marched down the length of Long Island and were ready to attack.

The Battle of Sullivan's Island
JUNE 28, 1776

From the British perspective, things went wrong almost from the start. Contrary winds held up the attack for two weeks. Second, Charleston and its defenses were more difficult to get at by direct attack from the sea than the attackers supposed. The Americans had exploited these difficulties to the fullest. The harbor was protected by narrow, low-lying

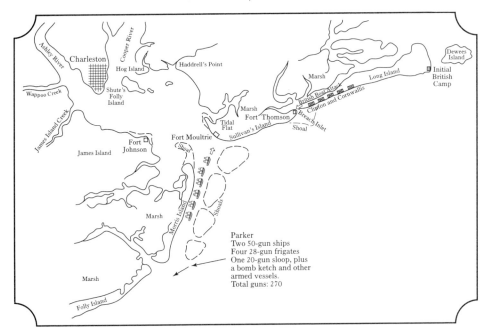

4. SULLIVAN'S ISLAND, JUNE 28, 1776

barrier islands, of which one, Sullivan's, had been well fortified at its channel end by the palmetto-log fort; and, at the other (or "Breach") end, by dug-in infantry and artillery. Many of the infantry, men from the backcountry, were equipped not with smoothbore muskets but with the far more accurate rifle of the frontier. And the channel itself, which cut through the barrier islands to reach the harbor, was narrow and shallow and required the skills of experienced harbor pilots to be negotiated with assurance.[10]

Parker had such pilots and he had the services also of Lord William Campbell, the former Royal Navy post-captain who was himself quite familiar with the harbor's waters. Campbell, at his own request, had been given a place of honor on the lower gun deck of the flagship *Bristol*—a point regarded as dangerous and likely to sustain high casualties in a sea battle.

At nine-thirty in the morning of June 28, Parker signaled the attack by loosing his topsails.[11] His ships, their flags flying, got under way the appointed hour later. At that moment Moultrie was conferring with Thomson at the Breach defenses and, on his horse, had to race back to the fort. He had time to remind his garrison of 400 (perhaps 453?) men—

and especially the gunners—to conserve ammunition and aim for the British ships as their helms were put over to anchor. Moultrie had a total of thirty-one guns available, a mix of British 18-pounders and French 26-pounders (captured by the British from a French warship nearly two decades before, and sent for the defense of the colony). By juggling ammunition, he had a total of twenty-eight rounds (some accounts give a lower figure) apiece for the guns positioned on the critical channel rampart and its bastions.

Parker's bomb ketch, taking up a position off the fort to the south and west, was the first vessel to open fire. The *Bristol* and her consorts sailed in line-ahead to their positions off the fort. Quickly dropping anchor, they fixed spring lines to anchor cables, devices that permitted them to slew about and shift firing position. By a little past eleven on a hot morning, both sides were thundering away at each other in what Moultrie later remembered as a continuous "blaze and roar" of the great guns.[12]

Parker's plan had called for three of his frigates to penetrate into the harbor and catch the palmetto-log fort in a crossfire—or perhaps to engage the American batteries on Haddrell's Point in Mount Pleasant. When the frigates set out to do this, however, two of them managed— probably while on a reaching tack, or sailing so as to gain a favorable angle for getting further into the harbor—to run afoul of each other. In the confusion all three ships ended up aground on the same shoal upon which the U.S. Army's engineer corps would, early in the next century, build Fort Sumter. Two of the ships soon were able to work themselves off. A third, the *Actaeon*, a new ship not a year in commission, could not. After fruitless efforts to pull her off, she was set afire by her crew and abandoned—only to have a party of the defenders later dart out in boats and take her flag, signals, and ship's bell. When the fire finally reached her magazine, the ship blew up.

For some reason, Parker made no further attempt to get any of his ships deep enough into the harbor to hit the palmetto-log fort from the other side. Moreover, the very potent bomb ketch, having sustained internal damage, shortly had to quit firing. Parker's ships instead settled down to firing into the fort, certain their broadsides would kill or ultimately drive the gunners from their guns. The British gunners found momentary encouragement when they saw the fort's blue flag, with its crescent-moon symbol, come fluttering down, its mast sheared in two by a cannonball. Now the flag—either the same flag or one like it that had been raised over Fort Johnson the previous September—lay on the ground outside the fort, directly in the full blast of shot cutting the air or thudding into the ramparts. At this point, Sergeant William Jasper— of whose origins little is known, other than the fact that he had signed up in Georgia—yelled something to Moultrie. Leaping down from an embrasure, Jasper ran forward to snatch up the flag, in full view of the ships and their fire. Jasper got through, his cheering comrades pulling him back into the embrasure. He and Moultrie attached the flag to a makeshift staff—perhaps a sponge or a rammer—and raised it, once again, over the fort. The exchange of fire continued.[13]

Meanwhile, at the other end of the island, Clinton's attack over Breach Inlet had gotten nowhere. Having long since discarded their earlier piece of misinformation that the inlet was fordable by infantry, Clinton and Cornwallis had assembled boats for an amphibious attempt. They had only enough boats to lift a portion of their force at one time. Still, supported by two armed vessels and their troops organized in three brigades, they made their move against Thomson's dug-in riflemen and artillery pieces—only to be repulsed with heavy losses. The tricky shoals in the inlet did their work, with one of the vessels that led the flotilla running aground. Together with the marsh, the sea contrived to funnel the attackers into a single, narrow avenue of approach, one the defenders could cover with rifle fire. At this point the generals either could not come up with or, perhaps more likely, could not get the commodore to cooperate in some workable alternative plan—bypassing the island altogether, for example, and moving against the mainland proper. There were no further attempts to get over the Breach, nor did Clinton try to attack Lee's forces in Mount Pleasant, an option he had earlier considered.[14]

Indeed, the attacks at both ends of Sullivan's Island had by now stalled. At the fort, the broadsides had slammed over and over into the sand-filled ramparts, but the spongy palmetto-log walls held up every time, absorbing these blows without splintering. The defenders had indeed taken casualties, including twelve men killed outright, but these were the merest fraction of the losses suffered in Parker's ships. Moultrie's gunners had concentrated their fire on the two largest ships, *Bristol* and *Experiment*, with grievous effect. Hot shot—metal balls heated red hot and fired from the fort to act as incendiaries—several times threatened to set the two vessels on fire. The *Bristol* suffered still more when a spring line to an anchor cable was cut by a roundshot—with the effect that the ship yawed around, exposing its stern to direct fire. On these two largest ships alone, Parker lost nearly seventy men, and almost 130 were wounded. He himself was twice hit, and two of his captains received wounds from which they would die after the battle. Lord William Campbell was also a casualty; never to recover from the wounds he sustained, he likewise would perish. The fortitude shown by the crews manning the British ships was on a par with that of such famous actions as Lagos and Quiberon Bay nearly two decades prior, or Trafalgar nearly three decades later. There was, as well, plenty of naval talent aboard Parker's vessels. A conspicuous example was Midshipman James Saumarez. One of a galaxy of British naval heroes in the war against Napoleon a generation hence, the teenaged Saumarez—the future Captain Sir James Saumarez and eventual Admiral Lord de Saumarez, Royal Navy—was promoted on the spot to lieutenant by Parker for his conduct in the action against the Americans' palmetto-log fort.[15]

As darkness fell, the commodore broke off the action. At length he recovered Clinton and the landing force—and sailed up the coast to join the British fleet and army gathering under the Howes for the main attack on New York. Neither he nor Clinton had sought ways to outflank Thomson's position or to land troops directly under the support of the squadron's guns. Coordination between the two had been poor or nonexistent. Campbell, knowledgeable of the harbor and better employed guiding the frigates in their all-important move against the fort, had instead been lost in an artillery duel with Americans who, firing from behind their walls, could give better than they got. In short, the advantages of sea power to maneuver, and the firepower that usually so well attended the British in the wars of that period, did not prevail at Sullivan's Island. Through their too-leisurely movements, and forfeiting the possibility of bypassing it to go after Charleston itself, Parker and Clinton had gotten hung up on Sullivan's Island—thereby losing a major opportunity for Britain.

The two generals, Clinton and Cornwallis, would return to Charleston nearly four years later. They would on that occasion take, with methodical, seemingly unstoppable efficiency, the city which had this time defeated them. But the Americans had won for now a huge victory for the Revolutionary cause in South Carolina and in the South. A potentially devastating counterattack had been beaten back, and the British had won no base from which to bring out the loyalists. The political revolution that South Carolina had made had been secured for the moment and an invader repulsed.

The loyalists were thus kept subdued and disheartened, and would remain so until British arms returned in strength to the South. Not so the Cherokees, however. Members of the Cherokee nation received supplies from British posts on the Gulf of Mexico and St. Augustine on the Atlantic. Supported by Crown agents, loyalists, and a handful of warriors from the Creek or other tribes, their decision to fight in summer 1776 would draw South Carolina into a larger frontier war that stretched, north and south, across a thousand miles of wilderness territory. It included as well the new "Over-Mountain" settlements in eastern Tennessee and the even more isolated settlements up the wilderness trails that led to Kentucky. These last were soon the targets of Indian attacks instigated from British forts as far away as the Great Lakes. The attacks against the southern Georgia-to-Virginia sector were mounted with a ferocity that forced many settlers to flee their homes. In South Carolina these settlers withdrew as far back as Ninety Six, until the line that defined the frontier lay on ground previously counted settled and safe. The Indians struck isolated points and did not always bother to discriminate between Whigs, loyalists, or blacks in their attacks.

Frontier warfare was small-scale, savage, and unsparing in its cruelty to combatants and noncombatants alike. Fighting of this type differed from the conventional or European style of the period in a number of respects. One was the remote, forested nature of the arenas where much of the combat took place. A second was that the Indians generally had better knowledge of the ground and of their opponents' movements. On the other hand, firepower and unit cohesion usually favored the whites, especially if the whites had shifted over to the offensive and could force battle. Indian tactics were hit-and-run, seeking to avoid pitched battles and preferring attacks on isolated locations or fighting from ambush. The Indians were elusive and hard to find. For this reason, the whites favored a reconnaissance-in-force approach. As developed during the colonial wars, this technique permitted them to go in strength after the Indians' towns and crops. Scouts and friendly Indians acting as auxiliaries helped guide the main column. This tactic played to the whites' advantage in firepower and forced the Indians to stand and fight—or abandon their villages and reserves of food.[16]

But most of all, warfare on the frontier was fought separate and apart from the conventions that generally governed European armies following the excesses of the Thirty Years' War, ending in 1648. Conventional battles to be sure were bloody, but European warfare of the eighteenth century remained limited as to ends and means. Rules, although frequently breached, at least in theory governed the application of violence, who could be a target, under what circumstances, and so forth. No such rules governed frontier warfare, where everything was fair game. In the war that soon surged across South Carolina's frontier, everything on both sides was fair game.

The Cherokee Attack on Captain James McCall's Camp
JUNE 26, 1776

The frontier war began amidst the various intrigues and diplomatic moves made by the two sides to win over the Cherokees. Two days before Parker hoisted the signal to begin the attack on Moultrie's fort, the Cherokees attacked a party of Whig militiamen and rangers which had entered their territory.

The party was in the process of looking for Alexander Cameron, a Scot, who was deputy to another Scot, the Crown's superintendent for Indian affairs in the South, John Stuart. Stuart, having had to flee Charleston for St. Augustine, had now arrived in Pensacola. But Cameron remained installed with the Cherokees, and the Americans wanted to do something about him before he could stir up trouble. The stakes were high enough that the Continental Congress sent commissioners. The month before, these same commissioners had held meetings with both the Creeks and the Cherokees at Augusta and Fort Charlotte. The meetings were remarkable for the broad promises the Americans offered regarding the security of Indian lands—and the quantity of rum they brought the Indians.

But Stuart had already trumped them. His trains of packhorses laden with powder and lead, sent north to the Cherokees via the Peachtree or other trails on the network of paths leading up from Pensacola, had already been received. By that time, too, delegations from tribes further to the north—Delawares, Shawnees, and the powerful Iroquois nation— had arrived to press the Cherokees to join them in a war that would erupt up and down the length of the frontier. Stuart's own view was that Cherokee participation in such a war would be a disaster for the Indians and a mistake for British policy. When it became clear to him that the Cherokees would go to war anyway, he did everything possible to ensure that their attacks would commence only when they could be coordinated with the effort Parker and Clinton were preparing for the South Carolina coast.

That Cameron was Stuart's chief means of exercising influence over the Cherokees was hardly lost upon the Provincial Congress; hence the decision to send the experienced Captain McCall after him. McCall led a small force whose specific mission was to penetrate the Lower Cherokees' (that is, the branch of the nation living in the foothills east of the mountains) country and find Cameron. Whatever their demeanor or initial reaction to McCall's questions, the Indians permitted the party to proceed through first one and then a second of their towns without incident. These were located in present-day Pickens County. After visiting still another village without incident, McCall's men made their camp some distance beyond, ready to press on next day in pursuit of Cameron.[17]

They reckoned without the Cherokees. A strong body of them fell upon the camp that night, managing to kill four of the militiamen and capturing their commander, McCall, at a cost of half a dozen warriors. The Indians had chosen to attack out of a sense of outrage. The sending of an armed party into their lands was a provocative act that could only have helped the arguments that Cameron and the loyalists were making.

Cameron remained free to continue his work among the Cherokees. On July 1, three days after Parker's and Clinton's unsuccessful attempt against the fort at the mouth of Charleston harbor, the Cherokees joined in a general Indian offensive that fell with particular fury upon South Carolina. McCall himself—who witnessed the death-by-torture of at least one white captive—eventually managed to make his escape, and would go on to play a prominent role in future backcountry operations.

The Cherokee Attack on Lindley's Fort
JULY 15, 1776

A Cherokee and loyalist force, subdividing into parties, swept into the western portions of the province early in July. Its attacks were mainly staged out of the nine Lower Cherokee towns situated in the eastern slope of the Blue Ridge. The raids first struck isolated farms, and next continued eastward into the region between the Broad and Saluda Rivers.

Many of the settlers fell back with their families to the fort located on Rabun (or Rayburn's) Creek, approximately six or seven miles southwest of present-day Laurens. The fort, called Lindley's (or Lyndley's), was one of a number of stockades left over from the Cherokee War of fifteen years before and was hurriedly put into a better state of repair by the refugees.[18]

These refugees were joined by nightfall on July 14 by a company of frontier militiamen. The whole force, now amounting to 150 men, was under the command of Major Jonathan Downs, a militia officer, justice of the peace, and member of the Provincial Congress.

Their attackers appeared before the walls of the fort by next morning. But the Indians had lost the advantage of surprise, and the advantage of the stockade's walls helped the defenders to get the best of the fight that followed. Indeed, Downs soon pursued the Cherokees and loyalists when these broke off to look for easier targets. A running battle ensued, in which the pursuers ended up capturing nine (some sources say eleven) of the loyalists.

It was discovered that these men had "painted up" in vermilion and dressed in the Indian fashion. This apparently was less an attempt to disguise their true identity than to show solidarity with their Cherokee brothers in arms. Moreover, it was a relatively customary practice: both sides sometimes did it. Such behavior was an aspect of the frontier and its type of warfare. It was a situation where two cultures had converged to form a composite one. The weapons, the musket and the long rifle, for example, were European in origin, but many of the techniques for hunting or fighting came from the Indians. The initial phase of white penetration into the wilderness was characterized by roaming groups of hunters making their living from the deer hides and furs they sent back to the settlements. The whites encroached on Indian lands, living sometimes in amity, sometimes in enmity, with the Indians and never greatly fettered by the ties of civilization. When settlers in small family groups moved in, the situation altered; the hunters either settled down or moved on, and the frontier pressed west. This early wild, free, and sometimes violent phase helped to create its own sort of distinctive, frontier-specific blending of Indian and white weapons and styles of fighting.[19]

This present group of "white Indians," as the militiamen referred to them, was marched under guard to Ninety Six. Real Cherokees taken had not gotten off so lightly, being shot out of hand or finished off with the hatchet. The successful defense of Lindley's Fort was indicative of South Carolina's ability to handle on its own resources alone—so long as there was present no substantial force of British regulars—the threat posed by loyalists or by Indians. The counteroffensive soon mounted against the Cherokees proceeded in the manner described above, a reconnaissance-in-force made into their country.

The expedition was small in comparison to the European-style battles that typified the war in more settled areas, but ruthless and without mercy to those caught in its blast. The Lindley's Fort fight was followed up by a campaign that, July through October, utterly destroyed the Indian towns and sources of food in that region. This effort was at the same time matched by Georgia, North Carolina, and Virginia troops who, in like fashion and composition to the South Carolina ones, marauded through other Cherokee holdings in a large sector across the South, laying waste the villages and the fields.[20]

The Ambush at Essenecca/Seneca Old Town
AUGUST 1, 1776

Horrific stories of Indian outrages swelled the militia ranks of the force moving against the Cherokees. The initial column sent out was under the command of Major Andrew Williamson, the same officer who had defended Ninety Six. He was again assisted by Andrew Pickens of the Long Canes region. Williamson and Pickens waited briefly to gather additional men at Dewitt's Corner (now called Due West), a point where the major trading path entered the country of the Lower Cherokees, and then commenced their campaign.[21]

Scouts soon slipped back to confirm that Cameron, accompanied by a party of loyalists, was still with the Cherokees and was camping on the Keowee River, perhaps two days' march away by foot. Williamson determined to go after him. Leaving the rest of the column behind, he took with him a force of 330 militiamen, all well mounted and armed. Accompanying this force were two loyalists the scouts had captured and brought back to use as guides. The plan was for the main body to follow as rapidly as possible.

Williamson moved out before dark on July 31, intending to use the speed of the horses and the cover of darkness to hit Cameron at daybreak. The route he chose was the most direct one, the Keowee Path—in some places a single trail, here and there a web of paths—that would deliver them to where Cameron was camped. Williamson failed to take into account either Cameron's foxiness (he had, after all, dodged the Americans before) or the Cherokees'. The Cherokees may have tracked the scouts back to Williamson's camp, or they may have been looking for just such a move all along. In any event, the Indians were waiting for Williamson at a well-chosen place on his route north. In the early morning hours of August 1, as his column approached the ford at Essenecca, Williamson ran into not just the Cherokees, but also the loyalists and Cameron himself.

The ambush point, Essenecca, apparently comprised two villages—one on the east bank of the Keowee that included the chief's house and other buildings, plus a larger, more populous one on the west bank, with most of the dwellings and a council house. The botanist William Bartram, the Philadelphia Quaker who was a friend of Benjamin Franklin and regarded as America's first naturalist-artist, had passed through Essenecca on the eve of the Cherokee trouble. According to Bartram, Essenecca amounted to 500 people and had relatively open ground, planted in corn, around it. This site was just to the west of what is now the Clemson University campus, and is now under Lake Hartwell.[22]

A wooden fence or palisade of some sort protected the east-bank village. It was from that point that a body of (according to Williamson) some 1,200 Indians—if the figure is correct, a force four times his own—now suddenly opened fire on the mounted militiamen. Firing from the darkness and yelling out war cries that added to the terror of blundering into a trap in the middle of the night, the Cherokees sent Williamson's troops reeling back. A first casualty—significant also because he was the first man of the Jewish faith to fall in this war—was Francis Salvadore (or Salvador), son of a British merchant. A promising individual, Salvadore had, in the period just before the war, become a planter in the Ninety Six area and had already won election as a member of the Provincial Congress. He was hit in the first volley and knocked from his horse. As the militiamen retreated, the Indians fell upon him. While he was still alive, they scalped him and hacked at him with their knives.[23]

Timely action by subordinates saved Williamson's panicked and greatly outnumbered force. First, a handful of men led by Captain (later Colonel) LeRoy Hammond turned and mounted a sudden counterattack. Yelling and spurring their horses, Hammond and perhaps twenty other South Carolinians galloped straight up to the Indians' palisade—

and fired their weapons point-blank at the men on the other side. This stopped the Indians for a moment and gave the rest of the column a chance to rally. Next, Pickens—whose men had heard the firing and came on the run—arrived with the remainder of the force. Taking position on a slight rise of ground in an open area, the militiamen were able to fire into the Cherokees with good effect. Indeed, the Indians chose to fall back after dawn. Presumably, Pickens's arrival had thwarted the Cherokees in their preferred tactic of circling around to hit from behind.

With daylight Williamson resumed his advance. His men moved cautiously back towards Essenecca and the ambush site of hours before. The Indians were by now gone. Reaching the first village, they burned it. They likewise crossed the river to burn the west-bank one as well, but only after the redoubtable Hammond had first ridden over on his horse to confirm that it also had been abandoned. They also put to the torch the Indians' reserves of food for the winter, some thousands of bushels of corn and peas. The Indians' cattle and hogs were either slaughtered or driven off.

Williamson's losses amounted to nearly twenty men killed or wounded. Salvadore was found where he had fallen the night before. He soon died of his wounds. The wounded Cherokee warriors found on the field were immediately scalped (although other Cherokee warriors may have been sold into slavery). The departure of the Parker and Clinton force after Sullivan's Island soon freed units—the Third Regiment or mounted rangers, for example—for service on the frontier, and the counteroffensive against the Cherokees moved into its final phases.[24]

The Destruction of the Lower Cherokee Towns and the Ring Fight
AUGUST 3–15, 1776

A force of Georgia troops also joined the column of militiamen commanded by Williamson and Pickens. When additional militia and provincial troops arrived, John Rutledge, president of South Carolina, advanced Williamson to colonel, the better to command this assemblage of farmers, planters, and frontiersmen now serving as soldiers. Their objective was the Lower Cherokees' eight remaining towns. They would also next attack any towns of the Over-hills or Upper Cherokees (those living west of the mountains) or the Middle Cherokees (those living in western North Carolina) that they could reach before the onset of winter.

Early in August, so reinforced, Williamson led an expedition of 640 men towards the mountains. Additional forces were to follow along when they were ready. Over the days ahead his troops carried out a plan of destruction that saw the main town of the Lower Cherokees, Keowee, burned to the ground. This particular town was located on the west bank of the river of that name, and was a place planted with peach and locust trees. There were numerous cornfields in the vicinity. All was put to the torch, cut down, or otherwise destroyed. Cattle and hogs were slaughtered for the troops' own consumption—or merely so that the Indians would not have them. Also destroyed were other nearby villages or hamlets. With their reserves of peas and corn gone, the Cherokees would have to get through the winter principally on game. Among the Cherokee towns were Chehohee, Estatoe, Eustash, and Tugaloo. Along with other towns and hamlets, these—all abandoned by their inhabitants, whose numbers of warriors could not hope to match the number of fighting men arrayed against them in Williamson's expedition—were likewise torched.

At this point, however, luck very nearly ran out for some of the militiamen. Guided by scouts, one of them half-Indian, Pickens left the expedition's main camp at first light on August 12 (or perhaps August 10 or 11) and set out to explore the territory to the west. His force amounted to twenty-five (some versions add ten more) men, each of them hand-picked for a dangerous mission. Pickens's care in choosing them was warranted. He soon walked directly into another Cherokee ambush, not two miles from Williamson's camp.

He and his men—a reconnaissance patrol acting in advance of the main body—had reached a point in the vicinity of Tamassee (also referred to as Tamassy, or Timossa Old Town), a village within sight of the elevation called Tamassee Knob. The militiamen were making their way across a cornfield, when perhaps as many as 185 Cherokees suddenly opened up from the trees with muskets and rifles. They then rushed forward to try to surround Pickens's men. He yelled for his men to form a circle. According to one account, it was actually a double circle. In this fashion, while the outer circle fired, those men in the inner one could reload weapons or themselves step forward to fire. The Indians likewise formed their own, larger circle in the cornfield, and the two groups blasted away at close range. Hand-to-hand fighting occurred when the Indians tried to break through. Some accounts say that muzzle-blasts on this scorching day set the brush on fire.[25]

This tactic of the "Ring Fight" was successful enough to win time for Pickens's brother, Joseph, to hear the gunfire and race up with a relief force. The Cherokees retreated into the woods after exchanging shots with the second group of militiamen. Pickens's own rifle had misfired or been damaged and he had had to use that of his Indian scout, fallen in the first exchange of shots. The fight in the cornfield had produced high casualties. Pickens lost six men immediately, and five more who died later of their wounds—a third of his force if the figure of thirty-five is correct, or more if the figure of twenty-five is the correct one. The Cherokees lost sixty-five men plus fourteen wounded warriors left behind. The day was by now approaching noon. Pickens's men buried their dead in the Indians' abandoned houses in Tamassee. They then set the village and all its buildings on fire. Regarding the fate of the Cherokee wounded left on the field, one of the militiamen who survived the fight told relatives years later that he had killed any Indians he could get a shot at and had scalped any he had killed.[26]

The full expedition resumed its campaign of destruction. The Ring Fight proved the largest clash with the Cherokees since the Essenecca ambush. Cherokee losses in these two actions were, as a proportion of that nation's warrior strength of some 356 men in the Lower Towns and approximately two thousand warriors in the nation overall, crippling. Williamson kept up the momentum, soon building a fort on the site of the destroyed Essenecca and naming it Fort Rutledge after South Carolina's president. In the months that followed, he pressed on westwards, ultimately joining forces with columns of North Carolina militia, the further to harry the Cherokees. Williamson's men eventually burned to the ground every Cherokee town they could reach short of the Overhills' capital of Chotee on the headwaters of the Chattahoochee. Counting the operations mounted by South Carolina, Georgia, North Carolina, and Virginia forces on both sides of the mountains, perhaps two thousand Cherokees—only a fraction of whom were warriors—perished, in the main from hunger and exposure to the cold rather than death in combat. Some who survived fled to take refuge with the Creeks. In the next year, 1777, a number of them sued for peace, and they eventually gave up their lands in South Carolina. Many who did not were joined by Creek warriors and continued to fight on. They remained a threat to the frontier for the rest of the war, but they could not win. Even supported by British supplies and occasionally by loyalists, they were too

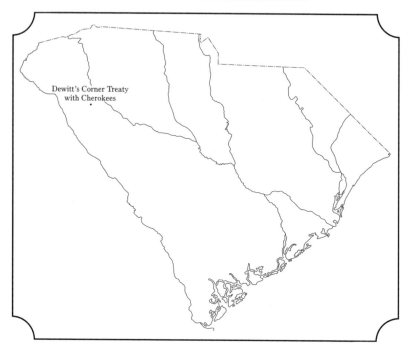

Dewitt's Corner Treaty
with Cherokees

5. ACTIONS IN 1777

few to prevail against the advancing wave of Americans lapping against
their territory.[27]

Another wave advanced in that summer of the Sullivan's Island and
Cherokee fights. The cause for which the war was being fought had
changed, marking a rising tide of American nationalism. South Carolina's
delegation to the Continental Congress was heard from. These men—
Arthur Middleton, Edward Rutledge, Thomas Lynch, Jr., and Thomas
Heyward, Jr.—joined with others to sign the Declaration of Independence, a step that followed the adoption earlier of a resolution for a
break with Britain. This action signified in clear and unequivocal terms
that the goal for which the Americans fought now was altered from
mere restoration of rights to separation from British rule altogether.

Also, South Carolina in this same period became not a colony but a
sovereign state in its own right. New constitutions adopted in 1776 and
in 1778 converted the Provincial Congress into a two-house General
Assembly. A substantial concession to the backcountry was the step of
disestablishing the Anglican or Established Church. This move, along
with representation and the provision of an effective system of courts

and jails, was very important to winning the support of that region. Together, these measures added up to no less than a hand extended, a way to try to bring the two regions together. It was a necessary step if the two areas, lowcountry and backcountry, were to be fused into one single—and loyal—whole. Nor did the new state balk at imposing this solidarity through measures harsh as well as soft. The legislature passed an act requiring all white males to take an oath in which they had to pledge their loyalty to South Carolina. Any male citizen who did not, but chose rather to keep allegiance to the British king, had to leave. Men in this category were given one year in which to sell their property and depart.[28]

From 1776 onward, with the failure of the British naval thrust at Charleston and the defeat of the Indians on the frontier, South Carolina was free to do as it chose in the work of building a unified polity by joining in purpose and goals the powerful men of the lowcountry with the new men of the backcountry. How well this process had worked, and the degree of unity it had achieved, would ultimately face the harsh test of British invasion. But that test was well in the future. For the majority, the news of independence rode on a surge of patriotic feeling and euphoria. In Charleston, both Independence Day and the victory at Sullivan's Island (designated Palmetto Day, June 28), were greeted with celebration, parades, and martial music. The seal of the new state showed a palmetto tree positioned above a horizontal oak, the oak symbolizing the British navy and, by its position, the American victory over it. Following a year of war, the British had been driven from South Carolina's soil and that state had joined a new, independent nation.[29]

The best part of a thousand miles to the north, however, all pretension to independence by South Carolina—or any of the Thirteen— nearly came to an end in the British offensives of 1776 and 1777. These began with the long-prepared attack on New York. Washington had never seen a pitched battle in the European style, and the quality of his generalship was not equal to the task of defeating the British as they maneuvered against him. The American army was nearly cut off, and the end of the rebellion seemed within the British grasp. When Washington at length retreated across the Delaware, the British awaited the onset of winter weather to finish off the rebel army. But Washington proved a more resourceful commander than that. On Christmas night, he and his soldiers struck back, recrossing the river to hit the Hessians holding

Trenton. The other part of the British plan—the move down from Canada via Lake Champlain—had likewise failed to achieve its intended results. By constructing a fleet of row galleys and other armed vessels, the Americans had forced their opponents to do the same. A single battle was fought—at Valcour Island in October—but by then the season was far advanced. The good campaigning weather was gone, and the British attack from the north had for the moment been halted.[30]

The 1777 offensive likewise focused on concentrating British forces in the valley of the Hudson River. This new version of the offensive, given additional forces and to be carried out by Major General John Burgoyne, found favor with the North ministry and with the king. A critical element was that British troops should advance up the Hudson from New York so as to support Burgoyne's main push as it came down from Canada. But the plan soon unraveled. Rather than vesting General Howe with the power of a true theater commander in chief, the North ministry, trying to run the war from London, permitted an alteration to the plan. Rather than acting to support Burgoyne as originally intended, British forces in New York would instead move by sea to attack Philadelphia, the American capital. Despite Washington's best efforts, he proved unable to defend that city or to retake it after the British had won it. But the Continental Congress simply reconvened at York, Pennsylvania, a place safely distant from the king's soldiers, and the war went on.[31]

It would be the thickly forested regions of New York below Lakes Champlain and George where the British plan would meet its final disaster. There, in a series of battles, Burgoyne and his army were isolated and trapped. His army reduced to half rations, he tried to break out but failed. In October 1777 he surrendered to the American general, Horatio Gates, at Saratoga. Burgoyne's army, a force in excess of five thousand men, did not capitulate outright; rather, it was technically handed over by the convention of promising not to fight again in North America: its soldiers laid down their arms and were to be shipped back to Britain. The fact remained, however, that the British had lost an army in the field. The victory at Saratoga was Britain's costliest loss of the war. It was also the single most important battle and, indeed, the turning point of the American Revolution. It was to prove the only large, unassisted American victory of the war.[32]

The victory converted the war from a struggle between an imperial mother country and her thirteen American colonies into a general conflict involving great powers. Early in the new year, 1778, the news of Saratoga helped sway the French, hungry for revenge after the Seven Years' War, to sign a treaty of alliance with the Americans. The war was now a colonial war that had expanded into a contest between rival powers, and Britain would have to confront far-flung military priorities in addition to those in America. Unlike during the Seven Years' War, there was no William Pitt in the ministry to forge an effective alliance with a Continental European power, as Pitt had done with Prussia. Instead, Britain stood virtually alone. Other powers, such as Spain in 1779 and Holland in 1780, would soon join France outright, or would confront Britain through a posture of chilly neutrality. Saratoga had changed the American Revolution into a world war in which the king's ministers were forced to look to the defense of other parts of the empire and of the home islands.[33]

In the face of this very great reversal, the war in America became for the British a secondary theater. They yet sought some new approach, some new strategy, by which they might still hope to win. Because of this, the war would again come to South Carolina, a place since 1776 free of war and where patriotic feeling ran high, but where the ranks of the Continentals were growing increasingly hard to fill.

CHAPTER 3

THE WAR COMES SOUTH

1778–1779

The English, controlling now the sea . . . determined to shift the scene of the continental war to the Southern States, where there was believed to be a large number of loyalists.

—Captain Alfred Thayer Mahan, *The Influence of Sea Power Upon History, 1660–1783* (1890)

The *coup d'oeil* of a general is the talent . . . of conceiving in a moment all the advantages of the terrain and . . . [being able to perceive] at first glance the weak spot of the enemy.

—Frederick II of Prussia

FACED NOW WITH a war against great-power rivals as well as the Americans, Britain stood on the defensive. The prospect of French invasion loomed. Ships and troops had to be shifted to cover a variety of threatened points: Canada, Florida, the West Indies—the British Isles themselves. Loyalists and a greater reliance on the navy were meantime to take up the slack in the war in America. For the first time the navy was directed to mount a full blockade from Maine to Georgia. French and Dutch ships had heretofore been able to run war materiel to American ports, Charleston in particular. Swarms of American privateers (armed civilian vessels acting as commerce raiders under a letter of marque) had likewise been able to prey from that port or others on Britain's merchant fleet.[1]

The British turned attention to their command structure. Surely defeat on the magnitude of Saratoga must have a culprit or two. The North ministry had long been under attack for its handling of the war; the loss of a whole army, however, was quite another matter. Lord George Germain, the Secretary of State for the Colonies, seemed an obvious target. Acting under North, he was the individual in the cabinet directly responsible for coordinating the war in America. He was as well a man whose own military past was not unassociated with controversy. Twenty years before, after the battle of Minden in the Seven Years' War, he had been court-martialed for disobedience of a direct order given under fire—a serious charge for an active-duty officer, which he, a colonel, then was. But Germain held George III's confidence and upon leaving the British Army, he began, through ability and effort, a rapid rise in political life. Success in that career had brought him finally to a secretary of state–level position and the ability to function as, in effect, war minister against the Americans. Most importantly, though, Germain continued to hold the king's confidence even after Saratoga. He thus held his place while General Howe received most of the blame. Soon the ministry replaced Howe with the supposedly more aggressive Henry Clinton, now a lieutenant general and wearing the red ribbon of a Knight of the Order of the Bath. North made no changes at the level above Clinton; thus the Earl of Sandwich, First Lord of the Admiralty and cabinet-seat head of the navy, kept his post.[2]

The new commander in chief had previously been Howe's second in command. He was familiar with America from his youth, when his father had served as a royal governor of New York. At age 48 in 1778, he was two years older than Washington. Some historians think he was the most capable general on the British side, a soldier of quick understanding and excellent grasp of the military situation. Certainly he put forward a thoughtful and promising proposal: that an overall commander be appointed, this individual with the power to direct all British forces in America and the Caribbean. Since the British were now having to operate in both zones at the same time, the idea made sense. Taking such a step would in theory have given them, for the first time in the American war, a true theater commander. But Germain would not hear of it. He continued instead to direct the war from London—an approach that had worked for Pitt in the French and Indian War, but in this one had resulted in Saratoga.[3]

Clinton had little time for such high-level policy considerations as the good campaigning weather of 1778 began. On the American side, Washington's army had suffered through its bitter winter at Valley Forge. Now, with recruits being trained, regiment by Continental Line regiment, in the new standardized methods devised by the self-styled

"Baron" Frederick William Augustus von Steuben of Prussia (given a general-officer's commission by the Americans), Washington's army was eager for battle. Clinton was not unready for battle himself. At the same time, however, he faced more problems than just dealing with Washington. The French might soon send a naval force of some strength across the Atlantic, and it was to be presumed that this force would endeavor to work closely with the Americans. Clinton would be in a fix should he be caught, forces divided, trying to hold New York and Philadelphia at the same time. Ultimately (and before the French threat materialized), the decision was made to abandon Philadelphia and consolidate forces at New York.[4]

It was towards that key base that Clinton and his army set out, marching across New Jersey. Washington moved forward in pursuit. He placed his lead elements under Charles Lee, the same officer who had informed Rutledge and Moultrie in 1776 that trying to hold the palmetto-log fort was lunacy. Lee made no plan and briefed no subordinate commanders. On June 28, two years to the day after the Sullivan's Island battle, his men blundered into the tail of the British column at Monmouth Court House. The redcoats quickly counterattacked to give the Americans the fight they had been looking for, and then some. Much of the fighting at Saratoga had been in deep woods, where Daniel Morgan's corps of Southern riflemen were in their element. This, however, was a battle in the conventional European style. The Americans had to shoot it out at close range and fight with the bayonet in the same linear formations as their opponents. This they managed to do, holding their line until the British chose to disengage and resume the march northward.[5] At the end of the day the Americans were left to take pride in their performance. Clinton and the British took pride in the fact that they had been able, despite being outnumbered, to stop their pursuers long enough to get to Sandy Hook and then by sea to New York.

With Clinton thus safely ensconced in a very strong base, Washington's hope was for the arrival of a French fleet. He had in mind a grand cooperative effort. That fleet was crucial to him, since sea power—in the classic sense of a battle-fleet navy able to dominate or "command the seas"—was a thing the Americans lacked. Only the French fleet could give Washington the sea power he needed to attack Clinton's strongly fortified, difficult-to-get-at position. Yet his hopes were to be dashed. A French fleet under Admiral the Count d'Estaing arrived in due course, but in a succession of efforts, it failed to defeat the British fleet (which it outnumbered). Count d'Estaing's fleet was able to gain victory neither at New York nor at Newport, Rhode Island, where a cooperative effort with the Americans was undertaken to gain that key position. Instead, the French fleet finally gave up on the Northern theater and sailed south to the Caribbean—and out of the Americans' war. D'Estaing was eventually successful in capturing St. Vincent and Grenada from the British in the West Indies, but Washington and his army were left to dig in at West Point on the Hudson, from which position they kept watch on Clinton in New York.[6]

And so, as matters stood while 1778 drew to a close in the North, the British had been able to deflect the French fleet and hang on to New York. While no one could have known at the time how events would develop, it turned out that Monmouth was the last major battle in which Washington faced the British without the presence of his French allies on the field; in fact, it was to be his last battle for three and a half years. The French fleet, upon which he had counted so mightily, had arrived but had soon departed. Absent this fleet, the Americans had little prospect of being able to attack Clinton. For his part, Clinton would not be lured into the hinterland and to a second Saratoga. The war in the Northern theater slowed to stalemate.

For that matter, it seemed to some in Whitehall that decisive victory in America was by now an outcome beyond Britain's grasp. Rather, the war appeared likely to end in negotiation. The right course was therefore to be in the best possible position when the parties came to the table. This meant holding as many chips as possible—*Southern* chips. New England might indeed be the epicenter of the rebellion, but by this point of the war it was a strategic nut too hard to crack. Amphibious raids might hurt its coast and the Royal Navy ravage its shipping, but the fact remained that New England was clearly lost.

Not so the Southern colonies. These—and again the ex-royal governors were heard from—offered hope of loyalists awaiting the call to arms. One group of Americans could be mobilized against another. An equally powerful attraction was that the Southern colonies produced commodities that Britain's economy needed: indigo, rice, tobacco, naval stores. The final factor was that it was now possible to move against these colonies. It had not been before, given the presence of the French fleet. But that fleet had departed, leaving the British the strategic beneficiaries of the situation. Their fleet once again enjoyed command of American waters, an advantage permitting free and widespread movement. It was recognized that this dominance might be temporary. The Royal Navy's first priority must be defense of the English Channel, leaving only a few ships for service in American waters. In this game of shifting ships between Europe and America, the French fleet would be able to return in powerful numbers. The British would in the meantime have to look over their shoulders in anything they did. But for now they could move at will—and retain the offensive. They could load up troops at New York and dispatch them down the coast to strike at any point they wanted.[7]

So, for a combination of reasons, the South was seen as an arena where military efforts might yet avail. If the British could seize these colonies from the bottom up, from Georgia to Virginia and then perhaps gaining control of the Chesapeake, they could come to the negotiating table in a very strong position indeed. It was a view greatly encouraged by early successes. In late December 1778, a British force from New York succeeded in capturing Savannah, capital and first city of Georgia. The officer in command boasted that he had been the first to "strip a star and a stripe" from the Americans' new flag.[8] Georgia was the youngest (founded in 1733) and among the least populous of the colonies. The British believed they could easily control it by holding two points: Savannah, its principal community and now theirs; and Augusta, located upriver at the head of navigation of the Savannah River and within reach of the country of the Cherokees and the Creeks.

This step set in motion Britain's new strategy of shifting the war to the South. It placed South Carolina squarely in the path of invasion. Clinton might toy with plans for defeating Washington in some decisive battle in the Northern theater, but his main effort was now to be made in the South. A second force, this one under Major General Augustine Prevost, was brought up from St. Augustine to reinforce the one at Savannah.[9] This action so inspired loyalists in Georgia and South Carolina that they began coming in to the British in substantial numbers. Might Whitehall's hopes for raising the loyalists come to something after all?

On the other side of the Savannah River, South Carolina by 1779 had enjoyed almost three years free of British rule and authority. Save in the form of occasional Indian activity along the frontier and Royal Navy

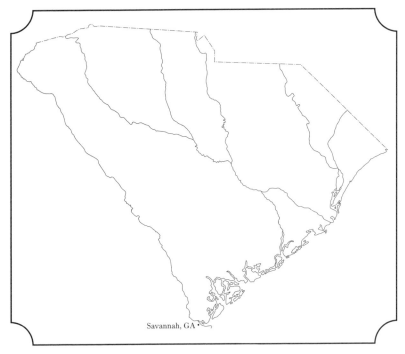

Savannah, GA

6. ACTIONS IN 1778

ships cruising the coast, it had been free of British menace as well. But now it had to confront the return of war. John Rutledge understood the peril and moved to stir the state's forces to activity. Militia units under Andrew Pickens soon took the field against loyalists trying to reach the British. A substantial body of these was intercepted and defeated at Kettle Creek near present-day Washington, Georgia. Five captured loyalists were hanged when they reached Charleston. This act established a precedent the British and loyalists would honor by paying back in kind whenever the occasion permitted. In this same period Congress acted to appoint a new overall commander for the Americans in the South. Major General Benjamin Lincoln was a Massachusetts man who had been wounded in the Saratoga campaign, and had a solid record as a planner and organizer.[10]

Upon his arrival he acted to gather forces at Purrysburgh, a point a dozen miles up the river from Savannah on the South Carolina side and twice that distance from Beaufort to the east. Lincoln soon had 3,500 men assembled. He contemplated a move against Prevost at Savannah.

Grays Hill/Port Royal Island
FEBRUARY 3, 1779

The capable Prevost, however, was too quick for Lincoln. Making the most of the small squadron of vessels available, he landed a force of two hundred redcoats under a Major Gardiner at Beaufort. The news that the British had outflanked him by this amphibious stroke against South Carolina's second oldest city forced Lincoln to send out the hero of the palmetto-log fort fight, William Moultrie. Certainly Moultrie knew the country and could be relied upon to get the best out of the local militia.[11]

Moultrie soon crossed the ferry over Whale Branch, the Coosaw River, to arrive on Port Royal Island. He had with him a force of three hundred men, the bulk of them militia plus a handful of Continentals. At least a few of the militiamen had earlier seen Continental service. His artillery consisted of two six-pounders and a smaller gun.

Gardiner, meanwhile, had moved over the island to occupy a position about three miles south of the ferry. This point, called Grays Hill, was a low hill that in the lowcountry amounted to a piece of high ground. Gardiner's own artillery comprised a single gun. He deployed his infantry and this one gun across the hill just inside the treeline and awaited the Americans.

The Americans began their attack with artillery fire, the infantry then opening up on redcoats they could see firing from among the trees. A hot fire at close range inflicted casualties on both sides (in fact, over 15 percent of the American force and perhaps even more of the British one) and knocked out the British gun. Running low on ammunition, both sides decided to withdraw at about the same time. The fact that the British withdrew first—and the excellent performance of the militia, which had managed to stand and fight in tight ranks against the redcoats—enabled the Americans to claim the victory. Commanding troops in the action were two captains, Thomas Heyward and Edward Rutledge (younger brother of the governor), who as members of the Continental Congress had each signed the Declaration of Independence over two years before.

Gardiner fell back with his men to Beaufort and eventually to Savannah. This boost to American morale encouraged Lincoln to try and recapture Augusta. But again, Prevost was too quick for him, deciding to take the bold step of advancing on Charleston itself. His army amounted to 2,400 troops, a substantial portion of them regulars. Left to oppose him was Moultrie, whose own numbers of 1,200 included two hundred

Continentals and the rest militia. Moultrie quickly abandoned the old position of Purrysburgh and fell back to the northeast to the Tullifinny River.[12]

Coosawhatchie
MAY 3, 1779

This new point offered the advantage of a slight rise near a bridge from which the road to Charleston could be watched. Moultrie was careful to leave a screen of outposts to cover other locations where rivers, including the larger Coosawhatchie to the south, could be crossed.

That critical outpost he entrusted to Lieutenant Colonel John Laurens, aged twenty-four, the highly regarded son of Second Continental Congress president (following John Hancock) Henry Laurens. The younger Laurens, educated in Switzerland, until the war began had intended to study law in London. He would, however, as a Continental Army officer prove a fire-eater in actions ranging from Brandywine to Yorktown. Moultrie reinforced Laurens with riflemen and, presumably, cautioned him concerning the tricky business of conducting rear-guard actions.[13]

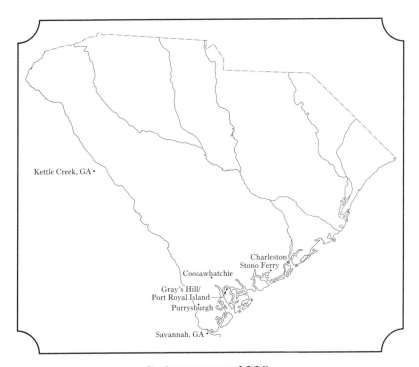

7. ACTIONS IN 1779

More to the point, he gave Laurens specific instructions about getting the outpost, now amounting to 350 men, pulled out and back across the river before the British could arrive in force to cut it off. What Laurens chose to do, however, was not to withdraw but to advance over the Coosawhatchie and meet the British head on. The British were soon able, by taking position in a plantation house and its outlying buildings, to fire with great effectiveness on the Americans. Laurens had deployed his men in the open, where they took heavy casualties but were able to inflict few on their opponents. At length, after Laurens himself was wounded in the arm, the American force withdrew across the river.[14]

Moultrie now began conducting a withdrawal up the road to Charleston. His was the only force between Prevost and the city. The Americans burned bridges or destroyed ferry boats in an effort to delay Prevost's advance and win time for Lincoln—at last recognizing the peril to Charleston—to give up on Augusta and return to the lowcountry.

The Attack on Charleston
MAY 11–JUNE 18, 1779

Prevost's redcoats took only five days to march from Port Royal Island to the west bank of the Ashley River. Crossing the river on May 11, Prevost the next day summoned Charleston to surrender. The arrival of a British army threw the city into consternation, and some leading citizens made an offer of neutrality. This offer Prevost promptly declined. Prevost had too few men actually to carry it off, but he—despite daily bouts with fever—opted to go through the motions of preparing to lay siege. Yet this second British attempt on Charleston soon ended. Lincoln arrived at last with superior numbers to push Prevost back.[15] Lincoln, however, and the pursuing Americans were to be brought up short in a vicious engagement fought in the third week of June.

If the British had found themselves somewhat unbalanced by South Carolina's coastal islands in their first move against Charleston in June 1776, this time they were quick to exploit them for their own purposes. Lacking the full force of warships and transports that had accompanied Parker and Clinton on that other occasion, Prevost had now only a small flotilla of vessels to rely upon. Not only did Prevost have only the smallest fraction of the firepower available to that other force, he had insufficient "lift"—vessels—with which to transport his forces; he could carry only a portion of his army at a time. The concern was that the Americans

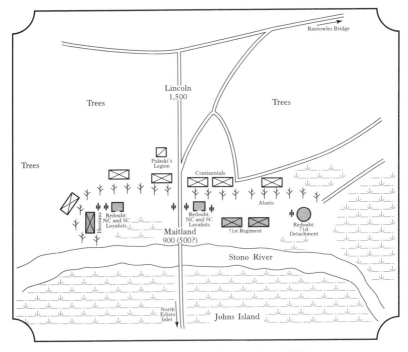

8. STONO FERRY, JUNE 20, 1779

would—just as he had hoped to do to them at Coosawhatchie—try to cut off a rear guard or some small fraction of his force before it could fall back.

His response to this danger was to use the islands and the small number of vessels available to improvise a route of withdrawal. By this means he could hope to let his army escape from Lincoln's superior numbers. He would do so by island-hopping back down the coast to Beaufort and, finally, to Savannah. Outposts would cover one island while his troops were, in stages, ferried over to the next, until at last the entire body was safely evacuated to the next point.

Stono Ferry
JUNE 20, 1779

By far the most critical of these outposts was the one guarding Stono Ferry. At most an hour's march from the bridge at Rantowles and the road coming from Charleston, this was the ferry by which the Stono River was crossed from the mainland over to John's Island. After Prevost evacuated his army from Charleston and over to James Island, John's

Island was his obvious next stop. Certainly the Americans recognized this fact as well. Lincoln had so far shown no particular zeal in seeking battle around Charleston. He now, however, moved with new aggressiveness in the hope of hitting the Stono outpost. His plan was to attack and overcome the British with overwhelming force. While he went for Stono Ferry from the mainland, Moultrie, given an additional force, would cross the river so as to cut off the British on John's Island.

Commanding the British rear guard at Stono Ferry was Lieutenant Colonel John Maitland. His force of nine hundred men included the Highlanders of the 71st Regiment, a battalion of Hessian infantry, quasi-regular units of loyalist volunteers from North and South Carolina, and six pieces of artillery. His position was located on the mainland bank of the river and was approximately seven hundred yards long. It was perhaps 175 yards deep, and protected on its right flank by marsh. Dense woods bordered the road coming from Rantowles Bridge. Maitland's men—and slaves pressed into service from local plantations—felled trees. These, with their branches sharpened and laid so as to point outward, formed a protective tangle or *abatis*—the eighteenth century's version of barbed-wire. Slight rises in the ground were likewise exploited by building wood and earthworks redoubts or strong points—two rectangular, the other round, for a total of three—from which infantry could fire from cover.[16]

Lincoln and the Americans, a thousand (or perhaps 1,500) strong, advanced on this point by a march conducted at night in order to achieve surprise and also to take advantage of the cooler temperatures. Moving through the trees near first light, the American light infantry exchanged fire with British sentries. With dawn, a general fire erupted all along the fort's perimeter. Attacking its left were light infantry, a large body of militia, and the mixed-forces, infantry-cavalry "legion" commanded by the Polish officer Casimir Pulaski; attacking its right were the Continentals and light infantry commanded by Brigadier General Isaac Huger of South Carolina. A force of Virginia militia made up the American reserve.

By now the artillery of both sides—the Americans had four guns—was in action and casualties began to mount. When the Americans under Huger reached the abatis and appeared at the point of swarming into the position, Maitland's Highlanders countered them. Huger was wounded. The Hessians likewise, at the other end, were bolstered by the

Highlanders, whom Maitland quickly shifted to threatened points. At length, and on a morning where heat and thirst felled men (one of them an older brother of Andrew Jackson) almost as effectively as artillery and small arms, Lincoln decided to withdraw. As he did so the fiery Maitland came after him with the Highlanders, until they were stopped by an American cavalry charge and the Virginia militia.[17]

Moultrie, with a second force, had meanwhile been unable to get enough boats to cross the Stono and advance in time to influence the outcome. Both sides paid a steep price for the battle: 150 (or perhaps 165) Americans killed or wounded, and 130 on the British side. The Americans had suffered a sharp defeat and the British were able to continue their withdrawal down the islands unimpeded.

Prevost fell back to Savannah but left a garrison—under Maitland—to hold the outlying position of Beaufort on Port Royal Island. The British had gained important information regarding the routes and southern approaches to Charleston. In London, Germain concluded from Prevost's ability to move so easily through South Carolina's hinterland that the rebel government lacked support among the people. American charges that Prevost's troops had looted plantations were met with British denials.[18] As the lowcountry summer came on in full force, the two sides settled into their respective positions to await the return of cooler weather in the fall.

Also returning in the fall was the French fleet under d'Estaing. Arriving from the Caribbean, its commander made the decision to assist the Americans in the southern theater rather than proceeding north to help Washington as originally planned. This was a courageous decision indeed, given that the height of the hurricane season would find his fleet on the Georgia coast. And yet he would prove no more successful in this theater than in the Northern one. His ships carried troops and substantial quantities of supplies, and he landed these to join an American force now moving to retake Savannah. South Carolina's investment in this force was considerable, and included Moultrie, Isaac Huger, John Laurens and Francis Marion. The French and the Americans, supported by d'Estaing's fleet and with the admiral himself leading a major assault, attacked on October 9. Though heavily outnumbered, the British managed to hold on in well-prepared fortifications. They counterattacked with grenadiers and marines. These managed to beat back their opponents, with heavy losses on both sides. One of those who fell was the same

Sergeant Jasper who had, under British fire, raised aloft South Carolina's flag at Sullivan's Island three years before—and had been given Rutledge's own sword in honor of his courage. In the end, the attackers had to fall back. D'Estaing had fought heroically and been badly wounded. Savannah was to be his last effort in America. With his ships he set sail to head, finally, back to France.[19]

The holding of Savannah was important to the British, but this second departure of a French fleet vastly more so. It opened the way for what came next: a full-scale effort against South Carolina. The situation obtaining in the North had not substantially altered. Washington remained fifty miles up the Hudson; Clinton was secure in his base at its mouth. But British fortunes much closer to home had meantime greatly improved. The entry of Spain into the war as France's ally had made it possible for these two powers to combine their fleets—and sail north into the Channel with the purpose of smashing the fleet that protected Britain. But no such invasion happened. The French and Spanish fleets botched the attack, wasting the summer maneuvering at sea. A Spanish attempt on Gibraltar was soon defeated. The Gordon riots in London—instigated by Lord George Gordon's railings against "Romanism"—were put down by redcoats, and this or that disturbance in Ireland or Scotland had been effectively dealt with.[20]

The center of their empire safe, the British could more easily turn to operations on its periphery. Clinton therefore, in autumn 1779, commenced the steps to send a fleet and an army south. He reckoned that the time available, even should the French try again with a fleet, would still be adequate to seize major objectives in South Carolina.[21] With those in his control, he could thereafter leave a strong garrison and return to New York with the balance of his troops. His deputy, a German general serving with the British, would meantime hold New York's fortifications with a force too strong for the Americans to overcome.

General George Washington and his commanders sought always to build an army of American regulars, the Continentals, able to stand up to the redcoats in terms of training, discipline, and unit cohesion. Any American general who sought to win in South Carolina, however, would have to devise means of effectively employing the large but not always reliable forces of part-time citizen-soldiers available, the militia. Illustration from John Grafton, *The American Revolution: A Picture Sourcebook* (New York: Dover Publications, 1975), p. 83.

The first rifles arrived in South Carolina by about 1750, carried south in the stream of backcountry settlement coming from Pennsylvania and Virginia. They were ideal weapons for frontier fighting, as depicted here. As weapons for infantry combat, however, their superior range and accuracy had to be weighed against the musket's superior rate of fire (perhaps three shots per minute against the rifle's one) and capacity to mount a bayonet for shock action. The musket could also shoot prepackaged "buck-and-ball," making it deadly for close-range fighting. Illustration from John Grafton, *The American Revolution: A Picture Sourcebook* (New York: Dover Publications, 1975), p. 140.

Major General William Moultrie, by Rembrandt Peale, oil on canvas, Gibbes Museum of Art/Carolina Art Association, Charleston, S.C. On June 28, 1776, Moultrie, then a colonel, was convinced that the palmetto log-and-sand fort that he commanded at the mouth of Charleston harbor could and should be held.

On June 28, 1776, Major General Henry Clinton commanded the British force that sought to attack Moultrie's fort by crossing over from Long Island (the Isle of Palms). An insightful strategist, Clinton nearly four years later achieved Britain's biggest success of the war in America—the conquest of Charleston and the supposed reestablishment of British authority in Georgia and South Carolina. He was, however, increasingly hampered by indecision and the convoluted command structure by which the North ministry conducted the war from London. Miniature portrait of Sir Henry Clinton, watercolor painting by Thomas Day, courtesy of The R. W. Norton Art Gallery, Shreveport, Louisiana, used by permission.

A View of the Attack Made by the British Fleet under the Command of Sir Peter Parker. Commodore Parker's ships—the largest two being the 50-gun two-decker "fourth rates," *Bristol* and *Experiment*—hammer the palmetto-log fort on Sullivan's Island, June 28, 1776. Royal Navy and British Army forces had in the previous war taken such formidable positions as Louisburg, Quebec, and Havana. But the plan that Parker and Clinton sought to execute failed to win the British a base in South Carolina, far less the conquest of its capital city, Charleston. Famous for his marine paintings of the Nelsonian era, Nicholas Pocock, although not present on the day of the battle at Sullivan's Island, was an English merchant skipper who was familiar with Charleston harbor. Engraving from a watercolor painting by Nicholas Pocock. Courtesy of the South Caroliniana Library, University of South Carolina.

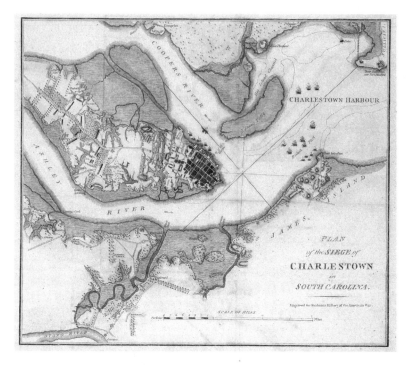

Plan of the Siege of Charlestown in South Carolina, 1780, by Unknown, hand-colored engraving, Gibbes Museum of Art/Carolina Art Association, Charleston, S.C. The map shows key American and British positions and location of Arbuth-not's ships after fighting their way into the harbor, April 1780.

Brigadier General Thomas Sumter. In the wake of the British taking of Charleston, the Gamecock, even when others were disheartened and the Revolutionary cause in South Carolina appeared lost, took up arms and rallied a group of partisans to join him. Engraving by H. B. Hall from a portrait by Charles Willson Peale. Courtesy of the South Caroliniana Library, University of South Carolina.

Opposite: A view from British lines of the siege of Charleston, April–May 1780. While the terrain relief bears little resemblance to the marshy, flat ground of Charleston and its lowcountry environs, it shows the city's skyline as well as the ships that the American defenders had scuttled in order to block British access up the Cooper River. Engraving from a painting by Alonzo Chappel. Courtesy of the South Caroliniana Library, University of South Carolina.

General Francis Marion's men cross the Pee Dee River. By late summer of 1780, the Swamp Fox's partisans had seized the initiative in the region of that river and beyond, moving against British outposts, lines of communication, and loyalist units. Engraving by C. Burt from a painting by William Ranney. Courtesy of the South Caroliniana Library, University of South Carolina.

Andrew Pickens. A proven frontier fighter in the 1776 campaign against the Cherokees, Pickens's solid leadership four years later ensured that the Americans' second line at Cowpens—the militia contingent made up of South Carolinians armed with rifles and muskets—poured a lethal fire into the advancing British infantry. Engraving by J. B. Longacre from a painting by Thomas Sully. Courtesy of the South Caroliniana Library, University of South Carolina.

Lord Charles Cornwallis, from a portrait by John Singleton Copley. An aggressive, hard-fighting general and able tactician, Cornwallis would go on to win resounding British victories in Ireland and India. Illustration from John Grafton, *The American Revolution: A Picture Sourcebook* (New York: Dover Publications, 1975), p. 101.

Gathering of the Overmountain Men at Sycamore Shoals, oil on canvas, by Lloyd Branson, 1915, Tennessee State Museum Collection, photograph by Jane Dorman. The Over-Mountain men depart their rendezvous at Sycamore Shoals in what is now Tennessee and head east. Joined by other riflemen from up and down a section of frontier stretching from Virginia to Georgia, they would catch up with Major Patrick Ferguson's force of loyalists at King's Mountain, South Carolina, October 7, 1780.

Daniel Morgan. Experienced in the fighting at Quebec and Saratoga, Morgan possessed the intuitive tactician's sense of ground, timing, and movement. At Cowpens, January 17, 1781, he was convinced that Tarleton would pursue with utmost speed, hoping to cut off the Americans before they could slip across the Broad River into North Carolina. He arrayed his forces accordingly, beginning the battle by letting Tarleton see exactly what he expected to see: a thin screen of riflemen apparently the rear guard of a retreating American force. Engraving from a portrait by Alonzo Chappel. Courtesy of the South Caroliniana Library, University of South Carolina.

The Meeting of Greene and Gates at Charlotte, N.C., by Howard Pyle (1853–1911), from "The Story of the Revolution" by Henry Cabot Lodge, *Scribner's Magazine*, August 1899, oil on canvas, Delaware Art Museum Purchase, 1912. Major General Nathanael Greene arrives in Charlotte, North Carolina, December 2, 1780, to relieve Major General Horatio Gates in command of the Southern Department. Greene's strategy soon forced the British in South Carolina to face a trying military problem to fight a war against American conventional forces at the same time that they tried to quell a partisan movement that stretched from the lowcountry to the foothills of the Blue Ridge Mountains.

Lieutenant Colonel Banastre Tarleton, by Sir Joshua Reynolds. Tarleton, the most talented cavalry commander of the war, made excellent use of intelligence and ruthlessly pursued retreating American forces or attacked their camps when such moves were least expected. Portrait, oil on canvas, National Gallery, London, England.

The partisan image greatly appealed to South Carolinians, particularly those of the planter class, who saw themselves as the functional descendants of the men who had ridden with Sumter, Marion, and Pickens. Writing to the Union army's Major General Henry Halleck in 1863, William Tecumseh Sherman considered "the young bloods of the South: sons of planters, lawyers about town, good billiards-players and sportsmen, men who never did work and never will. War suits them, and the rascals are brave, fine riders, bold to rashness, and dangerous subjects in every sense. . . . The men must all be killed . . . before we can hope for peace." Illustration from John Grafton, *The American Revolution: A Picture Sourcebook* (New York: Dover Publications, 1975), p. 96.

CHAPTER 4

IN THE PATH OF INVASION
1780

> The general naval superiority of the British . . . gave them decisive
> advantages in the South, in the rapid transport of their troops and
> supplies . . . [whereas ours could] be beaten in detail.
> —Lieutenant General George Washington

> . . . and with [our taking of Charleston] I think we conquer the
> southern provinces and perhaps much more.
> —Lieutenant General Sir Henry Clinton

CLINTON'S PRIMARY OBJECTIVE of course was Charleston. Not
merely the state's capital, it was regarded by the British as a place with
substantial Revolutionary elements—the "disaffected," as Clinton put
it—who needed to be dealt with. It was also through Charleston that
the Americans continued to receive war supplies. Moreover, Clinton was
immeasurably more knowledgeable about its watery maze of islands,
tidal marshes, inlets, and creeks than he had been three years before.
Prevost's thrust had yielded much useful information. So also had the
reconnaissances carried out by the hard-driving, ceaselessly active Captain the Honorable George Keith Elphinstone, Royal Navy. Elphinstone,
still in his early thirties, commanded the 20-gun *Perseus*, reckoned the
fastest of its class of ships in the British navy. Afterwards Admiral Lord
Keith, he had early gained Clinton's trust and indeed would consistently
distinguish himself in action both in this war and in the Napoleonic wars
of a decade and more later. Cruising the coast, he had recently taken
precise soundings of key estuaries and possible landing points around
Charleston. He had also put himself and a landing party ashore on the
sea islands south of the city. He reported to Clinton in person to make
a convincing argument that the mouth of the North Edisto River, some

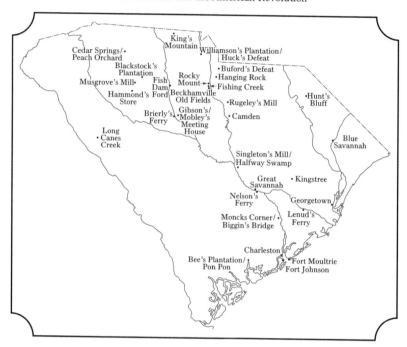

King's Mountain
Williamson's Plantation / Huck's Defeat
Cedar Springs / Peach Orchard
Blackstock's Plantation
•Buford's Defeat
Musgrove's Mill• Fish Dam Rocky Mount• •Hanging Rock
•Fishing Creek
Hammond's Store Beckhamville Old Fields
•Hunt's Bluff
Brierly's Ferry Gibson's / •Mobley's Meeting House •Rugeley's Mill
Long •Canes Creek •Camden
Blue Savannah
Singleton's Mill / Halfway Swamp
Great Savannah •Kingstree
Nelson's Ferry Georgetown
Moncks Corner / Biggin's Bridge Lenud's Ferry
Charleston
Bee's Plantation / Pon Pon •Fort Moultrie Fort Johnson

9. ACTIONS IN 1780

twenty-five miles southwest of Charleston, and a point used by Prevost's troops during their withdrawal, offered the most favorable location to bring forces ashore.[1]

Both were of the view that Charleston was too difficult to take by the direct, front-door approach attempted in 1776. Instead, Clinton planned to take it by the back door, landing from the sea to use the indirect approach. Thereafter he would go from island to island to get his forces into a position of advantage. Such an approach would let him dodge Charleston's protective batteries and envelop the city. Charleston's batteries were located principally on the Cooper River side of the city, oriented to repel a seaborne attack mounted across the water of the harbor. If his men could reach "the Neck," or the portion of the peninsula above Charleston, Clinton would be able to cut off the land approaches and lay siege. The British fleet could then fight its way into the harbor and put the stopper in the bottle. Charleston would be cut off and forced to surrender—in best case, without the need to mount a direct assault.[2]

The landings at the North Edisto were thus to be the first step of an effort that Clinton saw as phasing through fleet, amphibious, and siege-operation stages. The mobility of his nation's sea power enabled him to land an army at exactly the place he wanted—a thing the Americans would be almost powerless to prevent. His troops could come ashore on Seabrook Island and then proceed over the sea islands to hit Charleston from its least-protected point—the land side. Elphinstone also advised constructing a force of special row galleys. These were shallow-draft vessels that, manned by the Royal Navy, fitted with sails and sweeps (for rowing) and carrying light artillery, were ideal for operating in the tidal creeks and rivers of the lowcountry. It was known that the Americans already had a number of these, serving as part of the rebels' South Carolina state naval forces. The handful of British ones available had been helpful to Prevost. Now Elphinstone wanted even more of them. That way the British, not the Americans, could control the coastal waterways, with the galleys providing a nimble, hard-hitting strike force.[3]

British preparations for the move south were extensive, involving the bringing together of troops, ships, and a huge quantity of supplies. The day after Christmas 1779, a naval task force of five ships-of-the-line plus frigates and additional armed vessels stood out to sea from New York harbor. The warships escorted more than eighty vessels carrying troops, artillery, horses, food, and ammunition. The naval commander and Clinton's counterpart was Vice Admiral Marriot Arbuthnot, in charge of sea forces in the wake of Admiral Lord Richard Howe's return to Britain. The transports carried fully 8,500 redcoats, green-uniformed Hessian jaegers (German soldiers roughly equivalent to American rangers or British light infantry) and other German troops, plus an assortment of loyalist units. The plan was to sail south and then anchor off the appointed landing place. As the fleet reached Cape Hatteras, however, a severe storm struck the ships, dismasting a few and scattering many. Losses to the storm proved high in horses and artillery, especially the mortars and howitzers necessary for the siege.[4]

The planned rendezvous was not effected until the first week of February 1780, some six weeks after the voyage began. All this time Governor Rutledge, if not in possession of every detail of the impending moves against his state, was sufficiently clear about the situation to do everything possible to get help from other quarters. He had earlier—and unsuccessfully—done his best to persuade d'Estaing to remain after Savannah to protect Charleston. Now he requested all possible assistance from North Carolina and Virginia.

The invaders continued to collect themselves after the storm, with ships straggling into Tybee Roads off Savannah or Port Royal Sound. Water was replenished from Hilton Head and other local points. The galleys (some of which had been partially disassembled and carried on the decks of the larger ships) were made ready. These would proceed towards Charleston not by open sea but via the protected coastal waterways. The work of operating a plantation's boats for transportation purposes was regularly done by black South Carolinians, virtually all of them held in slavery. British preparations for this next move included not just reconnoitering the route (much of which forms the present-day Intracoastal Waterway), but also securing slaves of this sort, some by force, some not (some of them were happy to join the invaders), to serve as pilots.[5]

On February 9, Arbuthnot made signal and the fleet and its transports sailed north. After a day's sail, guided by Elphinstone's *Perseus*, the ships arrived off the North Edisto. If his first attempt against Charleston had been fraught with mischance and flaws in execution, Clinton this time left nothing to chance. While the deep-draft sail of the line and the frigates remained well out to sea, the transports, one by one, ran past the shoals to drop anchor inside the inlet. Captain Elphinstone supervised landing operations, with the light infantry going in first. Long boats landed these troops on the beach at Seabrook Island. Clinton and his second in command, Lord Cornwallis, soon joined them to move onto Johns Island proper. Other troops followed, until a whole redcoat column was snaking through the trees and along the sandy road paralleling Bohicket Creek. At the plantation houses the British found women, children, slaves, and elderly white males, but none of military age. These were gone, having taken arms and horses and joined the forces gathering in Charleston.[6]

Elphinstone acted as guide, naval liaison, and overall troubleshooter. He took soundings of the Edisto and Stono rivers to assist the vessels attending the army. By February 28, Clinton was ready for the jump over the Stono to James Island. The row galleys dominated the river, pouring heavy fire into American positions or landing troops to outflank defenders. Once ashore on James Island, British units fanned out to brush past American skirmishers. Reaching the harbor side of the island, Clinton's infantry for the first time could look across the water to see the actual objective, Charleston. Clinton then deployed most of his troops along

Wappoo Creek and its Cut, near which he located his headquarters. Wappoo Creek was a critical artery, enabling vessels to pass back and forth between the Stono River and Charleston harbor.[7]

The galleys were quickly moved up and collected inside this creek. The supply vessels, shifted from the North Edisto by sea to the Stono, were positioned so that they could better feed the army. Except for the storm, this campaign proceeded with a precision, an inexorable momentum, that made it seem a textbook example of eighteenth-century amphibious operations. But it was slow. The intricate moves ashore and the attendant evolutions of the supporting ships were beginning to tell on the admiral offshore. Elphinstone had already played the key roles earlier described; he now played one equally important. It became his task to go back and forth between the British commanders in chief on land and at sea, Clinton and Arbuthnot, who were increasingly at odds with each other. Arbuthnot's role was to keep Charleston blockaded and Clinton supported. He was apprehensive, though, about a sudden reappearance of the French fleet. Also, riding out winter storms so close to shore was fraying to the nerves (indeed, a 64-gun ship was lost during this period). So Elphinstone frequently had to sail from army headquarters to flagship and back, representing the needs of the one commander to the other. He performed this task well. Not only did he keep the admiral on station, he got him to send sailors and heavy guns from the fleet to assist the army now advancing on Charleston.[8]

For advancing it was. On March 7, Clinton's engineers were able to throw a bridge across Wappoo Cut. The sailors and large guns loaned from the fleet were placed in batteries erected to keep American vessels from looking into the creek from the harbor. Assorted longboats, flatboats, and other craft were positioned near the galleys. American cavalry patrols tried to reconnoiter but were driven off.[9] In this way Clinton's preparations remained hidden from view. Charleston's defenders knew their enemies were on the move but were unclear as to exactly where or in what strength. They remained transfixed by the presence of the British fleet, which, lurking just to the south, seemed poised to blast its way into the harbor at any moment.

The American commander, Major General Benjamin Lincoln, had already sought permission to withdraw his army from the city. Lincoln's preference was to retire into the countryside to fight another day, not to let his army be trapped at the end of a peninsula. He had seen what had happened to Washington at New York in 1776, when that general had nearly lost the cause by hazarding an army where the British could get at them with their sea power. He was also aware that Washington, despite such a risk, had made the decision to fight nonetheless. Washington had chosen to defend a place important to the American cause, and now Lincoln felt he must do the same in Charleston. And by now, it was almost too late to do anything else but stay. It happened that Washington himself also thought the best course was to save the army and abandon the city. But Washington, though commander in chief over Lincoln, was hundreds of miles to the north and without hope of influencing events in Charleston. The Americans thus were left to begin hurriedly erecting fortifications on the land side of the city, Charleston's most vulnerable point. Six hundred black South Carolinians were pressed into service as a labor force to begin working on a line of fortifications that would stretch across the peninsula, from the Ashley River to the Cooper.[10]

As noted earlier, Charleston on its harbor side was well protected, with fortifications and batteries studding the city along the Cooper. Much of the Ashley River side in that period was marsh, and thus naturally protected from attack by these barriers impervious to assault. Elsewhere, intensive effort soon produced a system of defenses consisting of redoubts (earthwork strongpoints), breastworks (chest-high earthen walls) and ditches. These ran completely across the peninsula just to the north of present-day Calhoun (then called Boundary) Street. A central feature was the "Hornwork," a masonry fortification that predated these new efforts (and upon whose site the original or "Old" Citadel would be erected early in the next century—and indeed which fortification was described by Clinton as "a kind of Citadel").[11] Two parallel sets of ditches were dug just forward of the line, again running river to river. The outer, closer-to-the-enemy one, supposedly able to be flooded at high tides, was intended to function as a moat. The second ditch was dry. Both were covered by abatis.

Other fortifications were located across the Cooper River at various points. There was also the palmetto-log fort on Sullivan's Island, fully completed and strongly manned. And there were warships as well. A full squadron of Continental Navy ships had arrived. These ships comprised three 28-gun frigates and a sloop. The vessels belonging to South Carolina's state navy (service in the state navy was the principal—until the

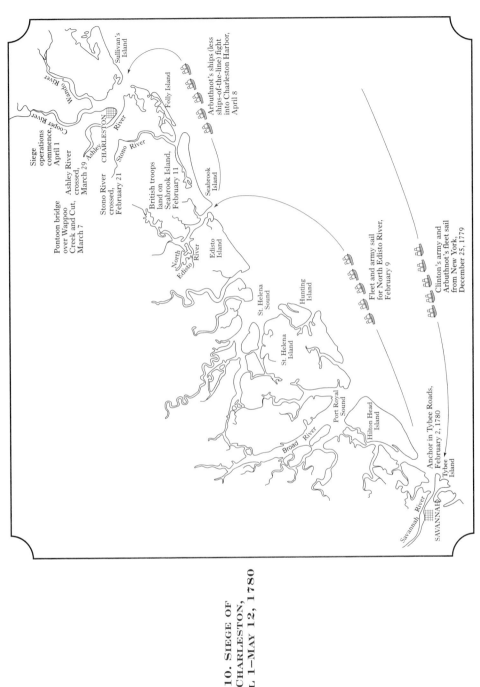

**10. SIEGE OF
CHARLESTON,
APRIL 1–MAY 12, 1780**

advent of the next or guerrilla phase of the war—military capacity in which free blacks were permitted to serve), as well as a handful of hand-me-down French vessels, were placed under the Continental squadron's commander, Commodore Abraham Whipple. Lincoln told Whipple that he wanted the ships to act aggressively. He specifically wanted to keep the British from being able to get over the bar with their fleet. Failing that, Whipple was to keep them to the outer portions of the harbor and away from the city.[12] Altogether, to defend Charleston, Lincoln had nearly four hundred pieces of artillery and almost 5,500 men. Approximately half of these were Continentals, the rest militia. In addition to a substantial share of Virginia's and North Carolina's Continental regiments, Lincoln had under his command the full array of the South Carolina Continental Line.[13]

More than six weeks had passed since Clinton's troops had stepped ashore. By March 28 he was ready to let the hammer fall: that is, to move his whole army up the Ashley, cross over to the other side, and push down the peninsula to trap the Americans—the envelopment. As before, Clinton's cavalry and light infantry drove back the American patrols—this time the ones covering the road that paralleled the river on its western bank. As quickly as he could, he moved the major portion of his army up that same road and into position for a crossing. The best and most likely point was Ashley Ferry, some dozen or so miles above Wappoo Creek.[14] He was careful to ensure that the Americans noted the concentration of British troops at this particular location.

Certainly what Clinton was about to do next—cross the river—was obvious. Lincoln again asked permission to get his army out of Charleston, but the fiery and persuasive Christopher Gadsden, the lieutenant governor, and others continued to demand that the city be held. Lincoln stayed. It was increasingly clear, though, that not all of Charleston's citizens still wished to fight. The year before, Prevost had threatened to free the slaves and give them arms if the city did not surrender. Now, with the appearance of this new and more powerful British army, more than a few were wavering: an occupying force of redcoats might be preferable to ex-slaves, armed and on the loose.[15]

Lincoln now shifted some units, placed under Moultrie and entrenched in breastworks, to cover Clinton's probable landing point at Ashley Ferry. In theory, if he could hit the British while the river-crossing was in progress, he might do some damage. But Lincoln kept his own headquarters in the city, making no effort to deploy any substantial element of his army out to a location where it could meet the British. He thus was in no real position to attack Clinton as that general came across the river. Instead, Lincoln let his time be taken up in long councils with the leading citizens. Few of these citizens were prepared to accept the sight of their defenders marching out of the city, no matter how pressing or legitimate the military purpose. The American army remained behind its walls.[16]

In the event, Clinton soon got his army over the river—but not at the place where the Americans had expected his attempt. Rather, Clinton managed to outmaneuver his opponents by crossing further up the river, so outflanking the Americans. He did this by adroit use of darkness and the row galleys and other boats earlier collected. Again, Elphinstone played a key role. The moves were intricately timed. First Clinton sent Cornwallis with the light infantry up the road towards Drayton Hall. This move brought the British to a point four miles above Ashley Ferry and fifteen or so above Charleston. Second, Elphinstone, coordinating the row galleys and the various boats collected in the Wappoo, prepared to move up the river. That night, under cover of darkness and staying close to its western bank, the boats got under way with muffled oars. Neither British movement, of boats or infantry, was detected by the Americans. At dawn on March 29 the boats, having reached Drayton Hall, loaded up the troops waiting there and quickly moved across the river.[17]

British and Hessian troops were now on the Charleston side of the peninsula. They advanced down Dorchester Road, driving back the screen of American dragoons and infantry guarding the way south. By noon the bulk of Clinton's force was over the Ashley and marching down the Neck towards the city. By late afternoon on March 30, his army was in position and deployed in a line across the peninsula. Clinton's right flank was situated at Gibbes's Landing on the Ashley, along the upper portion of today's Citadel campus. From there his line stretched diagonally across the site of what is now Hampton Park and over to the Cooper. The American lines were a mile and a quarter to the south. The supply line supporting Clinton ran from Gibbes's Landing back across the river to Linnings (now called Old Town) Creek, and from there to the ships anchored in the Stono. Munitions were brought in and British engineers began assembling siege equipment along a creek (since filled in) that cut across what is now the northern end of The Citadel campus.[18]

The American general, Lincoln, now confronted a British army larger than his own by three thousand men and ready to attack his defenses at their weakest point. Clinton had used his island-hopping and river-crossing phase to outmaneuver the Americans and get behind them. He now set out to commence European-style siege warfare against the city. The siege began on April 1. His men set to work digging redoubts—strongpoints from which artillery could shell the Americans—and parallels, trenches that would allow British engineers and infantry to inch closer and closer to the city's defensive works. Ultimately there would be three parallels, the last one angling towards the Americans' outer-defense wet ditch. The British artillery—some of it the large twenty-four pound guns borrowed from the fleet—was ferried over the Ashley. Slaves from area plantations conducted the heavy labor of moving supplies and equipment and digging fortifications. They were thus under fire, as were those doing the same thing on the rebel side of the defenses, and suffered accordingly.[19]

The Americans struck back at these British siege efforts with artillery. On April 6, while the British were still building their left-flank, first parallel redoubt, Continental Navy vessels sailed up the Cooper to open fire—but without doing enough damage to slow the process.[20] The Americans next planned to make a major sortie out from their lines but did not carry it out. That the besiegers, British and German, complained greatly of the sand fleas or gnats will surprise no one familiar with the lowcountry in that season. Much of the work of digging went on at night. The Americans tried to attack the British efforts. On some nights vicious fighting occurred when small parties encountered each other at close quarters—hand-to-hand struggles almost more characteristic of the no-man's land battles that would later be fought in World War I than most clashes that occurred in the American Revolution. By day and by night the two sides settled into an artillery duel, with the British concentrating their fire on the Americans' forward defensive works. The residential buildings of the city itself were scrupulously avoided. The British soon received new guns to replace those lost during the storm.

If the parallels advancing ever closer and the incessant shot and shell did not unsettle the defenders, what came next clearly did. Just past mid-March, Arbuthnot successfully brought his warships—minus his ships-of-the-line, which drew too much water—safely over the bar at the mouth of the harbor. To bring over the three heavy fourth- and fifth-rate ships (one with fifty guns and the other two with forty-four guns, respectively, and these three ships by themselves carrying a weight of firepower exceeding that of all the American guns defending Charleston), plus his four frigates, was a not inconsiderable feat of seamanship indeed. He had essentially to repeat the process earlier used by Parker, but on a larger scale. Arbuthnot first had to wait for a day with both maximum high-tide levels and favorable winds. Even under these favorable conditions, the ships still had to be lightened sufficiently to get over the bar, an effort that required (as it had for Parker) that guns and supplies be offloaded into transports waiting alongside while the ships rode at anchor. So lightened, the vessels were next sailed over the bar and brought to anchor again. The process was then reversed, with the big guns being reinstalled in their tiers of ports. Not all the guns had to be shifted about in this fashion, but of necessity the whole operation took place in open water. The vessels, their centers of gravity abnormally high because of the temporary removal of so much weight, were thus for a moment dangerously vulnerable to storms and heavy seas.[21]

Arbuthnot had earlier sent in Elphinstone on several nights to reconnoiter the inner-harbor channel and its approaches. He wasted little time after this step was accomplished. On April 8, just as the British ashore were completing their second main parallel, his ships weighed anchor to commence fighting their way into Charleston harbor. This time, in contrast to 1776, the British ships did not stop to engage the palmetto-log fort. Instead, they ran past it, firing as they came. Arbuthnot's ships, led by the 44-gun *Roebuck*, were well handled and made a brave sight that even the Americans had to admire. They stood in as close to the fort as possible to provide maximum cover for an accompanying column of auxiliary vessels. When these had safely passed, as a final flourish the last British warship, the 50-gun *Renown*, put her helm over to throw broadsides into the fort. She then sailed on, rejoining the others. Arbuthnot's ships had sustained damage (one transport ship was lost), but after a battle that had started in midafternoon and ended by evening, the defenders of Charleston looked out upon a harbor crowded with the masts, spars, and colors of British men-of-war.[22]

And in the other direction was a besieging army. Commodore Whipple had not done what Lincoln asked. His ships had neither attacked the British while their ships lay exposed at the bar nor tried to fight in close support of the fort—now bypassed and useless—on Sullivan's Island.

Rather, the American and French ships had pulled back into the harbor, no shots fired. Soon all but the three best frigates and some row galleys were scuttled. In this way they could at least block British entrance into the Cooper River channel. Cannon and crewmen ended up on shore, augmenting the land defenses at various points.

Only one escape route remained open to the Americans. The Cooper River, now protected by its new line of scuttled men-of-war, offered secure access to the Wando River and to the hinterland. Guarding the upper approaches was Moncks Corner, thirty miles above Charleston. This vital position was held by troops under Brigadier General Isaac Huger, and had recently permitted reinforcements of North Carolina and Virginia Continentals and critical supplies to be ferried by sloop down to Charleston via the Cooper. The route, still open five days after Arbuthnot had fought his way into the harbor, was used now to good effect: to permit the escape of the governor, John Rutledge, along with key members of his council. Rutledge had been voted special emergency powers (automatically to terminate once normal government could resume) by the General Assembly. The purpose of these was to enable him to keep the war going should Charleston, the seat of government, fall.[23]

Biggin's Bridge/Moncks Corner
APRIL 14, 1780

It was well that Rutledge got out when he did; the very next day a British force attacked the American garrison guarding Moncks Corner and Charleston's communication with the interior. Two British officers about to figure prominently in the war in South Carolina made their first major appearance in this action: Lieutenant Colonel Banastre Tarleton, commanding his British Legion, a mixed force of loyalist and British light cavalry and light infantry, plus troopers from a detachment of the 17th Light Dragoons; and Major Patrick Ferguson, commanding a force of loyalist rangers. A large column of British infantry followed. Tarleton's Legion was to emerge in this campaign as a hard-riding, hard-hitting force famous for striking where it was least expected and for cutting down its enemies without mercy.

Tarleton had, on March 20 (or perhaps the 23rd) and March 27, at Pon Pon on the Edisto and at Rantowles below Charleston, done well in skirmishes with the Americans. Just twenty-six, he had attended Oxford and studied law in London before taking a commission in the British Army. His record for aggressiveness and dash in the early stages of the war had won him command of the legion. Aided by excellent intelligence (he had intercepted a slave carrying messages), Tarleton now struck, surprising and routing a first-class American formation, the corps of cavalry and infantry units commanded by Huger. Supported by Ferguson, Tarleton's men hit the key position of Biggin's Bridge, on the forks of the Cooper River and just across from Moncks Corner, in a night attack. The legion charged, taking Huger's men by surprise, and captured four hundred prime dragoon horses, a wealth of supplies intended for the garrison at Charleston, and a hundred prisoners. A few of the Americans were able to escape into the nearby swamps.[24]

Lenud's Ferry
MAY 6, 1780

Some of these escaping Americans regrouped under Lieutenant Colonel Anthony White on the north bank of the Santee River. White soon had, counting the Biggin's Bridge survivors and local militiamen, on the order of two hundred or more men. The Americans camped and reorganized. White decided to concentrate on hitting the British foraging parties that were by now active in the area.

White's men soon picked off a twenty-man British detachment, taking the whole group prisoner. But he had reckoned without Tarleton who, flush from his success of three weeks before, was looking for another. White was by now on the south bank of the Santee and had arrived at Lenud's Ferry. He posted a guard and prepared to cross. Tarleton had learned of White's location and pursued at his only speed: very fast. Reaching the ferry in midafternoon, he and his dragoons swept past the outpost and charged White's main body. The Americans were caught by surprise and shot or cut down. White lost forty men killed or wounded. Tarleton captured over sixty prisoners and liberated the British foraging party originally captured.[25]

White and the remainder of his men were able to escape by swimming across the river. These actions of Tarleton's all but closed the British ring around the city. Left open to the Americans now were only the Wando and, directly across from Charleston, the area inland from Hobcaw Point. But not for long. Royal Navy crews, assisted by working parties of troops and pressed-into-service blacks, soon manhandled row galleys and other vessels overland from the Ashley and across the peninsula. British vessels were at last in the Cooper. With their support Cornwallis was able to capture Hobcaw Point and push up the Wando. The last way out was closed, and the Americans were trapped in the city.[26]

The British had already demanded their surrender. They opened up a full bombardment on the same day that Rutledge escaped via the Moncks Corner avenue. Lincoln held councils of war in which he proposed opening negotiations with Clinton. His goal was to obtain a convention similar to the one given Burgoyne at Saratoga. This might, in accordance with eighteenth-century protocols regarding the honors of war, enable him to get his army out after all. But Gadsden and others continued to demand that the city be held. The siege continued, the two sides firing at each other from their respective lines of works.[27]

By April 19 the British had closed to within two hundred yards of the American positions, and Arbuthnot's warships occasionally stood in to fire at this or that segment of the American defenses. At some point a stray British cannon ball knocked off the right arm of the statue of William Pitt, situated at the intersection of Broad and Meeting streets and raised a decade before. From their lines the British could see the church spires, the Exchange, and other buildings forming the Charleston skyline. The Americans could look in the opposite direction and see, up the peninsula, puffs of smoke as artillery was fired from a line of positions. Trees or buildings that stood between the lines had long since been taken down. It seemed only a matter of time before the city must surrender. The Americans soon received the bad news that recent reinforcements from New York and Savannah had raised Clinton's army to fully ten thousand men. Governor Rutledge's efforts to stir backcountry militia to action were without apparent result. Particularly galling was the surrender—without a shot being fired in defense—of Fort Moultrie and its entire garrison on May 6. This loss, to a landing party of sailors and marines, of the fort that had provided the palmetto-tree symbol on the state seal (and later, the state flag as well), and whose heroic defense had been celebrated on Palmetto Day by South Carolinians beginning the year following the battle, was a bitter blow indeed.[28]

The end really came when the besiegers were able to get close enough to penetrate the Americans' outer defensive line. They drained the wet ditch and seized the bridge running over it, and Clinton prepared for an assault. Hessian jaegers picked off American sentries and artillerymen. Next, on May 11, Clinton for a short period let his batteries fire hot shot into the city. Their goal this time was not the defenses but to set houses on fire. The two sides then shot it out in a furious artillery exchange. This proved the Americans' last hurrah. A day later, May 12, and after a month and ten days of siege, Lincoln and the American garrison surrendered.[29]

That body included seven generals, upwards of 450 other officers, and 5,100 men. Lincoln was on horseback, Moultrie beside him on foot, to receive Clinton at the gate of the Hornwork. British troops filed in, rapidly occupying the fortifications. The American troops, formed up, were marched out through the Hornwork, laying down their arms unit by unit in the space between the ditches. A Black Watch (42nd Foot, or Royal Highlanders) captain dismissed them: "as usual . . . a ragged dirty-looking set of people." Yet there was grudging respect as well, the Continentals having "more the appearance of discipline than . . . formerly," and some of their officers were well-turned-out, "decent-looking men" indeed. The concessions that Lincoln had been able to win from Clinton were only two. One was that the Americans could march out to hand over their weapons with drums and music playing— but with no flags flying, all colors cased. Second, men serving in the militia were to be paroled and allowed to go home. Not so, however, the South Carolina, North Carolina, and Virginia Continentals, some ten regiments' worth. These were to be kept under guard. The Continentals' officers were initially allowed to keep their swords. Soon, though, growing too rowdy for the British and raising toasts to Congress and to Liberty, they were disarmed and taken under guard to a camp across the Cooper.[30]

The taking of Charleston was Britain's single biggest victory of the war. It netted Clinton a bag in prisoners greater than the number of British troops taken at Saratoga. With the city fell the only American army in the South. Not merely the capital but the greatest part of the political leadership of South Carolina was lost. Resistance to British authority in the state—and perhaps the whole South—appeared crushed, with Georgia already taken and North Carolina and Virginia next on the list for invasion.

From the British perspective, the victory served to validate a basic faith that their regulars could beat the rebels in battle. Clinton, just as he had hoped, had captured an American army and taken a city without the cost of a frontal assault. His own casualties had been minimal. Not even the efforts of the excellent French military engineer, Louis Lebique, Chevalier du Portail, sent by Washington at the eleventh hour, had proved able to stop the British. Charleston also reaffirmed British faith in the capacity of sea power to bring the army to a point where an enemy could be attacked with advantage. The twentieth century would call these amphibious operations—or, to paraphrase Winston Churchill, the navy's ability to put the army ashore at the right place and at the right time. Clinton was clear about the linkage with the navy. He well understood that one of the reasons for defeat at Saratoga was that the redcoats had strayed too far from the firepower and support of the Royal Navy. By contrast, this new success suggested that the navy could help take even the most difficult point, thereafter helping to hold it as a secure enclave for the restoration of royal authority.[31]

British successes continued. On the Salkehatchie River at Morris's Ford, loyalists successfully ambushed Whig militiamen trying to link up with other Whig units. Worse, in the interior of South Carolina just two weeks after Charleston's surrender, the light cavalry leader Tarleton would catch up with and destroy the only organized force of Continentals left in the state.

Buford's Defeat/The Waxhaws Fight
MAY 29, 1780

By hard riding—his men would ride most of the day and into the night and sometimes all night, eating their rations and napping in the saddle, with only occasional short halts allowed for rest—Tarleton overtook Colonel Alexander Buford. Buford's command comprised the Third Virginia Regiment of the Continental Line, as well as militia and elements of Lieutenant Colonel William Washington's dragoons. These last units had recently escaped Tarleton's attack at Biggin's Bridge. Buford had arrived too late to join in the defense of Charleston and was now falling back towards other American forces in North Carolina. His lead of a week's march, however, was soon narrowed by Tarleton in his characteristic hard-riding pursuit. With Buford by now in the Waxhaws and about to cross over into North Carolina, Tarleton's troopers—who had ridden nearly 160 miles in just over two days—hit the Americans in a fight afterwards infamous for "Tarleton's quarter." As the British attacked, the Americans got off a volley at short range. A number of Tarleton's men fell, but the rest surged forward in a cavalry charge. When some of Buford's men, already overrun, raised their arms to ask for "quarter"— that is, to surrender—Tarleton's green-jacketed troopers instead and without mercy cut them down with the saber.[32]

While he would be ever after notorious in American eyes, this and the earlier fight with Huger assured Tarleton's reputation at home as a hero. Actions of this sort further convinced the North ministry that shifting the war to the South had indeed been the right course. The way seemed open for pacification of the countryside. British regulars would smash any organized American resistance. Thereafter, as the redcoats moved on to other objectives, a loyalist militia would remain behind to garrison the area and maintain the king's peace. South Carolina would be restored as a royal colony.

Clinton's days of enjoying his conquered city—whose houses and appointments struck one Hessian officer as by far the best in America— now drew to a close. He and Arbuthnot received intelligence that a new French fleet was on its way across the Atlantic. Indeed this new force— to include an army under General the Count de Rochambeau—was soon able to occupy Newport, Rhode Island, a point from which to threaten the British at New York. It was time for Clinton to return and see to the protection of his base. On June 5, after designating Cornwallis to command in the South, Clinton with a third of his troops, and Arbuthnot with his ships, sailed up the coast and back to New York.[33]

Clinton, however, had set in motion steps that would help to unhinge his cause in terms of the pacification of South Carolina—and ultimately of the war itself. It was at this time that Clinton began contemplating some major effort in the Chesapeake Bay. He had in mind establishment of a base there, particularly in the region of the York and the James Rivers in Virginia. In Clinton's eyes this was an appropriate move—assuming the Royal Navy could maintain their command of the sea. It would assert British power and also act to "curb the rebel trade," quite substantial, in Virginia and Maryland. It would likewise "favour the operations of Cornwallis" in his pacification efforts further south. The unintended consequence of this planning—when joined to actions by Cornwallis— was to be British disaster and Cornwallis's surrender at Yorktown on the fourth anniversary of Saratoga. But that event was nearly a year and a half and some of the hardest fighting of the war—much of it in South Carolina—away. Other actions by Clinton had more immediate effects.[34]

To this point, the British perception had been that the process of regaining South Carolina had begun well and was continuing to go well. But that process was now going awry. Former royal officers returned to the "colony"—but there was no effort to restore civil government as before. Rather, Clinton was inclined far more to the stick than to the carrot when it came to dealing with the rebels. To be sure, Charleston had not lacked for citizens enthusiastic to see the British back; a group had signed a document congratulating Clinton on his victory.[35] Others though, both in the city and in the backcountry, bided their time or adopted a posture of neutrality. But Clinton next acted in such a way that forced many South Carolinians to choose sides. The effect was to push them back to their old stance of resistance.

Whatever his gifts as a soldier, Clinton's abilities as a statesman were limited. He had earlier permitted former rebels to return home on parole—in return for their promise not to take up arms against the king again. This conciliatory gesture was more likely to achieve what the British wanted than what came next: Clinton demanded that these same citizens now take a new oath—one in which they not only had to pledge their allegiance, but had to promise as well to be ready to take up arms for the king. The implication of this new oath was that they might have to fight against their own countrymen and former comrades in arms. The reaction was hardly surprising. Many balked and began actively undermining British efforts to organize loyalist militia units, and some, finally, turned again to outright warfare.[36]

It was the backcountry where the effects of these various British policies, intended and otherwise, would be most critically felt. There, while Clinton sailed back to New York and Cornwallis dispatched columns to seize key points, both British units and loyalists acted to pillage or destroy the property of rebels. A few rebels were summarily executed. But at Beckhamville (or Beckham's Old Fields), near Great Falls, a party of militiamen soon managed to disperse two hundred or so men trying to take the Clinton loyalty oath to the king, in early to mid-June.[37] Other such events followed, particularly as American outrage over news of Tarleton's quarter displaced the despair attending the surrender of Lincoln's army at Charleston. Three clashes commenced what was to prove a long and bloody season of partisan warfare.

Williamson's Plantation and Cedar Springs
JULY 12, 1780

At Williamson's Plantation and Cedar Springs, forty or so miles apart, loyalists on the same day sustained defeats that, however small in terms of numbers, gave clear indication that the process of restoring the back-country to Crown authority would be more difficult than first conceived. In the first instance, at James Williamson's plantation, an American offi-cer of Tarleton's Legion—Captain Christian Huck, until the war an attor-ney at law in Philadelphia—was killed in an attack mounted at dawn by Whig militiamen. Huck commanded a detachment comprising Legion dragoons and loyalist militia. In his command were as well mounted infantry, the quasi-regulars of the Volunteers of New York. He had been sent into that area to cow the backcountrymen into not interfering with the administration of the loyalty oaths—or the king's business in gen-eral. But Huck and his men had also managed here and there to help themselves to property, or to use physical abuse on the farmers, planters, and their families. He had taken two men prisoner; these he intended to hang next day under accusation of being rebels.[38]

He failed to reckon, though, on the rest of the rebels. The best part of three hundred (some sources give half that number) of these, under local Whig militia officers William Bratton, Andrew Neel (or Neil), and Edward Lacey, struck next morning before the hangings could be carried out. Huck was killed in the first exchange of fire, and only a handful—perhaps forty or fifty—of his men, mostly the dragoons and the mounted infantry, escaped.

At Cedar Springs, located within the limits of what is now Spartan-burg, a courageous woman, Jane Thomas, brought word of an impend-ing loyalist raid and so alerted the Whig side to prepare an ambush. Mrs. Thomas had apparently traveled to Ninety Six to visit her husband. A planter and militia officer, he had been locked up for refusing to abide by the new oath.

The visit gave Mrs. Thomas the opportunity to hear talk of loyalist intentions against the rebel militia around Cedar Springs—the nucleus of what was the "Spartan Regiment" of the militia. Mrs. Thomas's son was the captain commanding one of these units; mounting her horse and accompanied by a servant, she rode without halt the sixty miles back to give warning. When the loyalists arrived, they were met with heavy fire and forthwith retreated with losses.[39]

Another southerner converting outrage over the new oaths and British heavy-handedness into active opposition in the field was Thomas Sumter. A former Continental officer and ultimately to be called the "Game-cock," he was, significantly, a member of the rising planter class of that backcountry region. He also had a new house, which a British-and-loyalist force—under Tarleton—now looted and burned.[40]

Rocky Mount
AUGUST 1, 1780

Sumter began organizing followers to attack loyalists and the lines of communication that reached inland to Cornwallis's newly established outposts. An early target was Rocky Mount, located near where Rocky Creek empties into the Catawba River just south of Great Falls; it was in fact an advanced post to the larger British base at Camden.

The position—part covered by a palisaded wooden wall, part by an abatis—comprised several wooden buildings. A force of 150 loyalist provincials, commanded by Lieutenant Colonel George Turnbull, Volunteers of New York, held it. Sumter's force of five hundred (perhaps six hundred) men mounted on horseback arrived with rifles or muskets at the base of the hill on which the position was located. With his men dismounted and under cover, Sumter demanded the position's surrender.

A hot fight developed when Turnbull refused, and Sumter's men—who lacked artillery to break up the British walls—tried to set the buildings on fire. The Americans had already lost eight men killed—among them the Andrew Neel who had two weeks before participated in the attack on Huck at Williamson. They now had to give up when a cloudburst doused the flames they had tried to light under British musket fire. Carrying their wounded and falling back down the Catawba, however, they ran into additional British troops on their way to relieve the post at Rocky Mount. In the action that followed, Sumter lost twenty more men but killed or captured three score of British or loyalist troops and took horses and weapons.[41]

Hanging Rock
AUGUST 1 AND 6, 1780

Sumter continued in this vein. Another nearby position was Hanging Rock, some fifteen or so miles east of the one just attempted. It was held by five hundred troops, a mix of detachments from quasi-regular loyalist units such as the South Carolina Rangers, the North Carolina Volunteers, and the infantrymen of Tarleton's Legion. A preliminary skirmish encouraged Sumter to try for a major assault, as did William Davie's daylight ambush of a nearby loyalist unit.

Davie led a force of militiamen from both Carolinas. Included in his ranks was thirteen-year-old Andrew Jackson, the future general and president, now variously a scout and message rider. Davie had attacked a unit of North Carolina loyalists encamped near Hanging Rock. There was little mercy shown to the loyalists who fell into their hands; Davie's men took no prisoners. Sumter and Davie now linked up, and together attacked the British position. In a hard-fought action on August 6, their men pushed the loyalists back but fell to looting the garrison's stores—not least the rum ration. The two partisan leaders had to break off their attack and ride away.[42]

Two infantry companies of Tarleton's Legion—dispatched from the garrison at Rocky Mount to help the one at Hanging Rock—were soon met and sent running. Despite the failure to take Hanging Rock, in two days of fighting the Whig militiamen had killed or wounded on the order of two hundred loyalist troops of the British, plus winning in the process a booty of arms, ammunition, and horses. Sumter's actual military achievements in this period were less important than the fact that he was willing to fight. The real significance was that Sumter's emergence—and those like him—signaled a general rising in a substantial portion of the state, very nearly the whole eastern one-third of it.

Nor did the rest of the states abandon South Carolina. When rumors circulated that Congress was prepared to hand over South Carolina and Georgia to Britain in exchange for peace, that body promptly passed a resolution pledging to fight on in order to win back all lost territory. To that end a newly created, second American army for the South was sent to replace the one lost at Charleston. In terms of Continentals only a fraction of the size of its predecessor, it was nonetheless commanded by Horatio Gates, regarded as the hero of Saratoga and the general who had gained the Americans their greatest victory. His troops included cavalry, artillery, militia from several states, and nine hundred Maryland and Delaware Continentals—the 1st and 2nd Brigades of the Marylanders, and a full regiment of the Delawares. These were commanded by Major General Baron de Kalb, a sixty-year-old German-born French professional serving with the Americans. The Marylanders and Delawares were usually regarded as the best line infantry in the American army.[43]

Gates had won at Saratoga not least because of slow, methodical organization and meticulous logistical preparation. Certainly the Americans in the South were greatly in need of such talents. But he chose, rather than careful preparation, to push ahead as rapidly as possible towards the British. This meant forced marches through summer heat and country that produced more loyalists than forage for his troops, and they suffered accordingly.

His hopes for an early engagement did not go unfulfilled. Hearing of this new American army, Cornwallis himself pushed inland rapidly, moving from Charleston to reinforce the British garrison at Camden in four days' march, an action of which Gates was unaware. The American force hurried south, moving as much as possible to take advantage of the nighttime cool. In mid-August, just north of Camden, the two sides would run into each other at dawn.[44]

The Battle of Camden
AUGUST 16, 1780

Cornwallis's force of some 2,230 or so men comprised troops from three excellent British regular units: two battalions of the 71st Regiment (Highland Scots) that had fought so well at Stono Ferry; the 23rd Regiment of Foot (Royal Welch Fusileers); and the 33rd Regiment of Foot. These were joined by units of volunteers and loyalists that had also performed well in the campaign to date: Tarleton's Legion, comprising both dragoons as well as infantry; Francis Lord Rawdon's Volunteers of Ireland; an infantry regiment of North Carolina provincials, and loyalist militia from South Carolina.[45]

In addition to the Continentals, Gates had Charles Armand's Legion of cavalry and infantry, and a first-class unit of Virginia light infantry. These, while not Continentals, were "state troops" and viewed as superior to the militia in training and performance. But Gates had also diluted his force by sending some of his best troops—a company of the Maryland Continentals, some artillery, and North Carolina militia—in an effort to help Sumter ambush the road leading to Camden from Charleston. He had likewise detached the excellent Davie, with his North and South Carolina mounted infantrymen, to cover the movement of the wounded from Hanging Rock to the Americans' hospital at Charlotte, North Carolina.

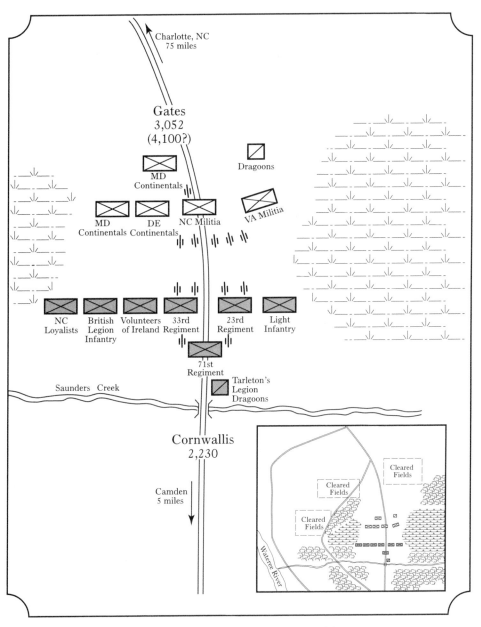

Charlotte, NC
75 miles

Gates
3,052
(4,100?)

Dragoons

MD
Continentals

MD
Continentals

DE
Continentals

NC Militia

VA Militia

NC
Loyalists

British
Legion
Infantry

Volunteers
of Ireland

33rd
Regiment

23rd
Regiment

Light
Infantry

71st
Regiment

Tarleton's
Legion
Dragoons

Saunders Creek

Cornwallis
2,230

Camden
5 miles

Cleared
Fields

Cleared
Fields

Cleared
Fields

Wateree River

11. CAMDEN, AUGUST 16, 1780

The battle began in the half-light when Tarleton's and Armand's dragoons—out in front of their respective armies—ran into each other on the road above Camden. An exchange of pistol and carbine shots erupted, followed by a charge from Tarleton that drove the American cavalry back. This charge was in turn stopped by the Virginia light infantry firing from the woods along the road. The two armies continued to move forward in column, finally flaring, contact made, to deploy into line. It was to be a European set-piece battle fought amid South Carolina swamps, the armies facing each other on a frontage determined by the ground available between the boggy areas flanking the road.

The artillery opened up. Gates outnumbered Cornwallis nearly two to one, but his troops were ill-fed, beset by stomach ailments, and done in from the push south. Far worse, he for some reason made the decision to deploy the Virginia militia, not de Kalb's proven Continentals, to hold the entire left side of his line. This would put them directly opposite some of the best troops available to Cornwallis, a regiment of highly disciplined regulars, veterans of Charleston and other actions—the 23rd Regiment of Foot. The 23rd fired a volley and then, yelling out their customary three huzzahs, advanced with the bayonet. It was too much for the militiamen, many of whom lacked bayonets anyway; their line crumbled and ran. The Maryland and Delaware Continentals and some North Carolinians were left to stand alone and their commander, de Kalb, to go down mortally wounded.[46]

To the derision of both sides, the hero of Saratoga rode off to safety on a fast horse, reaching Charlotte by midnight that same night. Cornwallis's generalship and the discipline and cohesion of his outnumbered redcoats had smashed the second American army in the South. The road to Charlotte was littered with abandoned gear, dead horses, and dead or dying American soldiers. Nearly seven hundred of Gates's men had fallen or been taken prisoner. The British had lost half that number. Two days later the audacious and never-tiring Tarleton surprised and hit the unprepared camp of Sumter and his men.

Fishing Creek
AUGUST 18, 1780

With news of the disaster at Camden, Sumter had pulled his command back, not stopping until he had put the Wateree River between himself and possible British pursuers. He had crossed at Wateree Ferry and was now camped on Fishing Creek just north of Great Falls.

He posted scouts and supposed himself safe for the moment. But Tarleton, who had captured Gates's baggage train on the road above Camden, had also picked up Sumter's trail and information of his whereabouts. Conducting one of his hard-riding pursuits, he drove his command to catch up with the Gamecock before the American believed that any British pursuit could possibly get so close. Tarleton turned his whole legion into a mounted unit by having his infantry ride double behind his hundred or so dragoons.[47]

He was aided as well by loyalists who knew the area. These helped Tarleton surprise and subdue the scouts Sumter had set out to watch the approaches to his camp. The Gamecock and his command were wide open. His men were milling about, cooking, cleaning weapons, and tending horses. Sumter himself was, according to one account, lying under a supply wagon or, according to another, bedded down in a brush lean-to. The British swept in and cut down the Americans. Sumter lost 150 men killed and 300 men captured. Tarleton lost sixteen men killed or wounded, but was able to free the equivalent of a company-sized body of British or loyalist soldiers that Sumter had taken in previous operations. He also recaptured British supply wagons likewise earlier taken.[48] The Gamecock—sans boots, hat, or saddle—managed to get away on his horse. So also did a handful of his men. The Americans had no body of organized troops left in South Carolina. Those who still had the will to fight could only do so as guerrillas.

CHAPTER 5

THE WAR IN THE BACKCOUNTRY
1780

The countryside . . . greatly enhances the effectiveness of an insur-
rection [because of] the scattered distribution of houses and farms.
. . . [A]bove all, the most characteristic feature of an insurgency in
general will be constantly repeated in miniature: the element of
resistance will exist everywhere and nowhere.

—Carl von Clausewitz, On War (1832)

[A Newberry District farmer named Waters had neighbors] who
were in favor of the King. . . . [At a store, one] insisted on Waters sub-
scribing an oath of allegiance to the King, which he refused to do,
upon which they came to words. Waters was in the act of starting for
home . . . when this neighbor seized a loaded rifle . . . and pursued,
saying: "I will kill you unless you subscribe to the oath." Waters . . .
snatched the gun from him and turned it upon him. When this fellow seized a stick and turned upon Waters, . . . [he] shot him. . . .
Waters surrendered himself to the civil authorities, and was put in
Ninety Six jail. Not long after . . . [his brother] and friends liberated
him by cutting down the door in a dark night upon which Waters
left immediately and took refuge in . . . North [Carolina] and there
joined the American army; and returning South with Green[e],
fought.

—P. M. Waters statement in John H. Logan manuscript,
A History of the Upper Country of South Carolina, Historical
Collections of the Joseph Habersham Chapter, DAR (1910)

PUSHING OUT FROM CHARLESTON five days after Lincoln had surrendered it, Cornwallis's columns had moved to establish outposts from
which to control their reconquered province. Garrisons were placed at
Beaufort (where the British had earlier established a toehold force) and
Georgetown on the coast and, inland, at Cheraw, Camden, Hanging

Rock, and Ninety Six. These latter formed a screen that guarded the approaches whereby help for the defeated rebels might come from North Carolina and Virginia. Their other purpose was to expedite the return of the interior to royal authority. Ninety Six, a settlement, court-house, and trading outpost within fifty miles of Augusta, anchored the western flank. It was a place doubly advantageous to British purposes because it eased communication with the Cherokees and the Creeks and also menaced the American settlements distant over the mountains. Further, as William Moultrie had acknowledged, its population was staunchly loyalist.[1]

In South Carolina, actions by the wealthy, polished elite of the low-country had won victory for the American cause in the first stages of the war, but only hard fighting in the backcountry could now save it. What followed was an extremely bitter episode. The war in the backcountry would prove integral to the larger struggle, but it was also a war unto itself—fratricidal, vicious, fought on its own terms and sometimes for its own reasons.

For the next year and a half and beyond, the conflict waged across the fields, forests, swamps, and hamlets of South Carolina was more a civil war than the one formally called that eighty years later. This one divided the people of a single state against each other. Rather than a war between two self-proclaimed sovereign entities or two geographic sections, as in the Confederate States versus the United States of America, this conflict was fought within the boundaries of a single state. No single determinism of class, section, political ideology, or religious affiliation easily explains how the sides chose themselves. The war split communities, districts, and families and set the fragments against each other. Fought for the larger purpose of supporting one or the other of the two sides, it was fought also to settle old scores or to best rivals. Payback took the form of loot-ing, physical violence, and outright execution of those who fell into the wrong hands. Crops and houses were destroyed, as was anything of value that could not be carried or driven off. The ebb and flow of the back-country conflict had everything to do with the rise and fall in fortune of the conventional armies of the two sides. Its mainstay, style of fighting, and option of immediate resort, however, was first and foremost guer-rilla warfare.[2]

Guerrilla warfare was a term only rarely and occasionally beginning to enter the language. It was one that European professional soldiers might use, but not the backcountry planters and farmers riding in the partisan bands. Not until thirty years later, during the Peninsula Campaign (1808–1814) of the Napoleonic Wars did guerrilla warfare become a standard term for the kind of hit-and-run combat that relied upon ambush, raids, and melting into the population before the enemy could react. Spanish for "little war," the term became notorious because the Peninsula Campaign—one in which Spanish irregulars preyed upon French lines of communication (and were in turn retaliated against themselves) —was conspicuous for the savagery that characterized both sides.[3]

Called also "partisan war"—a style of fighting that antedated the establishment of standing armies ordered by rules and regulations—it would acquire its own formalized, revolutionary strategy a century and a quarter later. In China Mao Tse-tung and in Vietnam Vo Nguyen Giap sought ways whereby forces of farmers could defeat armies equipped and operating in the Western way. Their people's-war approach involved the use of flexible levels of guerrilla organization and activity. In this way, in the basic stage the guerrillas concentrated on organization and preparation, with limited terrorist or small attacks. In the next phase, they expanded to coordinated operations to wear down and demoralize the enemy. Finally, in the last phase, scattered units of guerrillas fused themselves into an actual army. They then mounted the offensive that would give them victory.[4]

There was no carefully articulated theory for warfare of this kind in eighteenth-century South Carolina. Nor were the planters, farmers, and slave-holders (these last, politically and socially, were certainly anything but radicals) who would engage in this kind of warfare the products of some revolutionary school for guerrilla fighters; in the main they were inclined to admire the British, if not their current, hated policies towards the Americans. But all three stages of guerrilla warfare—even if lacking the twentieth century theorists' labels—would be present nonetheless. Many of these men had seen service in provincial regiments or, more likely, in the militia. Many had likewise gained their first experience of combat by fighting Indians—in the counteroffensive against the Cherokees four years before, and some in the Cherokee War a decade and a half before that. This first exposure to combat, accomplished within the ruthless, brutal pattern of the frontier, carried over to shape their approach to warfare.[5] The resort to the guerrilla style was not from the appeal of some grand strategic theory. It was from experience—and simply because there was no other way to fight. For the Americans, partisan warfare, the war of striking and then disappearing before the enemy could catch you, was their only option.

Thomas Sumter and a handful of others had been the first to take the field in this new partisan phase, hitting groups of loyalists and British positions in the wake of Charleston's fall. A host of factors, including self-preservation and the desire to hit back, motivated Sumter and his men to fight on the rebel side—and many of the same factors motivated the loyalists.

One of these factors was the Regulator movement, a dozen years in the past, whose effects were felt still. The Regulator movement, while it was occurring, had not reached the near–civil war proportions that the conflict achieved in North Carolina in the same period, but it gave clear indication of the rift between backcountry and lowcountry and of rifts in communities. By the late 1760s, although roughly half of South Carolina's population lived in the backcountry, that region had only a handful of seats in the lower house of the assembly. The lowcountry's plantocracy had balked at voting to appropriate funds for courts and jails for the backcountry, or taking other steps to combat the widespread lawlessness that became the immediate cause of the Regulator movement. Also, as previously noted, backcountry taxes supported the Anglican or Established Church, although Episcopalians were a minority in that region. In the eyes of backcountrymen, the lowcountry controlled government, courts, and the price of goods. It also made them pay for a church to which only a few of them belonged. The fact that it was that same lowcountry elite that would make the Revolution was cause enough for many to oppose it, choosing instead to stay loyal to the Crown. The Regulator period had been one of choosing sides. The chances were good that those same sides would be maintained in the war in the backcountry.[6]

The Indian issue was another dividing factor, most critically for the settlers along the frontier. For them, security against Indian attack was *the* issue; they looked to the Crown to keep the Indians quiet. So long as they acted in the role of protectors, the British could expect to keep a substantial element of such people loyal to them.

Yet the British did not. As noted previously, the Cherokee offensive of 1776 had helped to win many over to the Whig cause. The perception of a British-Cherokee alliance and belief that Crown agents were actively stirring up the frontier were all that it took. The British tie to these Indians could have but one predictable outcome: to drive frontiersmen into a camp that could protect them, the rebel one.[7]

This was the case in South Carolina. When the Cherokees chose to take up the hatchet in the king's cause in summer 1776, their decision proved destructive to themselves and far more helpful to the Americans than to the British. It converted neutrals or even allies into Britain's enemies. A small number of loyalists did choose to act with the Cherokees, but it was the Revolutionary cause, not the British one, that now promised to protect the frontier. South Carolinians had had a long and brutal experience of warfare in that sector. A decade and a half before, for example, the grandmother of John C. Calhoun, the future senator and vice president of the United States, had been killed and mutilated by a war party. In the first year of this current war, the parents of Wade Hampton, Revolutionary officer and grandfather of future Confederate general and post-Reconstruction governor Wade Hampton, had perished in like fashion.[8] Whitehall's involvement with the Cherokees cost the British side more than it ever could have gained in military advantage from the alliance. In the event, the Cherokees proved far more valuable to the Revolutionary Americans as enemies than they ever could have as allies.

Also playing a role were the steps lowcountry Whigs had taken—albeit haltingly—to reach out to backcountry areas and communities. The very modest expansion of representation for the backcountry, achieved with the Provincial Congress of 1775 and with the constitutions adopted a year later and three years later, respectively, was crucial. This expansion of representation came hand in hand with the act of disestablishing the Anglican Church, a step more important than it might at first appear; its real significance was not religious but political.[9] As a good-faith-intentions gesture on the part of the lowcountry, the region where that church was most firmly entrenched, it took the fire out of class and sectional arguments raised against those on the coast. It won friends where previously there had been suspicion, sectarian rivalry, and enmity.

And touching all these other matters was the fact that there were new men of rising economic and political ambition in the backcountry. Indeed, the Regulator movement had been led by such individuals. They wanted their region cleaned up and rid of any who stood in the way of prosperity and order, even if it meant using vigilante justice. Newly prosperous, these men were planters and owners of mills and stores and slaves. They were men of influence, persons around whose leadership communities in the backcountry naturally coalesced. Some became magistrates, others militia officers, and some both. These were positions of prestige and importance, a fact lost upon neither the lowcountry Whigs who had the power to hand the positions out, nor the new planters of the backcountry who wanted them. The relevance to the Revolution is clear. It was these men—an emerging elite that desired linkage to the older, established elite of the lowcountry—who made the determination of whether a particular area of the backcountry went rebel or loyalist. There would prove to be high concentrations of those with loyalist leanings between the Broad and Saluda rivers and, of course, around Ninety Six. But it was the Whig side that won the preponderance of the new men in other areas. The Revolution continued a process already in development before the war, in which the rising men of the backcountry and the lowcountry's plantocracy found common cause and forged bonds accordingly.[10]

But it was by no means that simple or tidy; the loyalist side found plenty of adherents as well. These were individuals of a more conservative frame of mind, or who had found perhaps their previous situation under royal-colony government a favorable one and wanted no change. Then too, some who had initially favored the Whig cause later reversed themselves. One who did so was Andrew Williamson. He had defended Ninety Six against the loyalists in 1775, the action that brought the first bloodshed of the war in South Carolina. But in 1780 his loyalties changed. He handed over to the loyalists that same Ninety Six for which he had fought them five years before.[11]

What might have induced him to take such a course remains unclear. What is clear, however, is that substantial areas of South Carolina, often following the leadership of local men, became a patchwork of hostile communities and districts ready to fight, or raid and plunder in reprisal. Nor did all families see things the same way. Some divided, with fathers and sons or brothers taking opposite sides. A notable example was the Moultrie family. On one side was General Moultrie himself, the patriot, and on the other his brother, a staunch loyalist. Dr. John Moultrie consistently held prominent office under Crown authority and did his best to draw other South Carolinians to the same cause.[12]

A century ago some historians believed that, with the coming of the Revolution, the white population of the Thirteen Colonies divided into thirds: one third rebel, one-third loyalist, and one-third indifferent. The current view is that the proportion of those neutral in the war should be revised upward at the expense of the other two groups, particularly the loyalist one. That said, whereas loyalists may not have constituted more than twenty percent of the American white population as a whole, the fact remains that in South Carolina their numbers were substantial. At the end of the war, when the defeated loyalists could seek reimbursement from the British government for property losses, those from South Carolina were, of all the former colonies, second only to New York in the number of claims honored.[13] The British problem was always one of how to mobilize and employ that strength. When it was employed but got out of hand, it contributed to a situation of social disintegration and chaos that played into the hands of the rebels, not the British.

On top of that, measures adopted by Clinton and Cornwallis would prove poorly suited to achieving British aims in South Carolina. Clinton's first stance of permitting militiamen to return home on parole—giving them time to reflect, as it was put, on the "returning beams [that is, the benefits] of Royal government"—started off well. But, as seen, he soon departed from this policy, requiring not just allegiance to the king but also to take up arms against the king's enemies. This step alone guaranteed that many South Carolinians would be king's enemies. Other harsh measures followed. Cornwallis's new-oath policy was soon accompanied by a decision to confiscate the estates of leading rebels. Other leading rebels were then either confined in Charleston or shipped off to St. Augustine, to be held prisoner in its old Spanish fort. But the imprisonment of these "rebel grandees," Clinton's term for them, did not break the Revolutionary cause in South Carolina. It fueled instead a sense of outrage and a willingness to hold on no matter what.[14]

Cornwallis was an able, resourceful, and energetic commander. Fighting during the Seven Years' War, he had been made a colonel at age twenty-eight. He remained hopeful of reconciliation with the Americans and had earlier, in sessions of Parliament, opposed some of the same policies that had helped bring on the war. His career after his time in America was characterized by great distinction—and an ability to fight through situations of military and diplomatic complexity and peril. In 1798 he would defeat a French army landed in Ireland and supported by Irish rebels. This success in a counter-insurgency struggle was matched by his role in India, where, as governor general, he defeated

French intrigue and substantial native forces. In this success, won at great distance from Britain, he both secured and expanded his nation's power on the subcontinent.[15]

His career in coping with the political and military realities he encountered in South Carolina in 1780 and 1781, however, was less successful. He did not, for example, prevent his troops from carrying out the excesses that soldiers of any army, unleashed on a civilian population, are capable of perpetrating. Such a laissez-faire policy toward his own troops was not likely to break either the South Carolinians or those ready to help them in the states to either side. A particularly notorious example was when one of Cornwallis's officers, acting in the belief that Presbyterian churches were "sedition shops," and that membership in the denomination was equivalent to being a rebel, proceeded to burn down as many such churches as he could. The effect of this on the Scotch-Irish, many of them of course Presbyterians, was predictable: they became rebels. Too, while both sides attracted a share of undesirable individuals, some choosing the British one had been, a dozen years before, specifically identified as outlaws by the Regulator movement. They were regarded as backwoods bandits pure and simple, a riffraff fallen in with the British because it was a license to steal and a way to get even. Some found their way into loyalist ranger units in East Florida, particularly those organized by Prevost on the eve of the advance into Georgia and South Carolina. Their operations now had British sanction. They offered scope to plunder property, from which slaves could be taken and resold at a profit. That these actions were connected to the British side was not lost upon the backcountry populace.[16]

But looming above all were Banastre Tarleton and his Legion of green-jacketed dragoons and infantry. These, more than any other British or loyalist unit, came to symbolize the cruel, hard aspect of Crown pacification. Neutrals came to hate Tarleton and his command; the rebels already did. Of course, many in the Legion were Americans, recruited from New York and New Jersey two years before. To the cutting down of Buford's men and the hell-for-leather rides that let them show up at times and places the Americans least expected, the Legion soon added another reputation: they became notorious for roughing up civilians and helping themselves to property they encountered along the way. There was more. In the hunt for Sumter, Tarleton and his men took time out to dig up the dead body of Colonel Richard Richardson. Richardson, only recently deceased, had been the commander in the Snow Campaign of 1775. Tarleton perhaps took his cue from Charles II's restoration of 1660—and the exhumation of the bodies of Charles I's main regicides, Oliver Cromwell, Henry Ireton, and John Bradshaw. Did he think to daunt, by such measures, a people who had endured a wilderness trek from Pennsylvania or Virginia and perhaps the savagery of frontier warfare along the way? Tarleton, conspicuously competent as a cavalry commander, was reckoned by some the most dangerous man on either side. To give him and his men free rein against the backcountry people, however, was not a good way to restore the "beams of Royal government."[17] Its effect was to catalyze people into resistance.

A hard core of such resistance had held out even when the Revolutionary cause appeared most hopeless. The governor, Rutledge, now seemed at his most determined. Scion of one of South Carolina's most distinguished families and trained in law at London's Middle Temple, he did not hate Britain but was implacably opposed to restoration of British authority. He traveled the state, working tirelessly to try to fan sparks into flames, sometimes merely a step or two ahead of the British cavalry sent to look for him.[18] Rutledge in this harsh period was the de facto Revolutionary government of the state—not merely the head of government but the *sole* government. Three key guerrilla leaders now emerged to wage irregular warfare at the same time that he carried on with the emergency powers granted him prior to the fall of Charleston. These three leaders, with Rutledge's sanction, and in three main regions of the state, prosecuted guerrilla warfare against their enemies from marshlands to mountains.

Two were to emerge as the most famous South Carolinians of the Revolutionary period, more remembered even than Rutledge, or than the victor of June 28, 1776, Moultrie. Thomas Sumter, already noted as the first to commence partisan activities on a broad scope, and famous as the Gamecock, was to operate mainly in what is today sometimes called the midlands of South Carolina—roughly the geographic midsection of the state—but mounting forays as well as far as the North Carolina border. The second leader to emerge—but usually accounted the most famous—was Francis Marion, the Swamp Fox. Marion's was the area immediately below Sumter's: the lowcountry and the coastal plain bordering it. Marion operated from a base protected by the swamps of the Pee Dee River. From this interior position he was able to move against his opponents in a zone stretching from Charleston to George-town, and inland to Camden and the area of present-day Columbia. A third leader, Andrew Pickens of the Long Canes Creek region, operated for the most part in the area not lowcountry or midlands but the foothills of the upper portion, or upcountry, of the state. To say that each partisan functioned in a particular zone is not to suggest that these were assigned by the edict of some general staff. Rather, Sumter, Mar-ion and Pickens simply took up arms and began fighting in the regions where they lived. All three had seen extensive service in militia, provin-cial, or Continental forces. Their careers and backgrounds are illustrative of the internal struggle going on in the backcountry, and give some sug-gestion of the crucial capacity of these three individuals to help deter-mine the outcome of that struggle.

Of the three, only Marion was a native of South Carolina; he was born the son of a planter in an area so heavily French Huguenot that it was referred to as the "French Santee." Sumter was born in Virginia, his parents recent immigrants from England. Pickens was born in Pennsyl-vania, moving with his family as a child first to Virginia and by stages finally to the frontier district of South Carolina. He was thus part of the large internal migration down the "Virginia Road" from Pennsylvania that helped carry people into the backcountry of both Carolinas and Georgia.[19]

Sumter's early career leaves little doubt that he might one day earn his title of "Gamecock." A product of the frontier, poorly educated but aiming to go high, Sumter by 1761 was a sergeant in the provincial troops Virginia sent against the Cherokees. He managed to win a hand-to-hand, single-combat fight against the Seigneur des Jonnes, a French-Canadian officer notable for his raids and other operations with the Indians. Sumter took the seigneur prisoner, delivering him finally to Fort Prince George, a British position within Cherokee territory (and now under Lake Keowee).

This occasion marked Sumter's first visit to South Carolina. He was highly enough regarded for his competence as a frontier fighter that he was next detailed, at the conclusion of the French and Indian War, to escort several Cherokee chiefs on an official visit to Britain. But the road ahead was not altogether a smooth one. After conducting them suc-cessfully to Britain and thence back to their own country, Sumter was imprisoned in Virginia for debt. He soon escaped. Impressed by his earlier visit to Charleston and other points, he made his way back to South Carolina, eventually marrying a wealthy widow who possessed a plantation. Through sagacious dealings, Sumter eventually joined additional lands, grist and saw mills, and stores to this plantation. He appears to have been a classic example of a rising backcountry planter; he was soon named a justice of the peace. When the war came in 1775, he was a member of the Provincial Congress and a mounted-ranger captain under the same Colonel Richardson whose body Tarleton exhumed. Promoted to lieutenant colonel in a rifle regiment, Sumter was active in the defense of Sullivan's Island in 1776. A case of malaria two years later forced him to leave Continental service, seemingly ending forever his military activities.[20]

He was still in convalescent status when Tarleton swept towards the region called the High Hills of Santee, just east of the Wateree River's basin and west of the city later founded and named for Sumter. As noted previously, Tarleton burned everything he could at Sumter's plantation, stole slaves and horses, and slaughtered or drove away the livestock. Whatever Sumter's feelings had been up to that moment regarding the return of British authority, the destruction of his property by Tarleton's dragoons infuriated and galvanized into action this man who had emerged as a leading planter in his district, and who had proven he could handle Quebecois seigneurs and Cherokee chiefs. Wearing a cock's feather in his hat—his trademark—and willing to take on anybody at anytime, Sumter would become Rutledge's first active partisan leader.

The Gamecock was forty-six in 1780. His comrade-in-arms, the Swamp Fox, was two years older. Francis Marion, like Sumter, had won distinction by his conduct in the war against the Cherokees. In 1761 he was a lieutenant in the militia company commanded by Captain William Moultrie, this unit part of a force of South Carolina militia and British regulars sent into the Cherokee country in the upper, western portion of the colony. Marion personally led a main assault against the Indians' principal position, a point defending their town of Etchoe. The militia and the redcoats carried the day. He returned thereafter to the life of a planter, eventually acquiring the plantation, Pond Bluff, located near present-day Eutawville (and since 1941 submerged under Lake Marion, completed as part of the Santee-Cooper Project). He was well enough regarded that he was among those elected when a Provincial Congress was called in 1775. Marion was considered serious and hard-working, and he had little to say about his considerable experience of frontier warfare. Appointed a captain in one of the new regiments of troops raised at the outbreak of the war, he participated in both the capture of Fort Johnson and the defense of Sullivan's Island. Raised to lieutenant colonel, he took part in the Americans' failed siege of Savannah in autumn 1779.[21]

He missed being captured when Charleston fell only by a lucky quirk—an ankle broken in a fall prior to the start of the siege. He got out before the British could close their ring. Thus, like Sumter, Marion was abroad in the country's interior and ready to do the British harm. Like the more flamboyant Gamecock, he also was willing to fight on despite the appearance of total defeat following the surrender of Lincoln's army.

The third partisan leader, Pickens, had been sufficiently discouraged by that defeat to accept British protection in 1780. By then he was forty-one years old, a well-off and respected figure in the frontier region of the backcountry, and a sober elder of the Presbyterian Church. His father had served the colony as a militia officer and had later become a magistrate. Like the two other partisan leaders, Pickens had gained military experience in the Cherokee campaigns. This circumstance was significant also in that it brought his first contact with lowcountry leaders who were Whiggish in outlook. This contact was followed by marriage to a daughter of the backcountry's Calhoun family, likewise of Whiggish outlook. By the eve of the Revolution, Pickens was regarded as a promising man with ties throughout his region—and contacts with the lowcountry. When the time came to choose, he and others would ensure that his district took the rebel side, despite the fact that they were close to loyalist Ninety Six.[22]

Over the next year, Pickens served extensively in the frontier campaigns that defeated first the loyalists and then the Indians. He participated in the Americans' pursuit of Prevost below Charleston and thereafter in a second frontier offensive against the Cherokees. Pickens was a man tied into a network of prosperous families, lowcountry and upcountry, whose political outlook conformed to his own. He knew the country and how to lead South Carolina militiamen in combat. The loyalists' taking reprisal—a unit of them plundered and destroyed his plantation—caused him to take up arms as a rebel again.

Marion had moved at almost the same time as the Gamecock, hurrying north to join de Kalb as soon as his broken ankle would let him.

He reached de Kalb—now under Gates—just prior to Camden. Marion and his handful of followers—sons of the plantocracy, woods-runners from the margins of the settled regions, black men free and slave, and Indians from the Catawba and perhaps other nations—presented an appearance so ill-shod and bedraggled as to be remarkable even by the ragtag standards of the Americans' Southern army. Gates was unimpressed by Marion and his men; he decided to send him off on a make-work mission of no importance to the upcoming battle at Camden. After that battle, however, Marion would be free to commence a program of attacks of his own design against British outposts and supply lines. And as he did so, other bands would arrive to help South Carolina from across the borders.[23]

Musgrove's Mill
AUGUST 18, 1780

Some of these bands came from as far away as what became Tennessee —the Over-Mountain or Watauga settlements. Hard-pressed as these settlements were by the Indian offensive that continued intermittently up and down the frontier, it had taken this long for news of Lincoln's defeat in Charleston to reach these men and to have them come east across the mountains. They were under Isaac Shelby and were soon joined by Georgia militia under Elijah Clarke. These two groups linked up with a force of South Carolina militiamen under James Williams. The three leaders, all lieutenant colonels, shared command of a force of mounted riflemen some two hundred strong.[24]

Their objective was the mill operated by Edward Musgrove on the Enoree River. This mill—including various outbuildings and a plantation house—was occupied by a loyalist force, much of it quasi-regular provincials, over twice as big as the one commanded by the three colonels. The loyalists' position was in what is now Spartanburg County, near the community of Cross Anchor.

The colonels settled on a plan that might whittle down the loyalists' numbers. A small mounted force of the Georgians was sent across the ford and pretended to stumble into the loyalist position. Falling back, it then led the pursuing loyalist infantry into a prepared position of logs and earth. A hot fight developed as the loyalists assaulted the riflemen. The assaults were determined and mounted with fixed bayonets. The Americans were pushed back into the woods. As they fell back, however, a lucky shot from one of them brought down the loyalists' commander. This turned the tide, and it was the loyalists who now fell back. The fight continued, with the Americans ultimately losing a dozen men killed or wounded. But the loyalist losses were far greater, amounting to about 150 killed or wounded and 70 men captured.

Although the colonels contemplated a move against Ninety Six, word at this point reached them of Gates's defeat at Camden two days before. They concluded that it was best for them to get away to the north and west—and thus they missed the disaster that befell Sumter at Tarleton's hands at Fishing Creek a few hours later on the same day.

Nelson's Ferry
AUGUST 20, 1780

Cornwallis had won decisively at Camden and certainly Tarleton's streak continued unbroken, but dealing with this or that band of irregulars was proving vexing for the British. It now proved even more so. Marion had dodged the fan of Cornwallis's cavalry patrols and went south to watch the road from Charleston to Camden. Through some means he learned that American troops captured at Camden, plus supplies, were being marched south to Charleston.[25]

These troops and some wagons were by now at Nelson's Ferry, a point on the main road where a ferry crossed the Santee River. A small British detachment guarded the prisoners and wagons, these last containing weapons and gear captured at Camden. Marion attacked at first light with his handful of men, killing or capturing two dozen British and loyalist troops. His prize, in addition to the horses, arms, gear and supplies, was the liberation of 150 or so Maryland Continentals taken at Camden less than a week before. Trained soldiers were in short supply and highly prized by both sides. Marion freed these—or most of them, since some refused to go with him—to fight again for the Americans. The news of this fight, conveyed to Gates and later to the Congress, proved, with Musgrove's Mill, bright spots in an otherwise grim picture. Marion dodged the British pursuers sent after him by dispersing and hiding out in the woods and swamps he and his men knew well. Cornwallis sent Tarleton to hunt him down. It was this task that eventually led Tarleton, fed up with the exertions of an unsuccessful pursuit—and the heat, insects, and reptiles of South Carolina's swamplands in summer—to give Marion his famous name. Supposedly telling his troops to turn back and resume chasing the Gamecock, Tarleton declared that, "as for this damned old fox, the devil himself could not catch him!"[26]

So the Swamp Fox escaped and continued to raid and harass his enemies' communications and positions into the fall. A particular target was the loyalist militia that served the British. To that end he moved to attack forces of these men at various points along the network of roads connecting to the interior.

Blue Savannah
SEPTEMBER 4, 1780

One such location was on the Little Pee Dee River, just below Galivant's Ferry. Marion's command had, with the advantage of the weapons and horses just seized at Nelson's Ferry, doubled to something over fifty men. But British and loyalist units were by now out looking for him in strength.

Marion resolved to hit back before he could be trapped. A loyalist force of two hundred or more mounted men was reported moving in his direction, south along the Little Pee Dee. In the first brush with this group, Marion's men sent the loyalists' van or lead element reeling back. It was clear, however, that the full force was about to charge and finish him off.

Marion fell back to Blue Savannah—apparently to a small island—and quickly hid his men in a stand of trees and thick brush. When the loyalists came into range, Marion's men sprang their ambush and opened fire to inflict heavy losses. Not only did Marion escape destruction by converging British forces, he won a significant victory: the fight at Blue Savannah did much to weaken support for the British cause in the country along the Pee Dee River. Never strong in that area, it was largely broken by this sharp action—and by the one that followed.[27]

Black Mingo Creek
SEPTEMBER 28, 1780

Marion had received information from Whig informants and scouts to the effect that a body of mounted loyalist militia—forty-six men, commanded by John Coming Ball, a substantial rice planter of that region—was encamped at Shepherd's Ferry. This, on Black Mingo Creek, a tributary of the Black River, was within a mile of Willtown. Willtown, which no longer exists, was at that time the most prosperous community in the vicinity. Marion particularly wanted to defeat its loyalist garrison—local men that he and his own men knew—and drive them from that section of the state.

Ball was likewise familiar with the local terrain, routes through the swamps, and so forth. He had positioned his troops back from the ferry, and they were camped on the edge of some woods. Ball's and Marion's groups were approximately equal in size, although Marion may have picked up a few additional men on his approach to Willtown. He resolved to attack under cover of darkness.

Ball's guards heard the clatter of Marion's horses' hooves as they crossed the wooden bridge at Willtown. So alerted, he and his men were ready when Marion arrived, and they opened up at short range. The effect of this fire—some of it buckshot—drove the attackers back. But the Swamp Fox quickly hit Ball and the loyalists with a charge mounted from three sides—and the loyalists at last broke, some of them escaping by running into the woods. Marion had lost nearly a dozen men, Ball twice that number. Marion also captured Ball's thoroughbred horse, which he renamed Ball and rode for the rest of the war.[28]

These and other operations netted him weapons (a few of his men may have had the sabers and pistols of cavalry in that era, but most carried muskets or rifles) and horses. Thereafter he dispersed his command, his usual course since he had no means of feeding more than a small number. But inland, both Sumter and Pickens were gathering men, and would soon strike. So again would Marion. By such sparks South Carolina—regarded in Whitehall as all but taken on May 12 with the conquest of Charleston—was flaming into conflagration.[29]

CHAPTER 6

PEGASUS GALLOPED

1780–1781

Never gallop Pegasus to death.

—Alexander Pope, *Satires, Epistles, and Odes of Horace.* I.I.14 (1733–1738)

We were formed [at the Cowpens] in the order of battle and . . . clapping . . . hands together to keep warm. . . . The British line advanced at a sort of trot, with a loud halloo. It was the most beautiful line I ever saw. When they shouted I heard Morgan say, "They give us the British halloo, boys. Give them the Indian halloo, by God!" and he galloped along the lines, cheering the men and telling them not to fire until we could see the whites of their eyes. Every officer was crying "Don't fire!" for it was a hard matter to keep us from it.

—South Carolina militia major Thomas Young

THE REBEL PARTISANS were not the only ones active in the countryside. An ace up Cornwallis's sleeve and one of his most trusted officers was Major Patrick Ferguson. A career soldier ten years older than Tarleton, Ferguson, son of a Scottish judge, had experimented with irregular warfare ever since his arrival in America. He first raised a group of riflemen in his parent regiment, then led the independent unit of loyalist rangers that acted in support of Tarleton in the capture of Moncks Corner. Ferguson had also invented a technologically advanced kind of rifle that could be loaded from the breech, as opposed to the then standard but slower method of sending a "patched" ball (that is, one inserted into a small piece of greased linen or other material) down the muzzle with the ramrod. Supposedly, Ferguson, at Brandywine Creek three years before, had had the American commander, George Washington, clearly in his sights. He had, reportedly, refused to pick off Washington on that occasion, pronouncing that to have done so would have been ungentle-manly.[1]

Most importantly, Ferguson was a highly capable officer who had proven his ability to lead Americans—loyalist ones—in combat. Cornwallis had promoted him to inspector of militia, meaning that Ferguson was in charge of organizing all loyalist militia in South Carolina. As Cornwallis now prepared to advance into North Carolina, he counted on Ferguson to make a sweep to his left, or through the western sector of South Carolina. His assigned mission was to win back the frontier people to the Crown, and then, gathering forces as he went, to link up with Cornwallis as the British advanced northwards. It so happened that Cornwallis pushed into North Carolina and ran into fierce opposition around Charlotte—including the William Davie who had proved so effective in the earlier fights in the Waxhaws. Davie had raided Cornwallis's column as it moved north, and at Charlotte successfully held off Tarleton's Legion (Tarleton himself was not present, being stricken with fever) for a time. Cornwallis pronounced Charlotte and its environs a hornets' nest. Clearly both he and Ferguson anticipated the fielding of a substantial force of pro-British frontier militia in South Carolina. Their belief was that such a force could secure that region as well as helping to defeat the partisan groups active on the rebel side—and so clean up the backcountry.[2]

They greatly misread both the situation and the success of their pacification program to date. Their miscalculation of the extent of frontier loyalist support would lead to the first real reversal in the string of British successes in South Carolina that had begun with the fall of Charleston—and would cost Ferguson his life. As Ferguson pushed into the western region, he was successful indeed in bringing men to the king's cause—better than a thousand of them, in fact. But he also found enemies. Some of the loyalists he had raised had been those drawn into the British reversal at Musgrove's Mill on August 18. Ferguson's message to the Over-Mountain settlements on the other side of the Appalachians —that they would have to declare for the king or else face attack from the king's forces—was singularly ill-chosen. It roused the independent-minded Watauga pioneers to fury. Not only had they just beaten some of these same king's forces, they had also suffered greatly at the hands of Cherokee and loyalist raiders in 1776. They now resolved to strike at Ferguson before he could strike at them. The Over-Mountain men—

leaving behind a handful of their number to guard the settlements, by their departure dangerously exposed to Indian attack—gathered at Sycamore Shoals. They then headed east over the mountains, coming through the passes in early snow and calling forth support from up and down the frontier.[3]

In fact, they soon formed the nucleus of a group of frontier riflemen drawn not just from Tennessee but from the isolated farms and tiny settlements of both Carolinas, Georgia, and Virginia. Some had fought at Musgrove's Mill. Mounted on horses for faster movement, they swarmed after Ferguson and his loyalists. This turn of events surprised Ferguson; he initially retreated. He soon, however, made the decision—although the safety of Cornwallis's base was within two days' march—to hold atop a sixty-foot-high piece of partially wooded ground called King's Mountain, located just inside South Carolina and west and south of Charlotte, North Carolina. The Americans by now were hungry for the kill. Fearful that Ferguson might slip away, they pursued him—and his loyalists—all the faster, sending forward their best-mounted men. The riders pushed all through a drizzly night, eventually reaching, by early afternoon on October 7, a position from which they could dismount for an attack.[4]

King's Mountain
OCTOBER 7, 1780

The Americans who tied or handed off their horses to holders and advanced up the hill in weather now clearing of rain were a coalition much the same as that which had fought at Musgrove's Mill a month and a half before. Their leaders were Isaac Shelby and John Sevier, who commanded the Tennessee Over-Mountain men (and both of whom Ferguson had threatened to hang); William Campbell, who commanded nearly two hundred Virginia riflemen; and Charles McDowell, Benjamin Cleveland, and Joseph Winston, who between them had some three hundred or so North Carolinians.[5]

The Americans had camped the night before at a place called Hannah's Cowpens—a location in South Carolina where cattle were regularly rounded up and herded, referred to as "the Cowpens" or simply "Cowpens"—and some thirty-five miles west of King's Mountain. At the Cowpens the American groups already described were joined by four hundred or so South Carolina riflemen under James Williams. The total

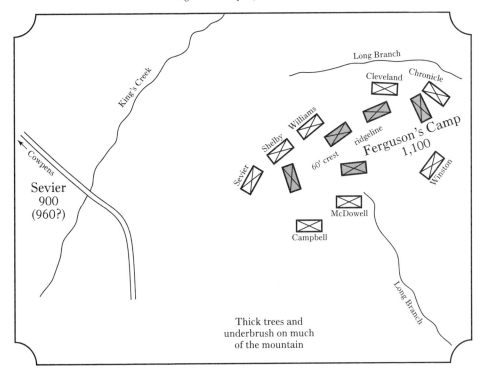

12. King's Mountain, October 7, 1780

force arrayed against Ferguson was nearly two thousand, although the number actually riding in advance to commence the attack—again, the best-mounted riflemen—was a little less than a thousand men (probably around 930 to 960).

Some maps show Ferguson's force as being situated all along King's Mountain, from a ridge beginning at its southwestern crest and running all the way to the broader portion that sloped to the northeast. If his men in fact occupied the southwestern point of the ridge at the beginning of the battle, they must have been pushed off in the early stages of the fight. What appears to have happened is that the Americans, under their coalition of commanders, divided the hill and its defenders into sectors before the attack and fanned out to commence their approach. In this way Shelby and Campbell, taking the southwestern portion of the ridge, attacked at opposite sides of the mountain. Williams, Sevier, and McDowell hit the next portion, which contained Ferguson's camp; and Cleveland and Winston hit from the northeast.

The battle thus appears one of encirclement. In fact, the Americans intended to fight it on a one-two punch basis, with Shelby and Campbell attacking first. The effect of this, once the attack had commenced, would be to draw Ferguson after these first two groups, leaving the others free to open up from the flanks and rear.

In the event, slipping through the trees, the riflemen managed to reach Ferguson's camp almost before his sentries could give the alarm. They opened up a deadly fire on Ferguson's ranks. Ferguson had not chosen to improve his position with breastworks or an abatis. He himself must have thought that his force, equipped with muskets and trained in the use of the bayonet in the British way, could smash the rebels. Certainly his men counterattacked aggressively, repeatedly pushing the riflemen down the hill. Each time, however, Ferguson's troops were driven back with heavy losses. In woods fighting of this bushwhacking sort, the long rifle was supreme, enabling the rebels to pick off their enemies with well-aimed, deliberate fire. When the riflemen were pursued down the hill, they fought in the frontier way, lashing out from behind trees with the hatchet and the knife. When they again advanced, they swarmed up the hill yelling what would come to be called in the Civil War the rebel yell. The loyalist ranks, receiving fire from all sides, began to flag. Ferguson, the rifle and irregular warfare theorist and expert, had lured himself into a situation where he could be destroyed by his own kind of warfare. He tried to lead a breakout charge. Mounted on a horse and swinging a sword with his left arm (his right one had been permanently disabled in the fighting before Philadelphia in 1777), he was hit by half a dozen rifle balls. He was struck down. So also were nearly a sixth of his men, not to mention the high number of wounded.[6]

The battle had been one between Americans. Ferguson had been the only actual British soldier present. The killed and wounded on the rebel side amounted to ninety men or just under 10 percent of the attacking force, and included two of the main commanders. Williams of South Carolina and William Chronicle of North Carolina both died in (or soon after) the battle. The British side lost roughly a third of the force, or 311 in killed and wounded. Approximately 660 of Ferguson's men were captured. The fight at King's Mountain, only an hour long, was a bitter fight, with the Americans continuing to pour in fire well after the point where the Americans on the other side had tried to surrender. Wounded loyalists were left where they had fallen, given neither food nor water. Dead loyalists were thrown into a long, shallow grave. Those captured were marched off toward Hillsborough, North Carolina, and were kicked or threatened with knives and hatchets along the way. As quickly as they could, the victorious rebels held a court-martial of their newly gained prisoners of war. Thirty-six were soon tried, a dozen sentenced to be executed, and nine immediately hanged. Additional numbers of the prisoners might also have been hanged had they not been able to take advantage of sleeping sentries to slip away during the night. The war in the backcountry carried a stiff price indeed if you were an American caught by other Americans on the wrong side.[7]

The loss of Ferguson was a personal loss for Cornwallis. But King's Mountain was much more even than the loss of a thousand-man force and a valued officer. It was a smashing defeat that showed in starkest terms the inability of British arms to acquire and employ a substantial force of loyalists. To raise loyalists in the interior of South Carolina had, after all, been a cornerstone goal of Whitehall's southern strategy. A defeat of this magnitude was hardly now likely to draw new numbers of loyalists flocking to the British camp. King's Mountain fell hard on the heels of the Swamp Fox's continuing operations near the coast and, inland, of Sumter's growing success in drawing men to the rebel side.[8]

Tearcoat Swamp
OCTOBER 25, 1780

Just under a month after his victory at Black Mingo Creek, Marion was again to achieve one of his greater successes in the general region of the Santee River. This one, against a loyalist force encamped at Tearcoat (also Tarcote) Swamp, was on the upper reaches of the Black River and about twenty-five miles north of the site of his summer victory at Nelson's Ferry.[9]

His object was the force of loyalist horsemen operating under Lieutenant Colonel Samuel Tynes. Tynes had assembled a sizable group and was looking to assemble even more men. Marion himself, using the arms and mounts captured from other loyalist forces since August—and on the strength of his growing reputation—could field some 150 men, his largest force to date. Still operating under the orders of Gates to harass the lines of communication that led to the British outposts in the interior, Marion continued to single out loyalist forces acting in support of the British for destruction.

As in other actions, he was aided by excellent intelligence from Whig families and their slaves in the area. He had sufficient knowledge of Tynes's location and strength to be able to arrive in the vicinity of the loyalist camp prior to midnight on the October 25. Marion again followed the approach proven successful the month before, organizing his command so that it could hit the loyalists on three sides simultaneously. When Marion's men thus charged in the darkness, firing pistols or muskets and carbines loaded with buckshot at close range, Tynes's command, relaxing about its camp (apparently Tynes had neglected to post sentries where they might give warning) and not ready for a fight, fell apart. The surprise was total. Marion's command suffered no casualties but killed three of Tynes's men and wounded a dozen others. Much of the rest of the loyalist force—two dozen men—was captured, leaving a like number of others to flee into the Black River swamps.

Two aspects of the action were significant. One was Marion's acquisition of eighty horses and that same number of brand-new muskets, plus accoutrements, useful for equipping additional followers, black and white.[10] The second aspect, in continuance of his earlier actions which saw loyalist support in the Santee–Pee Dee area of South Carolina all but smashed, was the ability of the Swamp Fox to reach out and strike British or loyalist outposts and units and then fade back into the swamps before he could be caught. Marion was building on success whereas Cornwallis's lines of communication in the interior were increasingly imperiled, a fact only too obvious to rebels and loyalists alike. This achievement was not, however, without personal cost to Marion. When loyalist horsemen in a subsequent action overtook his nephew, Gabriel Marion, they caught him and tied him to a tree at a crossroads. They then killed him by firing buckshot into his chest at point-blank range, leaving the body behind as a warning to those who might think to join Marion.[11]

But after King's Mountain, and given the ongoing defiance of the South Carolinians, Cornwallis had to pull back from further operations in North Carolina. He crossed back into South Carolina. An attempt by Marion to capture Georgetown was defeated, but it was known that other groups were rallying in the upcountry under Pickens. Sumter in particular needed immediate attention. Away from Marion's haunts in the lowcountry, much of South Carolina in that age, before widespread felling of timber, comprised the kind of good cavalry country that any horseman, British or American, prized. Substantial areas were virgin forest, largely free of underbrush or other impediments to movement. Beneath their canopy, the trees offered good avenues to freewheeling horsemen, whether actual cavalry or mounted riflemen. This latter mode, preferred by the backcountry militia and employed at King's Mountain, was one in which they rode to the battle but fought dismounted, using their rifles from cover to best advantage. Learning of the sizable force of this kind of militia gathering under Sumter, Cornwallis dispatched his dragoons before it could cause trouble.[12]

Fish Dam Ford
NOVEMBER 9, 1780

Major James Wemyss—the one who believed Presbyterian churches should be burned on the basis of their being "sedition shops"—was the officer appointed to chase the Gamecock. Wemyss's command comprised forty-five of Tarleton's British Legion troopers and a hundred infantrymen from his parent regiment, the 63rd Foot. Wemyss, the faster to chase Sumter, turned his whole force into a mounted one by putting the infantry on horses taken from the Americans or by letting them ride double behind the dragoons. It was his plan to catch the rebels at first light at their reputed camp at Moore's Mill on the Broad River.[13]

In fact, Sumter had shifted his camp some five miles down that same river to a point called Fish Dam Ford. The name derived from the man-made fishing weir of piled-up rocks that could be seen in the shallow parts of the stream. Sumter's force—also including some of the same South Carolina riflemen, those under Edward Lacey and William Hill who had fought at King's Mountain the month prior—deployed on both sides of the ford and put out sentries. This care in placing outposts was well taken in that, although Sumter was unaware at the moment that he was being chased, Wemyss had already learned from local loyalists and from his own scouts that the Americans had moved their camp to its present location. Wemyss had even designated five picked dragoons to be a team for killing or capturing Sumter.

The British force approached the camp in darkness, and, still in darkness, in early morning ran into the line of sentries placed to watch the approaches. In the exchange of shots that followed, Wemyss was wounded and put out of action. His second in command next led a charge down the road heading to the ford, taking fire all the while from the Americans camped in the woods on either side and by now thoroughly aroused.

As the action settled into a firefight, the Americans began to get the upper hand. The infantrymen of the 63rd, off their horses and fighting on foot, were pushed back with losses. So also were the troopers. The British at length disengaged, leaving behind the wounded Wemyss and other injured men under a flag of truce and near a fire; the wounded men were eventually paroled back to their own lines. In all, Sumter's command lost fourteen men wounded or killed. Wemyss lost a like number killed, but twice that number wounded or taken prisoner.

Sumter himself, as at Fishing Creek in the summer, only narrowly escaped capture or death. The team of dragoons sent to get him, guided by a local loyalist via an alternate route, quickly found its way to Sumter's tent. The Gamecock was surprised but, grappling with his enemies, managed to break away. He was without coat, trousers or boots; he said later that all that saved him from the night's freezing temperatures was the fact that he found and clung to an unsaddled horse.[14]

Sumter's lucky escape this second time encouraged the British to go after him all the harder. Cornwallis sent out Tarleton to conduct one of his hot-spurred pursuits across the interior in the direction of Ninety Six. It was Tarleton's plan to finish off the Gamecock by driving him against that point of loyalist strength. But this time there would be no repeat of Sumter's surprise and defeat of three months before, or of his close brush at Fish Dam Ford earlier that month. Instead, learning of Tarleton's intentions, Sumter planned accordingly, moving north as quickly as possible to dodge the trap. The fact that Wemyss had been captured caused the Americans to regard Fish Dam Ford as a victory, and new followers poured into Sumter's camps. Tarleton himself soon received word that Sumter was getting away, and decided to move even faster, choosing to pursue with cavalry alone and leaving the artillery. The dismounted portions of his command would hurry on as best they could. Sumter got as far as Blackstock's plantation on the Tyger River. There he stopped. Concluding that he was on good defensive ground, he prepared to fight. Altogether, reinforced by Georgia militia under Elijah Clarke, he had some four times the number of Tarleton's 270 mounted troops.[15]

Blackstock's Plantation
NOVEMBER 20, 1780

There followed a battle that the Americans should, given their numbers, in theory have won quite handily, but did not—in the sense that the

British were left holding the field. Yet they fought Tarleton to a stand-off. This was not least because American commanders were showing an increasing canniness about how best to employ their part-time soldier militiamen against their redcoat opponents. For the militiamen had heretofore often proved a poor match indeed for the well-trained and well-led infantrymen of the British Army in any fight requiring maneuver or standing up to heavy fire or the bayonet. And Sumter would know in advance that the force he would meet was precisely of this type: Legion infantrymen riding with the dragoons, and those of the 63rd Foot using captured horses. These last were veterans, tested in the siege of Charleston and recently at Fish Dam Ford. Upon reaching the battlefield, the group would dismount to resume its normal role of infantry, driving forward with the bayonet or firing disciplined, deadly volleys of buckshot and ball at close range. And of course there were Tarleton's dragoons. As at Buford's defeat in the Waxhaws, these would come charging, yelling and swinging their sabers down on top of the Americans as they tried to reload.

The engagement actually began two days before, when a party of Sumter's horsemen out on a reconnaissance exchanged fire with Tarleton's Legion and a battalion of the 71st Highlanders. The British were encamped at Brierley's Ford on the Enoree River. Casualties on both sides were light, and the partisans raced away to carry news of the contact to Sumter. Consulting with his commanders, Sumter planned a defense around the buildings comprising Blackstock's plantation. These were a main house and others situated on a hill overlooking the Tyger River on one side and, on the other, a small stream that emptied into the Tyger. Just to the north of this hill sat another, a ridge, covered mostly by trees and separated from the first by the road that led to the ford that crossed the Tyger. In the afternoon Mary Dillard—at obvious personal risk—rode in to tell Sumter that Tarleton's column, which had earlier passed by her house, contained cavalry and mounted infantry, but that the artillery and the rest of the British infantry, moving on foot, was some miles behind the mounted group.[16]

The Gamecock positioned Henry Hampton and his South Carolina riflemen to hold the main buildings at Blackstock's, supported by riflemen from Georgia. He himself occupied the ridge across the road, commanding units led by men already prominent in the backcountry war: James McCall, now a lieutenant colonel, who had gone into the Cherokee country after Cameron four years before; the Bratton who, with others, had attacked Captain Huck at Williamson's plantation in the summer; and the lieutenant colonels, Lacey and Hill, who had fought at King's Mountain, Fish Dam Ford, and other engagements. Sumter planned for Clarke's Georgians to attack in order to prevent the rest of Tarleton's force—the slower, dismounted portion, still some miles away—from being able to come up and support the mounted column. While the Americans were still occupying these various positions, Tarleton's mounted force arrived, coming up the road and deploying for attack.

It was now late afternoon. Rather than trying to "fix" the Americans—to hold them in place, that is, so that the rest of his force could come up in strength to finish them off—Tarleton decided to make an all-out attack with what he had. Despite odds of less than three hundred British or loyalist provincials against nearly a thousand Americans, the British attack began boldly and well. The redcoats of the 63rd Foot, now dismounted and fighting as the infantry they were, by their volleys and bayonet attacks drove back the American riflemen covering Sumter's left flank. But the momentum of their advance carried them into the zone of Hampton's riflemen, and these began picking off redcoats. Sumter meanwhile sent Lacey and his South Carolina riflemen through the trees to hit Tarleton's dragoons, at the moment quietly sitting their horses and awaiting the order to attack. The South Carolinians likewise inflicted casualties but were themselves driven back when the dragoons charged.

At this point, Tarleton decided to lead the dragoons in a charge that would either carry the Americans' main position at Blackstock's or else help the infantrymen to disengage. The dragoons spurred forward up the hill—and were stopped by Hampton's riflemen firing from their covered positions. As the British fell back, Tarleton with great courage picked up the 63rd's dying major and carried him—exposed to American fire all the while—on his horse back to British lines. Sumter likewise was exposed to enemy fire—from the 63rd, as he went forward to reconnoiter—and he was badly hit by buckshot in the shoulder, chest, and back. Covered by Lacey's riflemen, he was led from the field.[17]

Indeed, his whole force departed Blackstock's that night, crossing the ford and keeping fires burning as if still in occupation of the position. Tarleton, who occupied the hill next day, to his credit took care of the dead and wounded of both sides. The numbers told the story. The Americans had given up the position after dark and had lost three men killed and five men wounded. Tarleton was in possession of the field but had lost fifty-one killed and wounded (some accounts double this figure), and Sumter was still loose.

Both the nature of the pursuit—a high-quality but relatively small force of British regulars sacrificing available firepower (the artillery and infantry left behind) in order to move faster; and the nature of the battle—the tactical superiority enjoyed by British professional soldiers, in this case nullified by American numbers and rifles—were telling. The battle was small but illustrative of the nature of the problem confronting Cornwallis. As Tarleton was forced to lament to him in a message, he had taken losses that he could not replace. In a nutshell, this represented a British dilemma all through the war and especially in the South: the inability to replace losses in combat of first-class troops. The American militia had little hope of standing against the redcoats in a pitched battle—unless they could be employed in depth or by taking advantage of trees, brush, and cover. But if they fought in a way that minimized their exposure to linear formations of British infantry with bayonets, the militiamen at least had a chance. Tarleton, heavily outnumbered, claimed victory. Yet the Americans saw things differently. For the first time Tarleton had been stopped in a battle.

Long Canes
DECEMBER 11, 1780

Sumter's orders from Gates had been to harass the area of Cornwallis's new base at Winnsborough (now Winnsboro), a road-junction town situated in the hills between the Broad and the Catawaba rivers, and the loyalist stronghold at Ninety Six. This last was some forty-five miles distant to the west.

Having eluded Tarleton—and inflicted high casualties on British regular and provincial units in the process—Sumter's command, although he himself was recuperating from his wounds, was free to operate against these areas. Clarke with his Georgians and McCall his South Carolinians joined up with another Georgia force, this one under Benjamin Few. The Americans, numbering about a hundred men, set out towards Ninety Six.[18]

At the same time a British provincial and loyalist column moved out from Ninety Six, its purpose being to overawe the local Whigs and chase away rebel partisans. The column comprised 450 men, half loyalist militia and half the red-coated, quasi-regulars of the Volunteers of New York Regiment.

Clarke was in the lead of the Americans, and succeeded in ambushing the loyalist horsemen covering the British column. He then tried to hit the provincial infantry before it could attack, but was himself badly wounded in the ensuing volleys. In the end, the militiamen—who had taken nearly two dozen casualties—picked up the wounded Clarke and departed, having effectively shot up a substantial force that could make but little progress in subduing the Long Canes area. Indeed the loyalist column soon gave up on this task altogether and marched back to its base at Ninety Six.[19]

Halfway Swamp/Singleton's Mill
DECEMBER 12, 1780

The following day, over a hundred miles to the south and east across the state, Marion attempted his first action since being so heavily pursued by the British the previous month. His target was a column of British replacements intended for the 7th Foot or Royal Fusileers, now located at Cornwallis's headquarters at Winnsboro. These, amounting to two hundred men, were under escort of a detachment of the 64th Regiment.[20]

The escort was commanded by Major Robert McLeroth. Marion, riding north on the road above his old haunt of Nelson's Ferry, was about to hit the rear of McLeroth's column when the British officer quickly swung his command around and formed in battle array. At that point McLeroth made an unorthodox move: he formally challenged the Americans to a duel. Sending out a messenger under a white flag, he told Marion to choose an officer and his twenty best shots and he would do the same. The two groups would then shoot it out in a nearby field—and may the best side win.

Marion accepted the challenge. In reality, however, while these various preparations for the duel were being worked out, McLeroth was playing for time, using the delay to hurry his outnumbered troops (Marion had nearly seven hundred men; he had less than half that) further up the road to a better position. When Marion's picked team of duelists arrived as arranged for the event, they were surprised to see their British opponents suddenly do a turning movement and move off the field. Furious at having been duped, the Swamp Fox sent his men racing ahead to cut off McLeroth by a shortcut. The Americans arrived and installed themselves in a collection of buildings at a place called Singleton's Mill. When the British marched into range, Marion's men got off a volley. Then, to the surprise of the British, they were suddenly seen to be running for their horses. Puzzling over this strange behavior, McLeroth soon discovered what the Americans had just found out: the family that owned the mill all had smallpox. McLeroth and his command departed just as quickly as had the Americans.[21]

These various actions gave indication that Marion's and the other groups, even if not always successful, increasingly enjoyed the initiative. But if they continued to function solely in disparate guerrilla bands in this or that corner of the backcountry, the partisan units, though they might keep South Carolina stirred up from the lowcountry to the frontier, could not win by irregular warfare alone. Indeed, absent a viable American rebel army somewhere close enough to threaten Cornwallis— and so force him to keep his own army concentrated for a major battle— the British might yet prevail. They could disperse and act aggressively so as to hunt down the rebels, or so reinforce their outposts that the rebels could never take them (as would be indicated by Marion's repeated lack of success at Georgetown). On October 5, however, and two days before the King's Mountain battle, the Continental Congress had at last permitted Washington, the commander in chief, to pick the man he had wanted all along to command the Southern Department. That individual, Major General Nathanael Greene of Rhode Island, had been Washington's previous choice, but the Congress had instead selected Gates. At last Washington would have his way. Greene, perhaps the most talented commander available to the Americans after the commander in chief, proceeded to the Southern Department, reaching Charlotte on December 2 to relieve Gates.[22]

Greene found in North Carolina an American force comprising some 1,482 men, of which only a fraction were Continentals. It seemed probable that Cornwallis could move against him with more than three times that number of men any time he chose. The quality and quantity of weapons, food, and equipment available to the Americans were poor. So also was the level of their training. Greene received reports of the backcountry actions so far—most glowingly, of course, King's Mountain —but generally held little regard for these as the means of achieving victory over Cornwallis's army of disciplined regulars. Greene, like Washington, always endeavored to build a body of American regulars who, in terms of their own discipline, unit cohesion, and officer leadership, could go up against the redcoats on equal terms. On the other hand, he understood that he did not have such a force now nor was he likely to be able to field one in the immediate future. He needed time. Particularly he needed time to prepare, to bring in recruits and supplies, and to commence training and building the confidence of a force of Americans that for half a year had mostly tasted defeat.[23]

One way to do this was to keep Cornwallis occupied with the back-country guerrillas and not coming after him. At the same time, the delicate military calculus governing the survival of the partisan forces dictated that Cornwallis not be allowed a free hand against them. That is, he could not be permitted to disperse in a manner that would let him hunt down Sumter, Marion, and Pickens on a systematic basis. From Greene's perspective, Cornwallis needed to be forced to do two things at once: to keep chasing Gamecocks and Swamp Foxes, which meant a substantial degree of dispersion of forces on his part, and also to concentrate his forces—yet not so much that he was able to move back into North Carolina and destroy Greene's army before the American could have a chance to get it ready.

Greene thus had to threaten Cornwallis in a manner that would keep him dispersed and pursuing hit-and-run irregulars—but also sufficiently "massed" so as to be able to take on a substantial body of American regulars. He understood perfectly that Cornwallis would see an actual American army of Continentals as the real target—just as Greene himself would have had done had their roles been reversed. He therefore initiated his calculated risk for buying time by moving with the Continentals across the line and into South Carolina. The place he chose, the Cheraw area (or the "Cheraws") on the Pee Dee River, offered good positions, ample supplies of food, and a population overwhelmingly rebel in outlook. But the second step he took was the militarily unorthodox one of dividing his force—already inferior in numbers to Cornwallis's—into two even smaller ones. The smaller of the two he placed under Brigadier General Daniel Morgan. Numbering initially six hundred men, it was to move in the direction of Ninety Six in order to threaten that place so valuable to British interests. Also, he ordered Lieutenant Colonel Henry "Light Horse Harry" Lee (father of Robert E. Lee) of Virginia and his light cavalry/light infantry Legion into South Carolina to support Swamp Fox Marion. The news that the Americans, whom he outnumbered and had previously decisively beaten, had advanced into South Carolina and divided in two, with the second element now heading west towards the critical point of Ninety Six, was calculated to be unsettling to Cornwallis in terms of the practices of eighteenth-century warfare.[24]

It had the effect of forcing him to put off again a thrust into North Carolina—and also to have to divide his own army in order to deal with the American forces on the move. One part, the larger, he kept concentrated at Winnsborough, from which point he could move to block Greene should the Americans try to advance further. The other, a detachment of more than a thousand men, comprising infantry, cavalry, and artillery—his Legion plus reinforcements of British regulars and provincial units—was placed under Tarleton. This he sent after Morgan. The Americans called Morgan's force, which was unencumbered by artillery and thus able to move fast, the Flying Army.[25]

Nearly twenty years older than Tarleton, Daniel Morgan had seen some of the hardest fighting of the war. A cousin to Daniel Boone, Morgan had raised a company of frontier riflemen in 1775. He had participated in the American attempt against Quebec and, in the Saratoga campaign and commanding a special corps of riflemen, had played a key role in winning the battles that had helped defeat Burgoyne in 1777. A blunt, rough-hewn fighter, he had thereafter left the army in disgust when Washington selected another officer, Anthony Wayne, to command a larger, picked force of light infantry. But defeat in the South stirred him to leave retirement in Virginia in order to rejoin the fight. With his six hundred men—a nucleus comprising the excellent, proven regulars of the Maryland Continentals, plus dragoons under Lieutenant Colonel William Washington—he began edging towards Ninety Six on December 21. His mission from Greene, in addition to inspiriting the people and protecting them from British and loyalist raiders, was to raise all available local militia. He thus sent word to Andrew Pickens and to Sumter for support. He also sent William Washington's dragoons, reinforced by South Carolina militia, on raids intended to keep British attentions focused on him.[26]

Hammond's Store
DECEMBER 28, 1780

One of the most successful of these actions was fought three days after Christmas. Not only did Washington succeed in mauling a substantial force of loyalists, he also did so in an area of pronounced loyalist sentiment.

Hammond's Store itself was probably near the present-day community of Clinton, South Carolina, and within a dozen miles or so of Ninety Six. Washington's objective was not the store itself but a group of loyalist horsemen—some 200 to 250 of them, commanded by Thomas Waters from Georgia. The men had recently raided Whig areas and were now arrived in country they regarded as safe from pursuit.

Washington's eighty dragoons were backed up by just under two hundred South Carolina mounted militiamen under James McCall. McCall had been wounded at Long Canes the month before but had now recovered. Through good intelligence and by hard riding the Washington-McCall force managed to overtake the loyalists after a forty-mile ride. Catching Waters by surprise at Hammond's Store, the dragoons and militiamen managed to kill or wound some 150 men. The action turned into a running fight when Waters tried to get his command out. In addition to the casualties, a further forty loyalists were captured.[27]

A second force of militiamen the following day hit a fort north of Ninety Six, located at the Williams plantation. This action was successful in forcing the loyalist leader, Patrick Cunningham, to fall back to the safety of Ninety Six. The loyalists requested British protection to keep them safe from these raiders sent out by Morgan.

Cornwallis was looking forward to a meeting with Morgan, Greene, or both. He meantime awaited the arrival of Major General Alexander Leslie and 1,500 fresh redcoats from New York. These arrived in Charleston on January 8 of the new year and Leslie, wasting no time, immediately pushed into the interior. Leslie's arrival gave Cornwallis three forces. These amounted to a light, fast-moving British force under Tarleton that could hunt down Morgan and his Americans. A larger, slower-moving, but more powerful force of 3,300 men with artillery and supplies was under his own command; they would push up the valley of the Broad River. Finally Leslie, marching across the interior, would link up with Cornwallis and could help to smash Greene in battle. Cornwallis's particular hope was that Tarleton would be able to locate and hold Morgan in place. This would win time for one of the other two British forces to move up and finish off the Americans' Flying Army. They could next turn on Greene. Although Cornwallis intended for his and Tarleton's forces to stay within "mutual supporting distance" of each other—to be, that is, no more than a day's march apart—the reality was that the heavy winter rains and swollen rivers and creeks greatly slowed Cornwallis. This had the effect of allowing Tarleton to pull ahead. Supremely confident and ever aggressive, Tarleton now sought to do to Morgan what he had already done to a notable list of American commanders.[28]

The Cowpens
JANUARY 17, 1781

Morgan had reached the Pacolet River, at a point in the northwestern portion of South Carolina and some distance from where the river empties into the Broad. He was by now well aware that Tarleton was after him. At first moving to the south, he then faded back to the north. Perhaps he was not sure up until now that he was ready to offer battle. But he finally chose the Cowpens site.[29] It was familiar ground to some of his officers, and was—as it had been on the eve of King's Mountain—a main rendezvous point for the militia. Indeed some units continued to arrive there, one of them coming in just hours before the battle. These new units would swell Morgan's initial nucleus of six hundred to something over a thousand men.

Cowpens appeared good ground. Two roads coming from the south—one of them surely the way by which Tarleton would come—climbed up a slope and joined on top of a ridge. The ford over the Broad River was five miles to the north. Looking south from the hill, in the direction from which the British would likely attack, the ground on the left side fell off in a series of cuts; these became streams or branches of Thicketty Creek. Portions of the hill were wooded, others fairly open. Morgan was certain that Tarleton would come fast, determined to finish off the Americans before they could escape over the Broad River into North Carolina. Tarleton would come up the road keen to fight, take fire from the American troops along the hill, and immediately press home an attack—as at Biggin's Bridge, against Buford, and at Blackstock's.

Morgan listened to men who had fought at Camden, King's Mountain, and other points, but in the end took his own counsel regarding how to deploy at Cowpens. He devised a battle plan in three lines that would make best use of the capabilities of the units available to him—and that played upon Tarleton's bent for the bold attack.

From the point that Tarleton's column arrived at the bottom of the hill, Morgan planned a defensive arrangement that would force the

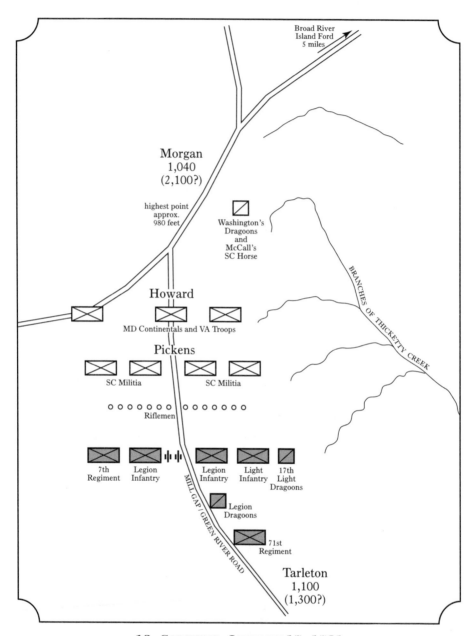

13. Cowpens, January 17, 1781

British to advance through concentrated rifle and musket fire coming from three successive lines of Americans. He himself had no artillery. Near the top of the hill, the third line of Americans—to be made up of the handful of regulars available, the Continentals—would meet the British in their own style, with volley fire and the bayonet.

By this plan the first Americans the British would encounter would be a line of sharpshooters. These, 150 Georgia, North Carolina, and South Carolina riflemen, would be deployed across the bottom of the slope, finding cover as best they could in the trees and brush. They were not to try to stand against the bayonets of the advancing British infantry. Morgan told them instead to get off two or three well-aimed shots and then fall back. Their purpose was to force Tarleton to halt his column and deploy for attack. They were particularly to aim for epaulets or other indications of rank—to hit, that is, the officers and sergeants by which the British maintained command-and-control and unit cohesion. The line of riflemen Morgan placed under Major Joseph McDowell of North Carolina—like many of his men, a veteran of Musgrove's Mill, King's Mountain, and frontier fights with the Indians.[30]

The next line up Morgan placed under Andrew Pickens of South Carolina. This line, amounting to perhaps five hundred men (some accounts give a lower, some a higher, number) was made up of militiamen. Some carried muskets, others rifles, but all operated in the mounted-infantry approach favored by the partisan bands—riding to the battlefield, but fighting on foot. Their horses were thus tied in the rear where, if things went against them, the militiamen could ride to safety. This line of men Morgan, with Pickens standing at his side, over and over told to get off three well-aimed shots and then retire.[31]

The final line—and upon which Morgan counted to be the hard core of the American position—would be made up of Continentals. There were less than three hundred of these, but they were good: veteran light infantrymen of the Maryland Line, commanded by the experienced Lieutenant Colonel John Eager Howard. Placed somewhat behind the Marylanders and in a position so that they could shift to cover several points were the eighty dragoons of Lieutenant Colonel William Washington's command. These in turn were backed up by South Carolina horsemen under James McCall, recently so effective at Hammond's Store. Some of these carried the pistols and sabers of cavalrymen, but many were essentially mounted riflemen acting in a cavalry role. The dragoons could charge in counterattack at the decisive moment or, if things went badly, charge to cover a retreat. They thus constituted a reserve for the Americans.[32]

To help Howard and the Continentals, Morgan assigned a battalion of Virginia militiamen under Major Francis Triplett. It was felt that these men, many of whom had previously seen service as Continentals, could operate to hold the flank of the Marylanders. It was abundantly clear to Morgan and to his commanders that if the British could break this final line, then the battle was lost, another Camden. The difference was that this one had a river a few miles away to block the Americans' escape.

Tarleton, meanwhile, came on with his customary speed and, hungry for a fight, was guided by a loyalist from the region. He drove men and horses to their limit. With good reason to be respectful of the accuracy of the long rifle, the British had developed tactics to beat it. The rifle, because it was slower to load than the infantry musket and did not carry a bayonet, remained essentially a hunting weapon employable in combat only under favorable circumstances. It could be used effectively from behind cover and when the rifleman had plenty of time to reload. The British therefore trained their cavalry and light infantry units in "immediate-action" tactics intended to exploit the rifle's slower, as compared to the musket, rate of fire. Such units were trained to advance and, if receiving fire, immediately to charge. The idea was to rush the Americans before they could reload. Also, British infantry armed with the musket (or its lighter, light-infantry version called the fusil or fusee) could get off three or more volleys per minute, whereas Americans armed with the frontier rifle could shoot only a third that fast. And, of course, facing charging bayonets and men—not to mention the standard practice of loading muskets or fusees from paper cartridges containing both ball and buckshot rounds, deadly at close quarters—would not have aided cool and deliberate loading, aiming, and firing.[33]

Tactics of this sort called for the cavalry and light infantry to move in advance of Tarleton's main column. The light infantry could effectively clear potential ambush spots, but in order to do so had frequently to deploy on line and sweep through to cover every ford along the way. Streams being plentiful in that hilly part of South Carolina, the January temperatures and dampness worked hard against the British soldiers. So also did the speed of the march, which prevented time for cooking or resting. In addition, Tarleton knew the country well from his chase after

Sumter the previous autumn, and he decided to steal a march on the Americans by moving all night. He did this by leaving campfires burning, a move that successfully deceived the American scouts watching from nearby and permitted his men to move closer and faster to Morgan than had been expected. Yet this level of exertion—the high-speed marches, the frequent stops to clear possible ambush points, the lack of hot food in winter weather—began to weigh heavily on the redcoats.

But Morgan's men by contrast were relatively rested and had fed well (at least some of them) on slaughtered beef taken (mostly) from loyalists. They also grasped the importance of the battle to come. A familiar story has Morgan passing around the campfires of his men on the night before the battle, stripping off his hunting shirt to reveal the scars he had received from a lashing—because of insubordination to a British captain—twenty-five years before. Morgan knew how to talk especially to the American militiamen, whose performance in battle likely would stem from considerations other than the drill and discipline thought to motivate regulars—the British, for example, with their long-term enlistments and fierce regimental pride. Morgan spent time with each unit, passing up and down the lines, explaining exactly what he wanted. He joked with them, but spoke with pride of their prowess with the long rifle. The militiamen would remember "Old Wagoneer Dan," his scars from the whipping—and about the three well-aimed shots.[34]

Tarleton's force contained some of the most proven British units in America. His infantry comprised a battalion of the 7th Foot (Royal Fusileers) and a battalion of the 71st Foot (Highland Scots). There were, as well, the veteran infantrymen of his own Legion. This gave Tarleton some seven hundred or more regular infantry troops as against the Americans' three hundred Marylanders—and perhaps another 250 or so if the ex-Continentals serving in Triplett's Virginia militia were counted. The British cavalry amounted to a troop (fifty men) of the 17th Dragoons, as well as the vaunted dragoons of his own Legion—fully some 250 cavalrymen in all. Two horse-drawn field pieces, of three-pounder-size, gave Tarleton a complement of artillery. In all his force—which also included loyalists, acting as cavalry and scouts—amounted to more than a thousand men.[35]

By the time his column reached the Cowpens after a wintry first light on the morning of January 17, Tarleton's men had been marching for five hours. Rifle shots and rebel yells suddenly erupted from the trees ahead. Men began to fall. Tarleton spurred forward, quickly waving the cavalry to charge and drive the Americans back. Instead, the screen of sharpshooters stopped the cavalry, inflicting losses in the process. Tarleton deployed, moving his infantry from columns on the road into line formation for an assault up the hill. The redcoats, huzzahing, moved forward with the bayonet and drove the riflemen back—perhaps bayoneting some of them to death, but again taking losses, especially junior officers, sergeants and corporals, in the process. The two British field pieces now opened up on the American position.

The British infantry continued its advance and next came within range of the second line of Americans, Pickens's militia. Waiting just down the rear slope of a small rise, the South Carolinians were ready. Picked marksmen walked forward a few paces and, raising their rifles, opened fire. Then the whole line opened up: firing, reloading and firing, reloading and firing again. Then they fell back to their left and, finally, around behind and to the right of the Continentals' line, a football field and a half to their rear. They fell back, not in a rout but in good order.[36] They had remembered about the three well-aimed shots.

The redcoats came on, volley-firing, cheering and charging up the hill—and smacked into the hard nucleus of the American main line, the Maryland Continentals. A misunderstood order to "refuse the flank"— that is, to shift around and block an enemy attack from the side—actually worked to the Americans' advantage. When a portion of this line, the Virginians, appeared to be falling back, the redcoats came on all the harder, thinking the Americans were crumbling. In fact, however, these turned about and fired pointblank into the attackers. Pickens's militia, likewise now established in their new position, threw in another volley from the flank, as did McDowell's North Carolinians, South Carolinians, and Georgians. The British charge faltered, losing momentum. Just then Washington's dragoons as well as the Continental infantry surged forward in counterattack. When Tarleton himself personally led a cavalry charge to try to save the situation, he was beaten back by the American cavalry. Much of his force, save for the battalion of Scots Highlanders, either held up their arms in surrender or ran. Accounts make it clear that only with great difficulty could officers prevent some of the Americans from giving Tarleton's men the same "Tarleton's quarter" he had given Buford the year before. The largest portion of Tarleton's force, including artillery, supply wagons, and a set of regimental colors, was lost.[37]

Tarleton had lost over a hundred men killed, over two hundred wounded, and six hundred men captured. Morgan had lost a dozen men killed and five times that in wounded. He had devised a defense in depth which endeavored to plan for, in realistic terms, the militiamen's probable performance against British regulars. He had used them in accordance with their capabilities—and backed them up with Continentals. By the time the redcoats reached the main line, the Continentals—the nearest approximation the Americans had to British regulars—could meet them on their own terms with close-range musket fire and cold steel. The militiamen and their commanders had kept good order, at several points on their own initiative seizing the moment to fire into the attackers with crippling effect. The Continentals alone could not have won the battle.

The news of the victory electrified Americans all across the South. Neither before nor after in this war would an American force so completely defeat a British one on the battlefield. Morgan, carrying with him wounded as well as prisoners almost as numerous as his own force, slipped that night across the Broad River lest Cornwallis catch him. South Carolina was once more open to the actions of rebel and loyalist partisans. Loyalist bands took reprisal in the days ahead against rebel militiamen who had been victorious at Cowpens, seeking them out and killing them in their houses, their families watching. Gamecock Sumter, dissatisfied with the sixty-day enlistment terms of his volunteer militia, came up with incentives of his own. Sumter's law, so-called, provided each man who completed ten months' service under him a slave and a horse plus other plunder, all to be taken from the loyalists. This could only fuel the civil war's reprisal and counter-reprisal, with the Americans' Greene noting that the backcountry was fought over by "little armed parties" acting against each other with "savage fury." The loyalists and the Whigs could be found "butchering one another hourly," and the war went on.[38]

But Tarleton and his force of regulars had at last been beaten. In three months' time British policy in the war had sustained two body blows. Cornwallis had first lost the hope of a loyalist rising in South Carolina. The numbers involved at King's Mountain had been small but the portents of the battle large. Now a second commander, hated and feared by the Americans, a hotspur who had galloped across South Carolina and time and time again had proved invincible, had been beaten in a battle where the numbers on the two sides were approximately equal. Major General the Earl Cornwallis said of the Cowpens engagement, "[the] affair has almost broke my heart."[39]

CHAPTER 7

AGAINST THE OUTPOSTS

1781

I will not say much in praise of the militia of the Southern Colonies, but the list of British officers and soldiers killed and wounded by them . . . proves but too fatally they are not wholly contemptible.

—Major General Lord Cornwallis

We fight, get beat, rise, and fight again.

—Major General Nathanael Greene

SOUTH CAROLINA was an easy country to invade but a hard one to occupy. To defeat rebels in South Carolina, Lord Cornwallis gave thought to methods that had defeated rebels in Scotland thirty-five years before. To put down the Highland clans that rose in support of Prince Charles Edward Stuart in the Jacobite rebellion of 1745, the British general the Duke of Cumberland had (1) sought to defeat his opponents in decisive battle, doing so at Culloden in April 1746, (2) placed, as his means of doing so, main reliance upon a conventional force of British regulars, (3) used loyal elements of the Scottish population to help defeat the disloyal ones, employing militia units as components of his army, and (4) the conventional battle won and the Highlanders routed, established garrisons and rooted out to destruction the infrastructure by which the clans were sustained.[1]

These approaches had proved highly—and ruthlessly—effective. The rebellious clans were smashed, Culloden was the last land battle fought in Britain, and the chief rebels were tried and executed for treason. Their severed heads, displayed on spikes at Temple Bar, were still visible decades later—a gruesome sight that did not fail to sober Americans visiting London on the eve of the trouble with Britain.

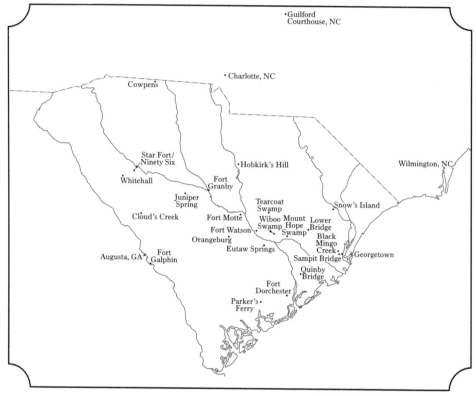

14. ACTIONS IN 1781

In Cornwallis's mind these two distant places, Scotland in "the Forty-five" and South Carolina after half a decade of rebellion, were not necessarily all that far apart. Rather, the two offered parallels instructive in terms of theaters of operations. In both cases there appeared to him the central and obvious military fact of dealing with a pack of rebels-in-arms. Against these as a category—as he would show again in Ireland in 1798—Cornwallis was prepared to move with whatever level of aggressive zeal the situation required. Also, both South Carolina and Scotland were close in terms of size, with 31,113 square miles for the former and 30,468 for the latter, inclusive of the Isles. Both had also received aid from an external great-power rival of Britain's, France, although South Carolina's share had been restricted to naval and logistical support rather than the actual troop units that had been sent to help the Scots in that earlier war.

And yet, apart from the obvious differences as to climate and terrain, the two cases differed in other fundamental ways that should have given pause to Cornwallis and the ministers in London, especially Lord George Germain, ever optimistic about the prospect of raising loyalists and of the war in general. One such area was basic geography. Scotland, of course, occupied the northern end of a European island whose sea approaches, over which outside help would have to come, could be controlled by British sea power. By concentrating military forces to take care of the land zone and naval forces the zones offshore, the British could effectively cut off and isolate Scotland. Not so South Carolina. It too, as demonstrated by the fall of its capital, Charleston, was vulnerable to British sea power, but only on one of its three sides. Triangular in shape, South Carolina possessed two other sides forming land frontiers that could not be controlled by sea power. The long, shared borders with North Carolina and Georgia had proved altogether porous when it came to the easy passage of rebel forces into or out of the state. Virginia also was a source of rebel forces, and not that far distant. By contrast, Scotland's insular situation afforded one border, south of which lay a historically more powerfully neighbor. South Carolina's situation was a continental one, with borders shared with (except for the Cherokees, who could be kept subdued through punitive campaigns) neighbor-states who in fact were sisters in arms.[2]

Moreover, in a land war fought on their own continent, the Americans could always hope to lure British military forces away from the advantages of their nation's sea power. It had been British sea power, after all, that had made possible the invasion of South Carolina the year before. Nearer the coast the British could fight the war by sea-based, amphibious means, and in that kind of war they enjoyed the inherent benefits of the interior position. That is, in an ocean war in the Atlantic, Britain was positioned not at the edges but at the center of such an arena. This position, along with the interactive support of their navy, offered shorter supply lines, a shorter radius of turn, and the ability to shift this way or that more rapidly to meet a threat. Above all, it meant the ability to bring overwhelming force to bear at a particular point. But the sea-power projection advantage fell away the further inland they moved. South Carolina may have represented a section of territory lesser in geographic extent than its neighbors to either side, but the fact remained that it was part of a huge continent, a piece of the main. It could not, by the methods which had worked so well against the Jacobites in Scotland, be cut off from help from its friends.[3]

Cornwallis had by now also had ample time to discern another basic reality of the situation: this time, as opposed to the Forty-five (and despite the exaggerated claims of the ex-royal governors and Germain regarding the Southern colonies and their loyalist populations), the numbers simply were not with the British.[4] Scotland's population at the time of the Forty-five was huge compared with South Carolina's white and black populations combined—and nearly twenty times its white population of only 70,000. But it was the relative proportions rather than the absolute numbers that told the story. Only a fraction of Scotland's population—the Highland clans, and by no means all of these—had risen in revolt. The more substantial element of the population, the Lowland Scots, had almost to a man had supported the Hanoverian king in London rather than joining the rebels. Of course, no such comparable overwhelming majority supported *either* side in the Revolution in South Carolina; however, the element actively supporting the British, at best a fragment of the overall population, was as a proportion of the whole nothing like as large as the clans that had chosen to take up arms for Bonnie Prince Charlie.

In 1746 Cumberland had moved into the Highlands with an army of 9,200 men to defeat the 4,100 or so that his opponent had mustered at Culloden. Counting Tarleton and Leslie, Cornwallis began his January 1781 offensive against Greene and Morgan with 6,200 men, both regulars and various loyalist units. The two American commanders together had at that point something under three thousand men, of which only the merest fraction could be counted regulars. So Cornwallis's numbers relative to his enemies' certainly looked as good as Cumberland's. But in this case looks could be deceiving. Cumberland had had the advantage of actually having more Scots on his side than Bonnie Prince Charlie had on his. But that was not the case with Cornwallis and the Americans. Cornwallis had only a relative handful of loyalists with him. Far more Americans were against him than with him—or were just neutral. Also, Greene's strength was as much in the potential as in the actual, since there were Americans ready to take the place of those lost to combat. And, by working feverishly, Greene's officers were able to recruit into the American camp men from Georgia, both Carolinas and Virginia.

Many loyalists had come out for the king when Cornwallis had invaded North Carolina—and paid a price for it when he fell back to Winnsborough.[5] Cornwallis's position was far from being as favorable as he believed it to be.

More than anything else Cornwallis wanted to bring Greene to battle and smash him as Cumberland had smashed the Scots at Culloden and as Cornwallis himself had already smashed the Americans at Camden. Battle was the payoff, and what general was ever heard to proclaim that victory in battle was not the ultimate test of his calling? Cornwallis believed that, had Morgan not been so quick to get over the Broad and away from him after Cowpens, he might yet have defeated him.[6] Above all, like virtually every other general officer before or since, he saw the conventional forces of his enemies, not the irregular ones, as his real target. So now he resolved to catch first Morgan and then Greene. He took from his army's earlier slow movement, and its inability to keep within supporting distance of Tarleton previous to the Cowpens battle, the lesson that his army would have to move faster in order to accomplish such a feat.

While he considered how best to do this, the American partisans continued to attack points all across South Carolina.

Georgetown
JANUARY 25, 1781

A week after the battle at Cowpens, Marion—assisted by Lee and the dragoons sent by Greene—mounted his second attempt on Georgetown. That post was the principal British garrison in the coastal portion of South Carolina above Charleston and, given the Swamp Fox's highly successful campaign in the Pee Dee of the fall, virtually the only main point in that region still left to the British.

Aided by excellent intelligence concerning the strength, disposition and numbers of the British garrison, Lee and Marion mounted an attack that soon gave them most of the town. In the process they captured the British garrison's commander, Lieutenant Colonel George Campbell. Yet loyalist troops continued to hold a strongpoint that commanded the town and which could be supported by vessels from the water. Marion and Lee lacked the artillery that could have reduced this position. In the end they had to give up on their attempt to take Georgetown—it was Marion's second try—and ride away.[7]

Wiboo Swamp
MARCH 6, 1781

Greene's idea—that sending Lee's dragoons to work with Marion would keep Cornwallis's forces stirred up all the more—was working well. Tarleton may have failed to catch the Swamp Fox the previous autumn, but other British soldiers were more than ready to try now.

Lieutenant Colonel John W. T. Watson, a Guards officer and a future general, commanded a force of loyalists, both horse and foot, and the battalion of a first-class British Army regiment, the 3rd Foot or Buffs. He envisioned a two-columned approach that would pin Marion at last and prevent his escape. Watson would move along the Santee River while Lieutenant Colonel Welbore Doyle, leading a second column made up of British regulars and loyalists, would proceed along Lynches River. The two forces could then either join each other or act in mutual support if one of them discovered the quarry. These two officers did not know the precise location of Marion's base in the swamps, but reckoned that this slow, methodical, double-pronged movement was a good way to find it— and probably better than Tarleton's unsuccessful hell-for-leather one.[8]

But the Swamp Fox was himself well aware that Watson and Doyle were looking for him. He used a screen of scouts and informers to track the progress of both groups. Marion decided to hit Watson's column along the Santee at a point in the Wiboo Swamp—a location part of the Santee-Cooper Project's Lake Marion since 1941, and approximately due south of the community of Manning. The advantage of fighting in this area was that British movement was restricted to the few causeways that crossed the swamp. These could then be defended by relative handfuls of men, who themselves could fall back if pressed too hard.

In this way Marion made Watson pay a stiff price for each causeway position he took. Watson used artillery to drive Marion's men back from one outpost, but this rearguard action won time for the bulk of Marion's command to escape across the swamp. Yet Watson still came on, chasing the Swamp Fox across the Black River towards Kingstree. Heavy rifle fire from the Americans at last caused Watson to give up trying to cross the bridge to catch Marion; he and his men rode away.

These various skirmishes—fought at Mount Hope Swamp, the Lower Bridge of the Black River, and at Sampit Bridge, where Marion slipped around to attack the rear of Watson's column—continued over several weeks. In the end, Doyle—a loyalist officer—managed to locate Marion's base at Snow's Island. Doyle's men attacked, killing seven and wounding fifteen of the partisans left behind to hold the camp. But there were few stores left to destroy, and the rest of Marion's men had long since dispersed. The failure of the Watson-Doyle effort to corner the Swamp Fox was more far-reaching than the number of casualties taken, or the fact that its commanders simply had to return empty-handed, might seem to indicate. Rather, it showed that the Pee Dee region, strongly rebel since the beginning, was still that way; it certainly had been for the last ten months since the fall of Charleston. And Cornwallis's predilection for seeking decisive combat with the main American army under Greene meant that fewer and fewer British troops would be available for running down the Swamp Fox or pacifying the backcountry.[9]

Cornwallis commenced his second invasion of North Carolina in the wake of Cowpens. That defeat was a humiliation that spurred him to new extremes of effort. He gambled on a race that would take him, before it was over, all the way across North Carolina and actually into Virginia. His object was to cut off the Americans, making them fight a battle Cornwallis had no doubt he could win. He first pursued Morgan, hoping for revenge and to regain the British troops taken prisoner at Cowpens. He made every effort to move as fast as possible, scaling down his troops' tentage and equipment, and burning extra supplies and most of his wagons. He also took the extreme step of ordering the casks containing his army's rum ration dumped out—as he did, by personal example, holding up his own flask to pour out its contents in front of the troops. The impact of this last step on his men's morale may not be known precisely, but the wet weather, grueling marches, and reduced rations soon proved galling to Cornwallis's army; nonetheless, they moved fast enough to close to within ten miles of Morgan. Cornwallis fought his way past North Carolina militiamen trying to hold a ford on the Catawba; the Americans' commander, William Davidson, fell in the process. Yet the Americans still kept ahead and, early in February, successfully linked up with Greene and the main army in North Carolina. So also eventually did Brigadier General Isaac Huger, who led a small force of South Carolina militiamen, some of them so poor off in clothing and equipment that they had had to march without shoes. Greene was initially inclined to wait for Cornwallis and fight. In the end, though, he decided to fall back to the north. This decision induced a second series of forced marches that was hard on both armies, but harder on Cornwallis's.[10]

Cornwallis, now down to under three thousand men, pressed on as before, pushing hard to try and cut off Greene before the American could get his army into Virginia and safely across the Dan River. Tarleton, with his old style, managed to hunt down and defeat a force of militiamen. In the event, however, the Americans again won the race and Cornwallis, lacking boats to get over a stream swollen from seasonal rains, had to halt. Eventually he fell back to Hillsborough in North Carolina.

His call for loyalists to join him brought only meager response. The loyalists, like those in South Carolina, needed assurance that the army had come to stay and not go chasing off in some new direction after Greene. Also at this time Light Horse Harry Lee—until recently cooperating with Marion in South Carolina—and Pickens's militiamen managed, on the Haw River on February 25, to ambush the small force of loyalists that did try to join Cornwallis. Lee's and Pickens's actions, along with Cowpens and King's Mountain, were having their effect. Few loyalists were ready to come out for an army whose numbers were down and showing the effects of a hard winter's march across North Carolina. Greene—whose own army was suffering problems regarding sickness and exhaustion—by contrast was able to use the time to bring in recruits and militiamen, for whom Cowpens and King's Mountain had had quite the opposite effect as upon the loyalists. Equally important, he received early in March additional Continental troops. Various reinforcements brought his total to 4,400 men (a force larger than Cornwallis's), a fifth of whom were regulars of the Continental Line. He moved south into North Carolina again, ready at last to take on Cornwallis in a drawn battle.[11]

Guilford Courthouse
MARCH 15, 1781

Greene chose to do so at Guilford Courthouse just under two months after Cowpens. Since essentially the same ingredients were present as at Cowpens—militiamen from the Southern states, riflemen, cavalry and the nucleus of Continentals on the American side, and the veteran British infantry and Tarleton's cavalry on the other—it was not surprising that Greene chose to fight in the same manner. He no longer enjoyed the services of Morgan, however, who had had to return to Virginia with crippling back pains not helped by the forced marches of February.

Cornwallis came on, pushing his men to march a dozen miles beginning at dawn to get to the field on the day of battle. Greene by this point outnumbered his opponent better than two to one; as had Morgan, he sought best to array his army according to its various fighting capacities. The Americans were thus positioned in three main lines on sloping hills that offered both trees and clearings. It was the Cowpens formula all over: the advanced line of militia riflemen to get off their lethal shots; a second, far more substantial body of militia to inflict further casualties; and the Continentals, as before making up the last line, to stop the British with volleys and counterattack with the bayonet. Cavalry—Washington's and Lee's—would attack from the flanks.[12]

Yet the Cowpens arrangement would not work so successfully again. Cornwallis was far too able a tactician not to analyze the reasons for the defeat in January. This time he ensured that his troops and their officers were well prepared for what the Americans were likely to do. In early afternoon he deployed his infantry in line-of-battle formation. The attack commenced. A first line comprising Highlanders, Hessians, and line infantry advanced, followed up by battalions formed by guards detachments from the 23rd, 33rd, and 71st regiments, and the light infantry and Tarleton's cavalry. This last formation, partially rebuilt to its previous strength, had proved very effective in the pursuit across North Carolina—managing, although Tarleton had not known it at the time, to come within an ace of capturing Greene himself. The provision by Cornwallis of these follow-on infantry battalions and the presence of Tarleton's cavalry would work to unhinge the Americans' Cowpens-style plans. The second line of infantry, by closely following the first, would help to keep up the momentum of the British assault, and the Legion's dragoons would deflect the American cavalry's counterattack.

In the event the militia riflemen got off their well-aimed shots as before, inflicting high casualties before being driven back. So also did the second line of militia—particularly the Virginians, some of them fighting to avenge their showing at Camden seven months before. Now, considerably reduced by fighting their way through these two lines but finally reaching the Continentals, the British were met by a bayonet charge. They fell back and then, quickly reforming, were hit from the side by another attack: Washington's dragoons and the Cowpens-veteran Marylanders. A melee ensued. Cornwallis had only three pieces of artillery, but at this point ordered them to fire grapeshot into the Americans—all but certain as he did so that some of their shot must find British soldiers as well as American. The British charged but were again halted.[13]

Greene outnumbered Cornwallis (although it was true that the British commander had him in the critical category of regular troops), he was on ground of his own choosing, his men were better rested than their opponents, and he was carrying out a plan he had had time to prepare. This would appear to have been the moment to order the decisive, battle-winning counterattack to gain an even greater Cowpens. But Greene held back. Instead of attacking, he ordered a general withdrawal; the Americans, their way covered by Virginia Continentals and riflemen, fell back in good order. The British were in possession of the field, the Americans leaving it. Cornwallis had beaten a second American army in the field.

But had he? By the standard indicator of who was left holding the field, Guilford Courthouse was clearly a tactical victory for the British. Yet it was no Culloden, no decisive victory over an enemy force. Cornwallis's troops held the ground. They were, however, so done in by the march and the combat itself that they were scarcely able, after the battle, to tend to their own wounded. Many lay on the ground where they had fallen, suffering as well from exposure to rain and temperatures that plummeted during the night—and perished. Also, the earlier destruction of the extra rations, so that the army could move faster, meant that each soldier's share was at best a few ounces of beef and flour. It remained far from clear where the next day's rations, or those the day after that, would come from.[14]

Cornwallis had lost over five hundred men—better than a quarter of his army in killed or wounded. Losses had been particularly high among some of his best units—the Highlanders, for example—not to mention the high cost in officers and sergeants. The Americans, he remarked later, had fought like demons. Not only had Greene's army not been destroyed, it had not actually been all that badly hurt. In actual numbers, he had lost about 250 fewer men than Cornwallis, and he had every expectation of being able to replace these within days of the battle.

A Culloden-style victory may have been Cornwallis's goal, but such by this stage of the war was not a likely outcome. Of the American commanders in the South, the successors to Lincoln and Gates had learned the hard way that they would have to—and in fact had—come up with new and innovative tactics and ways of fighting if their men were to have a chance against the redcoats. Their problem was the same one that

Washington faced: Americans would show up for the battle, but it was hard to keep them around long enough to turn them into a trained force. Some means was therefore needed by which to offset the limitations they faced as part-time soldiers—the successive lines of militia in a defense in depth, anchored by the nucleus of Continentals, for example. Greene ordered a withdrawal out of a realistic assessment of what his men—and his relative handful of actual regulars—could really do. He was well aware that Cornwallis still had Tarleton in reserve, and while Tarleton may have lost his reputation for invincibility, no one on the American side regarded him as a force not to be reckoned with.

For the reality was that Greene had sustained a tactical defeat that was a strategic victory. Greene's was a defeated army that, in relative terms and as replacements came in, was stronger after defeat than before it. Cornwallis's victorious one, though, was just the other way around. He was short on supplies; he judged that he had insufficient troops to take on Greene again, and at length chose to follow the Cape Fear River down to Wilmington, North Carolina. This move put him in touch with the Royal Navy and its capacity to bring messages and replenish supplies and equipment. His mission from Clinton had not altered: to ensure the pacification of South Carolina and its restoration as a royal colony. Cornwallis had won no sweeping Culloden victory, and the rebels to his flanks and rear appeared more powerful than ever. Given his mission and this situation, his priority now should have been not conquest of a new arena but to solidify existing British gains in an old one.[15]

But Cornwallis had fixed his sights on Virginia. By attacking that most populous of the thirteen American colonies, he believed he could force Virginia to keep its troops at home rather than sending them south to help the Carolinians. He could also hurt the Americans economically, and there remained the allure—if he could gain reinforcements—of some new battlefield victory. In April 1781, he and his column of troops, now rested and re-equipped, left Wilmington and began marching, not south to look after the British outposts in South Carolina but north, to what he hoped would be new gains in Virginia.[16]

By this choice he exposed those outposts to attack by the same partisan bands as before. The various bands and groups opposing him and raiding his communications were now supported by an American army that he had already beaten. Against this same "beaten" army, however, Cornwallis reckoned that he could not move with the numbers presently available to his own army. Greene's idea, by contrast, was to employ the irregular forces of Pickens, Sumter, and Marion with Continentals in a cooperative effort that could capture the main British garrisons and outposts across South Carolina, one by one. Had Cornwallis remained in place and kept well supplied by the advantages of sea power, this approach would not likely have worked. Rather, Cornwallis could have waited for the Americans to show their hand—and drawn them into battle more on his own terms, precisely as Washington had recognized.

Fort Watson
APRIL 15–23, 1781

Greene began by sending Lee back to act with Marion. Their objective was Fort Watson, named for its British commander, the same Lieutenant Colonel Watson who had recently been chasing the Swamp Fox. It was located on the Santee River where the main road to Camden came up from Charleston. American control of Fort Watson would assist Greene's own efforts to take Camden, the main British outpost in the central part of the state, by helping to isolate the latter. While these moves were afoot, Greene sent Pickens to stir up trouble around Ninety Six, the further to dishearten the loyalists after Cowpens and the subsequent departure of the main British army in the South to North Carolina and Virginia.

Fort Watson—surrounded by an abatis and unique because it was built atop an ancient Indian mound—had, two months before, already bested an American force under Sumter. The fort was in Sumter's neck of the woods, and the Gamecock had apparently eschewed carrying out any sort of reconnaissance before attacking it. The British and loyalists beat him back with heavy losses. The defeat apparently so enraged some of his men that they later, having ambushed a supply convoy on its way to the fort, invoked Tarleton's quarter to shoot down some of the surrendered British troops—a favor the British themselves soon returned when they captured some of Sumter's men. Lee and Marion now faced only a handful of British and loyalist troops—but had neither artillery nor picks and shovels by which to attack the thick walls. Moreover, the bulk of the fort's garrison, out again on another foray to hunt down guerrillas, was expected to return at any moment. In the end Lee and Marion captured the fort by building a log tower—named after militia Lieutenant Colonel Hezekiah Maham, whose idea it was—by which riflemen could fire from elevated protection into the fort. Unable to fire back, the fort's garrison surrendered on April 23.[17]

Hobkirk's Hill
APRIL 25, 1781

The fact that this effort had now cut off Camden, Greene's objective, from British help from the south should in theory have greatly aided the American commander. It did not prove so in practice, however. Greene's opponent was Lieutenant Colonel Francis, Lord Rawdon, who commanded a force smaller than the American one but which enjoyed access to a number of previously and well prepared defenses. Moreover Rawdon, while only twenty-seven, was no pushover and had soldiered in America since the beginning of the war. The future Earl of Moira and Marquess of Hastings, he was to serve with distinction a quarter of a century later in India—and would, as governor general of Britian's vast holdings on the Asian subcontinent and as commander in chief, act to defeat numerically superior forces of sepoy (Indian soldier) enemies. Two days after Lee's and Marion's victory at Fort Watson and while Greene waited for reinforcements, Rawdon seized the moment and went after Greene.[18]

Greene's army, about 1,200 or so (some accounts say 1,500) men in all, contained a brigade each of Maryland and Virginia Continentals, two squadrons of cavalry, including William Washington's dragoons, a small component of North Carolina militiamen, and three artillery pieces. Rawdon's force of approximately nine hundred men consisted of the regulars of the 63rd Foot and an artillery battery, plus a number of loyalist units: the Volunteers of New York, a South Carolina regiment of provincials, the Volunteers of Ireland, and the King's American Regiment. His cavalry, likewise a provincial unit, comprised New York loyalist dragoons.

The Americans were situated on a ridge just north of Camden, called Hobkirk's Hill, and Rawdon's force slipped through the woods to catch them by surprise. Hard fighting followed in which the British, copying the American practice, used riflemen to pick off officers and sergeants. Rawdon's hope of achieving surprise over the Americans was only partially fulfilled, however, since Greene had placed outposts that held up the British long enough to win time to array his force. The process of getting through the woods had kept Rawdon restricted to a narrow

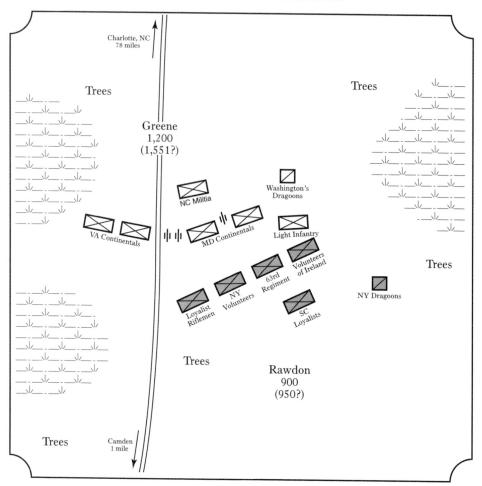

15. HOBKIRK'S HILL, APRIL 25, 1781

front. Greene tried to overlap both sides of that front, but the British commander quickly brought up a second line to cover the first. In this fighting at close range, a key officer in one of the Maryland units went down early and, to overcome the confusion, the regimental commander attempted to reform the line. But this maneuver exposed the flanks of other American units, and Greene ordered his artillery to fire into the British. This slowed his opponents' momentum and won him some time. He was, however, as at Guilford Courthouse, eventually driven from the field. Yet the costs to Rawdon were, like those of Cornwallis at Guilford Courthouse, also very high. Thanks to Rawdon's audacity and skill, the British had gained another tactical victory at Greene's expense—but at the forfeiture of high-quality troops. Greene, in addition to those missing, had lost 132 men in killed and wounded. Rawdon had lost in killed, wounded and missing 262, or a bit under a third of his force.[19]

Greene sidestepped a second encounter with Rawdon but the British commander, although reinforced early in May, ultimately decided to give up Camden altogether. His goal was to let some outposts go in order to consolidate available forces into a new British field army for South Carolina and Georgia. Apparently neither Clinton nor Cornwallis saw fit to take steps at this time to ensure that a British officer of general's rank be appointed to command, and into Rawdon's able but youthful hands fell this new effort.

Fort Motte
MAY 8–12, 1781

Lord Rawdon did not fail to let his men destroy Camden's fortifications —or for that matter, much else of the town as well, including its courthouse, all other public buildings, and every large house in sight. He began moving south towards Charleston. As he did so, a point on his route of march was Forte Motte—essentially the Motte family's house at Mount Joseph Plantation, improved by the British with the addition of palisaded walls, earthworks, and an outlying ditch. The place was located on the Congaree near where the river joined the Wateree, and where the road from Charleston came by.

A 140-man force of British, Hessians, and loyalists held the position. Lee and Marion, three weeks from their Maham-tower success at Fort Watson, were soon hard at work conducting deliberate siege operations to take it. It was to their considerable alarm, therefore, that they observed campfires burning on the High Hills of Santee, only two days' march or so distant. These belonged to Lord Rawdon's force, now on their way south from Camden, and signified that the British were within range of being able to relieve Fort Motte—and perhaps catch its American besiegers from behind. If the siege were to achieve results, it would have to be soon. Lee and Marion had already discussed using fire arrows or some other means to try and set the roof of the house on fire. The mistress of the plantation, Rebecca Brewton Motte, was a backcountry Whig who without hesitation agreed to the attempt, according to one account going so far as to volunteer the actual bow and arrows to be used. In short order the Americans shot their flaming arrows, attacked, and the British garrison surrendered. The two sides somehow managed to put out the fires before the house was lost. In best plantation style, the lady of the house then set down the officers of both sides to dinner.[20]

Learning that Fort Motte had already fallen, Lord Rawdon decided to push on and try and save others of the posts yet in British possession. Lee and Marion themselves soon rode on to other opportunities.

Orangeburg
MAY 11, 1781

Fort Motte fell on May 12. The day before, Sumter had managed to take possession of Orangeburg, its British and loyalist garrison, and its ample stores of supplies. Orangeburg was a key link on the network of roads that connected Charleston with Augusta, Ninety Six, and other points. By aggressive action the Gamecock, after his slow and painful recovery from the wounds received at Blackstock's, had been able to make a show of strength that overawed the garrison's commander. He had only fifteen regulars and a handful of loyalists, and Sumter's horsemen—their ranks swelled by the considerable appeal of Sumter's law—caught them before they could prepare a proper defense. The booty acquired at Orangeburg helped bring in additional men.

Fort Granby
MAY 15, 1781

Sumter also tried but failed to take Fort Granby, another important British post, this one situated on the Congaree River below present-day Columbia at Cayce, where the road between Ninety Six and Camden reached it. After cooperation with Marion in the taking of Forts Watson and Motte, Lee had pushed west so as to support operations that Greene envisioned for Ninety Six. The Swamp Fox remained active in his own Pee Dee–Santee region. He specifically, as ordered by Greene, intended to go after Georgetown again.

Fort Granby, also referred to as the Congarees, was a plantation house and former storehouse for the Indian trade improved by fortifications into a strongpoint. These improvements included a parapet, batteries, redoubts, and a ditch. Most of the position was covered by an abatis. Sumter had come close to taking it by surprise, but an informant had given Lord Rawdon warning and time to reinforce it. The garrison was potent—nearly three hundred loyalists, sixty British regulars, and an artillery battery.

Lee expected a difficult and lengthy siege operation. Apparently declining the chance to take the fort by surprise, he set to work emplacing his own light artillery pieces where they could fire on the building and the walls of the fort. His men captured the outlying pickets and a patrol returning to the fort.

The fort's commander, a loyalist, soon began talks with Lee under a white flag. His demand was that he and his garrison, plus a rich quantity of supplies and personal property, be allowed to march away—in return for which Lee could have the fort. Lee agreed to these terms. It was well that he did so, since Rawdon, by now alerted to the danger facing Granby, was leading a relief force to the fort's rescue. But the terms had already been agreed to and signed, and he and his force had no choice but to honor them and turn back. The Americans had won another outpost in the backcountry.[21]

Fort Galphin
MAY 19–21, 1781

Four days later, one of Lee's officers, Captain John Rudolph, gained another. This one, on the Savannah River a dozen miles south of Augusta, was useful to the British as a point where goods destined for the Creeks and the Cherokees could be stored before being distributed. It was garrisoned by loyalists and provincials, and occasionally reinforced by other British units passing through.

Part of the American forces now gathering for an attack on Augusta drove boats and their covering force of British troops into the fort. When Captain Rudolph—soon backed up by the rest of Lee's Legion—finally took Fort Galphin on May 21, the Americans acquired a considerable haul in arms, equipment and supplies. A British and loyalist force of something under two hundred men surrendered with the fort.[22]

In just over six weeks' time the Americans had taken or acquired five inland points on the British line of outposts: Camden, Orangeburg (although the British were for a short time to regain its use later), and Forts Motte, Granby, and Galphin. Two major points at opposite ends of that line in South Carolina, Georgetown and Ninety Six, as well as Augusta in Georgia, now remained. Greene had already sent Marion (the Swamp Fox at more than one point risking his life to pass through enemy territory in order to hold coordination meetings with the commander of the Southern Department) against Georgetown again. Pickens and his South Carolina militiamen, some units of them elevated to the designation of full-time state troops, and backed up by Lee's Legion and an assemblage of Georgia militiamen, would go after Augusta. Greene himself would take Ninety Six, the loyalist strongpoint that had been long—and unsuccessfully—the target of rebel attempts at capture.[23]

Augusta, Georgia
MAY 22–JUNE 5, 1781

Two British forts, Grierson and Cornwallis, defended Augusta. Pickens could only have harbored ill feelings indeed against the loyalist elements of the town, since a younger brother of his, earlier captured by loyalists and Indians, had been burned at the stake near there. Lee and his Legion crossed the Savannah River to link up with Elijah Clarke. An additional detachment of riflemen, under Isaac Shelby, comprised veterans of King's Mountain. Clarke, a resolute fighter and a veteran of Musgrove's Mill, Blackstock's, and Long Canes, had—assisted by James McCall of South Carolina—already made a previous attempt on Augusta in September 1780. That attempt was unsuccessful, but it nonetheless gave Clarke useful information regarding the British defenses.[24]

A conspicuously effective component of those defenses was the body of loyalist rangers commanded by Colonel Thomas Browne. Browne, a merchant from England, had come to Georgia to make his fortune in the Indian trade. The force of rangers he raised after 1776 enjoyed the services of Cherokee and Creek warriors. Clarke, in his first attack, had been forced to abandon a number of his wounded. These were either hanged by Browne or handed over to the Indians to meet the same fate as Pickens's brother.[25]

But this new American attack was much more numerous and better organized. Pickens, Lee, and Clarke began with Fort Grierson. When the defenders of this position tried to fight their way out, a substantial portion of them fell in a running firefight. As at King's Mountain, the Americans shot some wounded or surrendering loyalists out of hand. This left Fort Cornwallis, the larger of the two forts, to the British and loyalist garrison with Browne in command. The American forces lacked artillery in any quantity, so they gave thought to a Maham tower. This device proved successful, its elevated, protected cover letting riflemen pick off anything that moved inside Browne's fort. Unable to get help from Ninety Six or Savannah, Browne at length had to open negotiations. Fort Cornwallis finally surrendered on June 5. With Augusta now in American hands, Browne and his force of over three hundred men, the bulk of them loyalists and accompanied by their families and whatever possessions they could carry, were marched under guard down the river to Savannah.

The Siege of Ninety Six
MAY 22–JUNE 19, 1781

The other point that Greene wished to take, Ninety Six, would not prove so easy. This most important of the British inland posts—indeed it covered the single most populous district in the entire colony—was held by a garrison well equipped and determined to hold out.[26]

The British had worked extensively to improve the position. It was no longer the makeshift of barns-expanded-into-forts of the Cherokee War or of Williamson's defense in November 1776. Rather, it now incorporated a set of fortifications as extensive, this far inland (with the possible exceptions of those at Pittsburgh or the forts guarding Lakes Champlain and George in the far North), as any in America. The fort comprised a central work as well as outer ones. Its central feature was an earthworks fortification called the Star Fort or Star Redoubt. This, to the east and north of the village of Ninety Six, comprised an embankment, more or less in an eight-pointed star shape, replete with the fraise (pointed stakes emplaced in the wall) cut-slope, parapet with firing steps and ports, and banquette features specified in European military engineering manuals (in fact, much of the fort had been designed by Lieutenant Henry Haldane of the British Army's Royal Engineers). The earthen wall that incorporated these various features was surrounded by a dry ditch. This in turn was further covered by an abatis. The Star Redoubt was the strongest feature at Ninety Six, but in fact the whole village was fortified. The masonry jail had been expanded into a redoubt, and earth had been heaped up—by a labor battalion of blacks pressed into service by Cruger—around its stockaded walls. Two strong block houses covered opposite points of the town. An abatis circled the wall. The position was well supplied with food and ammunition. Water, on the other hand, was a critical issue, and it was clear to the garrison that the Americans might try to capture the main source, a point just west of the village.

Ninety Six was held by one of the best of the loyalist officers, Lieutenant Colonel John Harris Cruger, from New York. His force of 550 men was made up of a battalion of de Lancey's New York provincials and others from a New Jersey loyalist battalion. These were joined by more than two hundred South Carolina loyalist militiamen under Robert Cunningham, brother of the Patrick Cunningham who had contested Williamson for the fort four years before. This present Cunningham, a judge before the war, had been given a brigadier general's commission in the loyalist militia by Lord Cornwallis.

A great irony for Greene—given the way his effort against Ninety Six would turn out—was that Lord Rawdon had actually sent word to Cruger to abandon the fort and fall back to Augusta. But the Americans had intercepted the messenger; Cruger never got the word. He decided to fight, doing everything in his power to improve his position until the Americans arrived to begin their siege.

Greene's army amounted to just under a thousand men, including about nine hundred or so Continentals from Delaware, Maryland and Virginia, plus North Carolina militiamen and a scouting detachment. This force was nearly twice as large as Cruger's, but hardly sufficient to undertake full-scale siege operations against such excellent fortifications. Of great benefit to Greene was the fact that his staff included Thaddeus Kosciusko, the Polish engineer serving with the Americans who had, five years before, designed the defenses which stopped Burgoyne's offensive of 1777, as well as the defenses that guarded the Hudson River at West Point.[27]

Kosciusko recommended to Greene an approach that would maximize the Americans' limited numbers by concentrating on the Star Redoubt. Greene accepted his recommendation although this would mean beginning at the enemy's strongest point. The Americans would build a succession of parallels—trenches and earthwork embankments covered from enemy fire and connected by zig-zag trenches—with the final one being actually inside the ring of Cruger's abatis. A Maham tower erected at the second parallel would let riflemen fire over the fort's walls and cover the Americans constructing the final parallel.

These various preparations commenced. When the siege was something over two weeks along, Greene received reinforcements: Pickens and Lee, fresh from their conquest of Augusta, arrived with their commands. This enabled the Americans to concentrate on more than just the central feature. Lee began trying to take Cruger's main water supply. But Cruger proved a master at using what he had in order to frustrate the besiegers. He mounted the only artillery he had on a platform from which his three small guns could sweep the American lines. He managed as well to send out a raiding party that destroyed a tunnel being dug under the British position and other works already constructed by Kosciusko. The Americans tried the tricks that had served them so well at previous sieges. But neither the flaming arrows nor the Maham tower availed, the loyalists countering the one by pulling shingles off houses so that they could not be set afire, and the other by raising the height of their walls with sandbags.

Worse still, the Americans had managed to dither away enough time to give the untiring Lord Rawdon opportunity to act. Rawdon had also recently received not just replacements but actual reinforcements—as a commentary on Whitehall's policies, the first sent out by the North ministry in three years. With these new troops he could not only match but outnumber Greene. Sumter's cavalry patrols picked up Rawdon's movement north from Charleston and sent warning to Greene. To win time, Greene sent Pickens and William Washington to join Sumter and do everything possible to slow Rawdon's way to Ninety Six.[28]

The siege, now in its fourth week, was conducted in hot weather made worse for the loyalists by their constant shortage of water. With his time running out, Greene made one more attempt to crack into the fort—and failed. An assault led by the same Captain Rudolph who had taken Fort Galphin managed to get inside one of the fortifications but was driven back by the loyalists and a ferocious counterattack. Greene withdrew next day, June 19, after twenty-eight days of siege efforts.

Lord Rawdon and the British relief column arrived two days later. Greene moved north, ultimately crossing the line into North Carolina. The march through South Carolina's summer heat had proved killing to Rawdon's men—some of them Irish troops who had gone straight from a sea voyage to a fast-paced, exhausting push across nearly the breadth of the state. He had no hope of pursuing Greene. Even such expedients as letting his troops' wool uniform-coats be transported in supply wagons, or permitting standard headgear to be replaced by the cooler, broad-brimmed straw hats of the lowcountry, could not save the British column from casualties to heat exhaustion and sunstroke that were nearly the equivalent of casualties in battle.[29]

The heat was hardly more sparing to the Americans. Dysentery and malaria wore the ranks thin. Greene had no money to pay his troops or buy supplies, and the Americans acquired much of what they needed by the simple device of taking it from their countrymen—and not always the loyalist ones. In truth, Greene's troops were bad enough off that they were described as being barefoot, clothed only by pieces of blanket belted around their middles, and having to use hunks of gray (Spanish) moss to pad equipment straps on bare shoulders. Rawdon fell back with his army, now exhausted, towards Charleston, and Greene re-entered South Carolina. He decided to let his own army rest in the relatively cooler temperatures of the High Hills of Santee, a point from which he could keep an eye on his opponent. Rawdon himself, his own health wrecked by the heat and hard campaigning, had to order at last that Ninety Six be abandoned. Its garrison and the loyalists of that area commenced their sad march towards Charleston. Ultimately Rawdon took ship for England, only to be captured at sea by a French fleet on its way to Yorktown. He was later exchanged.[30]

Georgetown
JUNE 5–6, 1781

Marion at last took Georgetown. He had decided to approach the town and attempt it not by surprise but by proper siege-warfare methods that could help negate the power of the bastion that had caused him so much difficulty on his previous attempt. In the ensuing period, his ranks had been made larger by his reputation for success—and by the clear appearance of a drubbing he had given the Watson-Doyle forces as they had chased after him through the swamps in March and April. And just as Greene had hoped, the combination of Cornwallis's departure for North Carolina and Virginia and British exertions elsewhere in the shade had left only a handful of men in the Georgetown garrison.

The Swamp Fox's siege operations had scarcely begun before this remnant chose to abandon their position and sail safely away to Charleston via Winyah Bay and an inland passage of tidal creeks and bays. Georgetown would be raided two months later by a party of British and loyalists landed by ship. The raiders would proceed to burn much of the town—including forty-two houses—but Georgetown would remain in American hands for the rest of the war.[31]

CHAPTER 8

THE STRUGGLE FOUGHT OUT

1781–1782

For my part I am convinced that . . . though we may conquer, we shall never keep. How the experiment has failed in the Carolinas I cannot judge.

—Lieutenant General Sir Henry Clinton

Greene's wretched force . . . [was] almost naked, swarming with vermin, thinned by . . . battles, and scrawny with famine. . . . [His soldiers] needed everything.

—Philip Edward Pearson statement in John H. Logan manuscript, *A History of the Upper Country of South Carolina,* Historical Collections of the Joseph Habersham Chapter, DAR (1910)

Greene remained camped in the High Hills. Another capable officer, Lieutenant Colonel Alexander Stewart (some accounts have him as Stuart), took Rawdon's place. A coalition of partisan horsemen under Marion and Sumter, backed up by Lee's dragoons, soon drove a British garrison out of Moncks Corner. Thirty miles from Charleston, Moncks Corner had fallen to Tarleton and Ferguson, reinforced by Lieutenant Colonel James Webster's infantry, in April of the previous year and following the attack on Huger at Biggin's Bridge. Ferguson and Webster were both now dead. The one had been killed at King's Mountain, the other at Guilford Courthouse. But despite the loss of these and other talented officers the British remained quite capable of taking on the Americans and doing well in the fight.

Biggin Church and Quinby Bridge
JULY 15–17, 1781

Sumter had gained reinforcements from Greene—Lee's Legion and Marion's horsemen, now styled a brigade—and had also gained permission to carry out a plan that would let him go after Moncks Corner. But the British, either through informants or guessing what was afoot, abandoned the position before Sumter could strike. They pulled back to the parish church of St. John's Berkeley, locally known as Biggin Church from the name of the creek that flowed by. The original building had been lost in a forest fire four years before. Now rebuilt, the British had expanded it into a strongpoint.[1]

Sumter, Marion, and Lee and their forces were camped not far away. Before the Americans could attack, the British struck, hitting the American camp in a surprise attack in late afternoon. The largest portion of the British force was loyalist rangers, all mounted, who were from South Carolina and knew the territory. The loyalists were commanded by Major Thomas Fraser, and he formed his men for a charge. Just when it appeared that Sumter's men might be driven out of their camp, Lieutenant Colonel Edward Lacey, veteran of the Williamson's plantation and Blackstock's fights and King's Mountain, had his riflemen open fire to force the attackers away.

All this time Sumter had been hopeful of avoiding a direct attack on Biggin Church, although a group of horsemen—probably from his command—had earlier approached it and been driven off by heavy fire. The position had not only the church's thick masonry walls, it had also been improved by the British by the addition of a double abatis and some earthworks. Sumter's preference was to threaten the roads around and behind the church, hoping to get the British to abandon the position. He wanted to catch them while they were on the road and falling back rather than when they were dug in.[2]

He got his wish, for the British commander, Lieutenant Colonel James Coates, with elements of the 19th Foot, did just that. He fell back on the night of July 16, having placed any supplies and equipment that his men could not carry into a wagon or two and left the rest in the church. The church building, only recently reconstructed, was set afire.

Viewed another way, Fraser's preemptive attack on Sumter's camp and Coates's departure in the night from a prime position were intended to disrupt and delay the Americans and win some time. Sumter's command set out in pursuit in the early morning hours, when the flames from the burning church were sighted in the distance. Coates divided his command as he moved back, sending Fraser and the mounted South Carolina loyalists over the Bonneau Ferry road in the direction of

Charleston while he proceeded towards the bridge over Quinby Creek with the infantry. The Americans also divided, with Lieutenant Colonel Wade Hampton's South Carolina mounted riflemen chasing the loyalist South Carolinians. Lee's and Marion's horsemen pursued the 19th Foot.

It was Coates's plan to get over the bridge and then destroy it before his pursuers could cross. Posting a detachment to guard his rear, he got the rest of his command over. He was in the act of placing his one piece of artillery where it could fire over the bridge, when the Americans rode up. They overpowered Coates's rear guard but paused when they came to the bridge. The British had already pried up some of the planks and were rapidly trying to pry up more. There was already a considerable gap in the bridge. Light Horse Harry Lee rode up, furious that his dragoons were slow to charge over. Led by Lee, they now did so, their horses just managing to make the jump. The dragoons were followed by a contingent of Marion's horsemen—led by Lieutenant Colonel Hezekiah Maham, inventor of the Maham tower useful at Forts Watson and Cornwallis.[3]

A causeway lay on the other side of the bridge. The Americans began a determined but disorganized series of charges against the British infantrymen who had rallied around Coates. The Americans captured the British gun; the British captured it back. Coates now moved his men the short distance to the main house and outbuildings of the Shubrick family's plantation.

The two cavalry commanders, Lee and Marion, considered the situation and decided that it would take infantry to go after the infantry so well positioned in these buildings. The infantrymen in Lee's Legion and dismounted men from Marion's command began moving into position. Lee and Marion also wanted to wait until their one piece of artillery—left behind when the pursuit started, in order to let the pursuers move faster—was brought up. At that point Sumter rode up and decided upon an immediate attack. Lee and Marion pointed out the obvious fact that the British had a gun and they did not, but Sumter was determined; the attack commenced.

It lasted until nearly sundown, but the Americans were unable to dislodge the British. Now low on ammunition, the various units of Sumter's and Marion's brigades finally withdrew. There was recrimination in the American camp that night, with blame attaching to Sumter for the botched attack made without artillery. Losses had been high. Of the approximately six hundred Americans engaged, the number of killed and wounded amounted to sixty or so—roughly ten percent of the force. Marion's brigade had taken many of these losses. The Swamp Fox, cold-silent in his anger, departed with his remaining men. So also did Lee, marching back to the High Hills to rejoin Greene's army.[4]

Thus depleted in strength, Sumter gave up on the idea of a second attack against Coates. The fight at the bridge and at Shubrick's had been costly for the British side as well, Coates losing forty-four men plus the full company of infantry captured when the dragoons first arrived. The British had clearly gotten the best of the fight, but, as on other occasions, at a cost they could ill afford.

Quinby Bridge and Shubrick's was to prove the Gamecock's last fight with the British, as opposed to operations against the loyalists. When Governor Rutledge returned to South Carolina from the American capital at Philadelphia, he chose this particular moment to declare Sumter's law—the recruiting inducement of letting volunteers take property, especially slaves, from loyalists as payment for their service—illegal and reprehensible. The Gamecock, who was also worn down from illness and the rigors of campaigning, felt he had no choice but to hand over his command to someone else. He returned home briefly to the plantation burned by Tarleton the previous summer. Rutledge, however, soon sent him on forays against loyalist bands still active in the interior of South Carolina. Of that whole state, soon only Charleston and its surrounding enclave remained in British hands.[5]

This situation did not lessen the brutality of the war. Marion's nephew had already been killed by loyalists. Pickens had lost a brother under horrific conditions, and some of the Gamecock's men happily continued on with Sumter's law even after Rutledge's repudiation of it. The British garrison in Charleston next hanged thirty-year-old Lieutenant Colonel Isaac Hayne, on grounds of spying and treason. Hayne had been captured while leading a raid against the outskirts at Charleston. He was run down by the same Major Fraser and his South Carolina loyalist rangers who had attacked Sumter's camp near Biggin Church the month before.

It was true that Hayne, a planter and militia officer, had accepted parole after the fall of Charleston—only to return, as did hundreds of others, to the field on the Revolutionary side. The espionage charges were considerably more wanting in substance. But the British military court of inquiry—presided over by an American loyalist—lost no time in passing sentence. On August 4, after being held prisoner in the Exchange in downtown Charleston, Hayne was publicly hanged. Clearly neither side had been overly scrupulous when it came to the matter of executing someone who had changed sides and oaths a time or two. But the execution of Hayne—a popular member of the planter class, a breeder of thoroughbred horses, and a community leader—drew particular outrage. The rage was directed at Lord Rawdon, unfairly so, since it was the garrison commandant at Charleston, Lieutenant Colonel Nisbet Balfour, who had in fact been in charge during these proceedings.[6]

Anger over the incident brought a surge of militiamen into Greene's camp in the High Hills. Just as welcome to Greene—who had done his best to turn many of the South Carolina mounted militiamen into foot soldiers—was the arrival of a new force of Continentals. This gave the American commander of the Southern Department something in excess of two thousand men. And although his numbers were roughly equal to his opponent's—not altogether promising odds for an American commander whose strength in regulars was still inferior—Greene decided to attack. Screened by mounted South Carolina riflemen under Hampton, his men began marching south towards Charleston in the second week of August. British Lieutenant Colonel Stewart quickly shifted to block him, choosing a strong masonry structure, the plantation house at Eutaw Springs, improved with additional works, as his main position.[7]

Parker's Ferry
AUGUST 13, 1781

At the same time Marion set out to avenge Hayne. When word reached him that Fraser and his men were operating in the area of the North Edisto River, he prepared an ambush at Parker's Ferry. The advantage of this point was that a single causeway led through swampy ground. Marion placed his men in the trees where they could fire onto the causeway.

He also sent out a small party to lure Fraser's South Carolina loyalists into the trap. When Fraser spotted Marion's horsemen, his command surged forward in pursuit. The waiting partisans fired into the loyalists with muskets loaded with buckshot. Fraser tried to charge into the trees after Marion's men but was driven back. His losses may have been as high as ninety men (some accounts triple that figure) killed or wounded. Marion fell back only when a British infantry unit marched up to support Fraser.[8]

Eutaw Springs
SEPTEMBER 8, 1781

Marion then moved north to link up with Greene for the advance towards Eutaw Springs. The battle there would prove to be the last pitched battle fought in South Carolina in the Revolution. After letting his men rest for a month and a half in the High Hills, Greene moved north to Camden and then shifted over to cross the Wateree River. He turned south with every confidence that he could beat Stewart. His army included two battalions of Maryland Continentals—one of which, under Howard, had fought so well at Cowpens—and five more battalions of Virginia and North Carolina Continentals. A company of Delaware Continentals—under Captain Robert Kirkwood—was also highly regarded for its excellent performance in previous engagements. There were, altogether, just over nine hundred Continental troops available. Greene's cavalry included both the mounted portion of Lee's Legion and William Washington's dragoons, as well as other cavalrymen or mounted infantry from Sumter's old brigade or those of Marion and Pickens. Sumter's and Pickens's brigades were combined under Pickens's command. Apart from a unit of North Carolina militia, the rest of Greene's army was made up of South Carolinians serving in either militia units or full-time units of state troops. His artillery amounted to four guns: two three-pounders and two six-pounders. Greene's numbers overall were somewhere between 1,900 and 2,100 men.[9]

His opponent, Stewart, had perhaps 2,100 to 2,400 men. Many of his regular troops had faced the Americans before: the 3rd Foot (the Buffs), and the 63rd and 64th regiments. Stewart pulled the flank companies—the grenadiers and light infantry—from three regiments and placed them under a well-regarded officer, Major John Marjoribanks. Stewart had as well plenty of Americans in his army: two battalions of New York loyalists (one commanded by the John Harris Cruger who had held Ninety Six until relieved) and one of New Jersey men. His cavalry comprised South Carolina loyalists. He had the same number of guns as Greene (four), but had a slight edge in the weight of shot they could throw. Stewart's position was on the south side of the Santee River and commanded Nelson's Ferry. Charleston was fifty miles to the south and east.[10]

Scouts and informants brought Greene excellent information regarding the British position. At first, all went well for the Americans as they advanced. Greene achieved surprise, managing in midmorning to brush

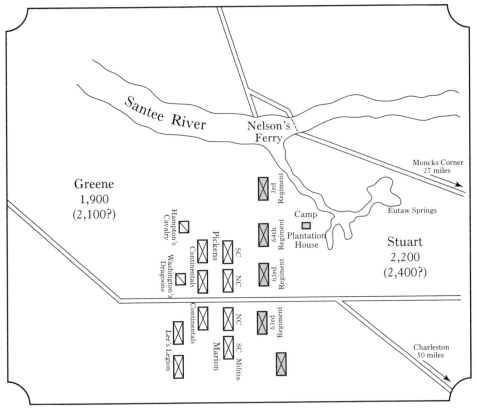

16. Eutaw Springs, September 8, 1781

past some of the South Carolina loyalist cavalry. The plan was for the main body of the Americans to attack in two lines with the militia—some North Carolinians plus the South Carolinians of Marion's, Pickens's, and Sumter's units—moving forward in the first line. This line was to be followed by one made up of Continentals.

In the event, both lines, the one behind the other, advanced on the stockaded plantation house through trees interspersed by fields. Despite their surprise, the British quickly formed their own line and began firing by volleys. The militiamen performed well in this action, managing to inflict considerable losses on their opponents. At the point when the militia line began to lose momentum, however, Greene sent forward the second line, the Continentals. This had been his plan along. It was a step he presumed would drive the British back and win him the battle.

It worked—initially. The redcoats fell back, but in good order. Greene appeared on the verge of victory when two things happened to unhinge the American advance. The first was that his "tatterdemalion" (Greene's term) troops, as they pushed the British back, got into the considerable provisions and supplies the Eutaw Springs camp offered—including the rum. Forward motion was lost as troops who had lived through a hard spring and a worse summer began breaking into boxes, barrels, and casks.

Most accounts of the battle refer to this occurrence, and undoubtedly it proved a factor in the outcome. But a specific tactical move by the British played a much more discernible role. Either on Stewart's order or because he seized the moment himself, Major Marjoribanks—the officer commanding a grouping of several regiments' flank companies—took the action that would cost Greene the battle. Marjoribanks's troops, situated to the right of the British line, had already done considerable damage to the American cavalry units that Greene sent against them. Indeed, they captured no less than William Washington, who was wounded and unhorsed. What Marjoribanks did that proved so telling, however, was to pull his units back and reform them in a new position, one of considerable tactical advantage. In this way they were partially protected by the plantation house's garden wall and a portion of the palisade. Most of all, from this point they could fire directly into the Americans' left flank. They now opened up a heavy fire, managing to hit in the process some of the American soldiers who had stopped to help themselves to the riches of the British camp.

On this move the battle turned from an American victory into at best a draw. Marjoribanks' action jolted the attackers, caused confusion, and helped set up a British counterattack against the other flank of the Americans' line. Instead of advancing, some of the Americans began to fall back. Greene may have already lost control of his attacking units and, in the face of this sudden British move and its withering fire, had no choice but to fall back. Stewart and his redcoats still held Eutaw Springs.[11]

The battle had lasted three hours and been fought in the scorching temperatures of early September. Both sides had fought hard, and casualties were high. The killed and wounded for the Americans amounted to more than six hundred men out of the approximately two thousand engaged. Nearly a hundred men were missing. Perhaps they had thrown down their arms and simply run. On the British side, with slightly higher numbers engaged, the losses were somewhat smaller, with just over four hundred in killed and wounded and another two hundred-plus missing. The British had also lost Marjoribanks, the officer who played such a key role in helping them turn a near disaster into something approaching a victory. He died of his wounds after the battle.

Stewart received reinforcements from Charleston but soon decided to withdraw. Greene had no reinforcements and decided to take his army back to the High Hills. Of the four battles he had fought since taking over in the South—Guilford Courthouse, Hobkirk's Hill, Ninety Six, and now Eutaw Springs—he had won not a single one. And yet the end result was always the same for his opponents: bravely fought, hard-won tactical victories that were followed by decisions to withdraw, with the victories being purchased at a cost that could not be sustained.[12]

Greene's army returned to the High Hills beset by malaria, malnutrition, and the stomach maladies that were its constant companions. Morale was rock-bottom. Much of the militia had already dispersed home to farms or plantations devastated by a year and a half of war and pillaging. Some of the Continentals were angry to the point of mutiny. They had not been paid in two years. To maintain discipline, Greene had one soldier—a South Carolinian—publicly shot for continuing to shout encouragement at angry Maryland Continentals whose officers were trying to talk them back into ranks. But he held at least a fragment of the army—less than a thousand men—together until the weather could cool.[13]

Meanwhile, events four hundred miles to the north were unfolding that would place not just Greene's army but the whole struggle in South Carolina in a new context. The year before, at his departure for New York from Charleston, Sir Henry Clinton had begun consideration of establishing a base in Virginia. Clinton by now had little faith in the ability of the British, no matter how hard or well they fought, to win a battle or battles that could compel the American rebels to conform to the will of the British. Rather, he believed that holding a series of enclaves and bases, supported by the navy, offered the best solution. He was no optimist on this point; however, he still believed that the loyalists, properly bolstered, could be of use.

Lord Cornwallis, his subordinate, was diametrically opposed to this view. He believed in action, in winning battles, and had now come to regard Virginia as the key to the South—and perhaps to winning the whole war. Cornwallis was contemptuous of the enclaves-bases idea and thought it a waste of time for British soldiers to hold these when they could be out seeking decisive battle with the rebels. A further difficulty was that relations between the two men had long since grown strained. Clinton had instructed Cornwallis in clear terms that protection of the outposts and the pacification effort in South Carolina and Georgia—the taking of which amounted to Britain's biggest single gain in the war—was his first priority and one not to be neglected in favor of an invasion of Virginia.[14]

But Cornwallis had persisted in the course already described. In the three-way correspondence going on between Clinton and Cornwallis in America and Lord George Germain in London during the spring and summer of 1781, Clinton was increasingly the odd man out. He had steadily grown disheartened about the war and the prospects of ending it favorably, and had even threatened resignation to Germain. At the same time Germain by now considered Cornwallis to be exactly the kind of aggressive general who could win the victory he still believed was possible. He also wrote a dispatch to Clinton to reassure the British commander in chief, North America, that the new French fleet and army now sailing to the Caribbean from European waters would be carefully watched by Admiral Sir George Brydges Rodney, Royal Navy. Germain assured Clinton that Rodney would in no wise permit the French fleet to come north and threaten the British in America.[15]

But Germain's approach of trying to run the war from London, the dichotomy in view represented by Clinton and Cornwallis, the split in British forces between Clinton's base at New York and Cornwallis in Virginia—and, ultimately, the failure of Rodney's fleet to prevent the French fleet's doing exactly what Germain had promised it would not—were about to cost them America. For the French and the Americans—who would march two armies south to combine them against Cornwallis and have the French fleet come north from the Caribbean and cut off Cornwallis from British help—their whole vast and complex operation, extending across a thousand miles and involving the movement of thousands of men, would come off like clockwork.[16]

Initially, all went well with Cornwallis's move into Virginia. Thomas Jefferson, the governor, excoriated Greene for moving into South Carolina with his army—instead of coming north to defend Virginia from Cornwallis. Early in June Tarleton and his dragoons raided Charlottesville and narrowly missed capturing Jefferson. Tarleton did, however, manage to catch half a dozen members of the Virginia general assembly, and his raids continued. Other actions were fought as Cornwallis turned his army south and east towards the Chesapeake and the peninsula formed by the York and the James Rivers. There, at the location of Yorktown, he established a base.

By that point the Americans—operating under the twenty-four-year-old Frenchman, the Marquis de Lafayette, major general in the American army, were shadowing Cornwallis's movements. Lafayette dispatched a message northwards, reporting Cornwallis's movements and new location at Yorktown to Washington.

The French naval cooperation with the Americans—so frustrating to Washington in the past—would now proceed to work with almost perfect cohesion and timing. The events that led to Yorktown unfolded in a sequence that would make the most of both the divisions within the British command structure and British bad luck.

The background to this victory was that in due course Washington had learned of the arrival of a new French fleet in Caribbean waters—this one from Brest and under Admiral the Count de Grasse. At a conference with Rochambeau, French commander in America, Washington had continued to press for French naval cooperation in an attack on Clinton in New York. But with Rochambeau's persuasive assistance, Washington's thinking gradually shifted. Ultimately it was decided that Cornwallis at Yorktown, not Clinton in New York, would be the target. Thus it was that the newly arrived French fleet eventually proceeded not north to New York, as Washington had originally wanted, but instead to the Chesapeake to cut off Cornwallis from the British navy's help from the sea. Despite Germain's promise, Rodney—in Mahan's phrase, a great tactician but not always a great admiral—failed to prevent this movement. Washington and Rochambeau meantime went through the motions of assembling forces for an attack against New York. This was a feint. Its purpose was to pin Clinton in the defense of that place. It would open the way for the French and American armies to move rapidly south. The goal was to concentrate against Cornwallis at Yorktown.[17]

While these moves were in progress, de Grasse's fleet duly arrived from the Caribbean in the Chesapeake. Later on September 5, three days before Greene and Stewart fought at Eutaw Springs, a Royal Navy force—outnumbered and also hampered by internal coordination and signaling problems—tried unsuccessfully to break the French naval blockade of Yorktown. In a battle fought off the Virginia Capes, the British force sustained damage to its rigging and had to return to New York for repairs. A second French naval force managed to slip in, this one made up of frigates and carrying the heavy artillery essential for the siege.[18]

These guns pounded Cornwallis's positions; they soon had their desired effect. So also did a serious of French and American assaults. At last, on October 19 and after an unsuccessful breakout attempt, Cornwallis, incapacitated by dysentery, was forced to surrender. He did so as Clinton was at last trying to bring a relief force to save him. Counting soldiers, sailors, and marines, there were more Frenchmen present at Yorktown than Americans. The victory had been a gift of French command of the sea in a crucial sector of American waters, American tenacity and perseverance in holding on, Washington's willingness to go for the bold stroke, severe strategic miscalculation by the North ministry—and almost incredible good luck on the part of the French and the Americans.[19]

It was well that this victory had been won, for the American cause at that moment was showing signs of strain. Washington had even used the phrase, "end of our tether." The Articles of Confederation form of government was now in effect but hardly equal to the task of paying Washington's troops. Trouble arose as it had with Greene's army in the High Hills. Some of Washington's regiments, long unpaid, chose to mutiny. Ultimately, to restore order and discipline, Washington had had to resort to execution of the ringleaders by firing squad. It had appeared that this infection might spread to destroy the army while the British, yet holding their bases, could merely bide their time while the American cause fell apart. And in South Carolina, Greene's own army was but a fraction of its Guilford Courthouse size of seven months before.[20]

In South Carolina, the war dragged on. Greene, quite conscious of his decline in numbers, nonetheless commenced a campaign to reclaim as much of the South as possible. The key ports—Wilmington in North Carolina, Charleston and Beaufort in South Carolina, and Savannah in Georgia—remained enclaves sustained by British sea power. He resumed the offensive on November 8, hopeful also of receiving reinforcements from Washington's army, victorious after Yorktown. As he did so, the loyalists struck out from Charleston with their own program of partisan raids.

Clouds Creek
NOVEMBER 17, 1781

One of the most destructive of these was led by William Cunningham, a member of that staunchly loyalist family. He led a force of several hundred horsemen. This particular Cunningham was sufficiently hated by the rebels for his merciless treatment of them that he was called Bloody Bill. Mounted on a thoroughbred horse named Ringtail, Cunningham picked a route that let his men slip into the backcountry undetected.

He knew the country and personally knew many on the opposite side. On November 17, he struck a group of rebels camped around a log house on Clouds Creek, a point in Edgefield County. This group, approximately twenty or thirty men strong, was unprepared and had neglected to post sentries. Cunningham had the advantage of surprise. The rebels fought from the house but eventually gave up. That proved a mistake. Only two of them survived; according to their account, Cunningham and his men shot or stabbed the rest to death.[21]

Hayes's Station
NOVEMBER 19, 1781

Cunningham was aided by the fact that, in the wake of Eutaw Springs and the wonderful news of Yorktown and the defeat of Cornwallis's hated army, a growing sense of war weariness prevailed. It was growing difficult to get militia forces into the field. He himself was manifestly on a mission of vengeance; he had no difficulty finding targets. He continued with his force, soon crossing the Saluda River. Two days after annihilating the party he had surprised at Clouds Creek, he located another group, this one smaller than the first.

It comprised fifteen militiamen, commanded by Lieutenant Colonel Joseph Hayes. These men defended a plantation house which, improved by a palisade and its own thick walls, was known as Hayes's Station. Cunningham this time either did not achieve surprise or else it little availed him, since the rebels fought back hard and effectively. But Cunningham's numbers told. After a three-hour exchange of fire, Cunningham's men drove the defenders out by setting their building on fire. The rebels surrendered.

They met the same fate as the Clouds Creek group. Cunningham held a trial on the spot, and sentenced Hayes to be hanged. The loyalists put the noose around his neck and kicked a platform out from under him. But the pole holding the noose broke. The enraged Cunningham finished off Hayes—still alive, but whose neck probably had already been broken—by running him through with a sword. The same was meted out to the other rebels. The backcountry war continued in its familiar patterns, and other loyalist raids reached as far as North Carolina.[22]

But on December 1, Greene drove the British out of Fort Dorchester, just fifteen miles from Charleston. The fort's garrison threw artillery and supplies into the Ashley River and fell back towards the defenses of Charleston. Early in 1782 reinforcements sent south by Washington forced the British garrison out of Wilmington, North Carolina. They then continued on to join Greene. He meanwhile repositioned his army at Round O, some forty miles inland from Charleston, but also sent some of the reinforcements—under Major General Anthony Wayne—into Georgia.

Wambaw Bridge
FEBRUARY 14, 1782

A particularly aggressive leader of the loyalist raids was Lieutenant Colonel Benjamin Thompson. Thompson fused volunteers from a variety of British and provincial units into a mounted strike force. At one point he contemplated a raid intended to capture the American commander, Greene. Fortunately for the Americans, the plan was foiled by events. Thompson also made effective use of slaves who had escaped from plantations to provide intelligence and serve as guides.

In this way he slipped into the region of the South Santee River. This was Swamp Fox country, but Marion—and in testimonial to the high regard in which his fellow citizens held him—had recently been elected to the state senate of South Carolina. He was now on his way back from his legislative duties. In the interim, Thompson got the best of a disorganized segment of Marion's old brigade in a sharp fight on February 14. He got his men away before the Swamp Fox could return to organize a pursuit. The Americans had lost two-score men in the engagement.[23]

Tydiman's Plantation
FEBRUARY 25, 1782

Thompson, leading about four hundred men, struck another blow the following day. Marion was by now back. He and Maham were looking to cut off the British force, which had acquired a herd of cattle and was

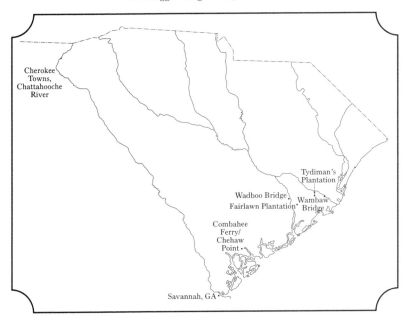

Cherokee
Towns,
Chattahooche
River

Tydiman's
Plantation

Wadboo Bridge
Fairlawn Plantation
Wambaw
Bridge

Combahee
Ferry/
Chehaw
Point

Savannah, GA

17. ACTIONS IN 1782

attempting to get back with it to the garrison in Charleston. The action
was fought at Tydiman's plantation not far from Wambaw Creek.

Marion sent a detachment to block Thompson. But confusion in the
American ranks turned the action into a second setback for the Ameri-
cans. Thompson, who later—as Count Rumford—gained renown in Britian as a scientist and inventor, led a charge that inflicted heavy losses on
Marion's men. Moreover, the British succeeded in getting the cattle to
Charleston. A final action remained to Marion—to be fought at Fairlawn
Plantation, to the east of the Cooper River, in August. In his last fight he
was bested by the same Thomas Fraser and his loyalist South Carolina
horsemen who had proved a nemesis at Biggin Church and captured
Hayne. At Fairlawn, Marion's men had initially gotten the best of the
action. However, when the horses pulling the ammunitions wagon
spooked and ran off, he had to order a retreat.[24]

But these raids—intended as much to steal food as to embarrass the
Americans—could not alter a process already well along. In July the
British were forced to evacuate Savannah as they already had been from
Wilmington. Charleston, however, continued to hold out as a British
base, with strong forces established in positions around it, including Johns

Island and James Island. Yet Greene's army offered sufficient protection for the South Carolina General Assembly—to which, as mentioned, Marion had been elected—to meet. This meant that South Carolina again had civil government—for the first time since the fall of Charleston in May 1780. The temporary capital was Jacksonborough (now Jacksonboro) on the North Edisto River, where a new governor, James Mathews, was elected. Christopher Gadsden, previously the lieutenant governor, had chosen not to stand for the chief office.[25]

The legislature quickly passed punitive measures against the loyalists gathered in Charleston. The message of these was that their property would be confiscated and they themselves banished. Irrespective of these laws, however, loyalist partisans continued to mount their raids and armed British foraging parties to sortie out to take slaves, supplies, and horses. A skirmish with one of these, on the Combahee River between Charleston and Beaufort, would cost the life of Lieutenant Colonel John Laurens.

Chehaw Point, Combahee River
AUGUST 27, 1782

Greene, trying to draw the ring around Charleston even tighter, had sent forces out to try to prevent these foraging expeditions from gaining what they were after. One such force, a brigade commanded by Mordecai Gist, had established a position that guarded the Combahee River. This was an excellent waterway, one the British had used before to get at area plantations.

The British force operating in the area comprised five hundred men and was supported by a flotilla of vessels. Though ill, the younger Laurens insisted on volunteering for the effort along the Combahee. He thus ended up in command of a detachment assigned to move in advance of Gist's brigade. Perhaps Laurens intended to set up a position so as to be able to fire artillery at British ships as they tried to get back down the river. Before he could establish such a position, however, he himself encountered a force of British infantry. Unbeknownst to the Americans, the British had landed a battalion—probably with the intent of ambushing Gist when he came up with the main body of his column. Instead, it was the twenty-seven-year-old Laurens who ran into these troops, and he sprang the ambush. He paid for his decision with his life. He was killed when he led a charge that he must have thought would win Gist some time or else drive the British back. The British force captured an American gun and inflicted, in addition to the loss of Laurens, about twenty other casualties in terms of wounded men. Laurens, however, was the only one killed.[26] Thereafter the British force returned to their vessels and continued foraging operations.

The elder Laurens had been captured at sea and for a year held prisoner in the Tower of London. After Yorktown, he was exchanged for the recently captured Lord Cornwallis. Occasional clashes here and there—not unlike the one in which the younger Laurens was lost—continued almost until the British evacuation of Charleston. These, rather than formal battles in the style of Eutaw Springs, formed the last actions of the war in South Carolina. The North ministry had fallen four months after Yorktown; a new one had by now opened negotiations for peace. Sir Henry Clinton had been succeeded as commander in chief, North America, by Sir Guy Carleton.[27] By this point, only New York and Charleston still remained to Britain as bases in what had been the Thirteen Colonies.

Greene kept up the pressure on the latter city; Washington watched the northern one. In fact, the British troop transports and escorting warships necessary to conduct an evacuation had arrived in Charleston harbor in September 1782. There they waited out the rest of the hurricane season. In addition to the sizable British garrison and all its stores and equipment, there were the loyalists—and the considerable population of black South Carolinians, most of them slaves—who would have to be evacuated as well. An untold number of loyalists—particularly from around Ninety Six or the Broad and Saluda fork—had already elected either to melt quietly into the population or perhaps to seek refuge in new settlements over the mountains or in British Florida, especially around Pensacola or what became Jacksonville. But fully 3,800 South Carolinians (plus at least some from Georgia, North Carolina and Virginia who believed as they did)—Americans who chose allegiance to British rule or perhaps feared reprisal at the hands of their countrymen—now made the decision to leave Charleston. Many would be transported to New York. This was Britain's last base in America south of Canada and north of Florida (Florida itself was soon to be ceded to Spain). A few would end up in Britain or perhaps the Bahamas. Most, however, would arrive finally in Nova Scotia, in Quebec, or in the portions of Canada eventually to be called Ontario and New Brunswick.[28]

Leaving also in the British and loyalist evacuation were the 5,500 black South Carolinians in Charleston. Some were free men who had fought in loyalist units, the rest were slaves. Some of these also may have fought in British units. All told, at least 25,000 black South Carolinians, amounting to no less than a fourth of its prewar labor force, left South Carolina between 1775 and 1782. Many settled in Nova Scotia or other parts of Canada. Not freedom but slavery, however, remained the lot of a substantial number of the black South Carolinians who left. They were as likely to end up back on American plantations as on British ones in the Bahamas or West Indies.[29]

The British were ready to evacuate Charleston by the second week of December 1782. They loaded up their ships and pulled in outlying units, with these soon embarked in transports. Their last troops out would be those holding the across-the-peninsula line of fortification (those parallel to and just north of present-day Calhoun Street) built two years before by the Americans, and of which the Hornwork was the central feature. On December 14, the final British troops left that fortification and marched through the city to Gadsden's Wharf, located at the eastern end of Boundary Street. There they loaded up in boats to be rowed out to the nearly three hundred ships lying at anchor in the harbor. As the redcoats pulled out, Greene and the Americans moved in on a sunny Charleston afternoon, marching down the sandy track of King Street towards the city. They were still in scarecrow uniforms and no better off in food than they had been during the summer of the Eutaw Springs battle. Yet they marched erect. Many, though, had to limp along shoeless to the beat of fife and drum. At three in the afternoon, Greene and his troops, escorting the governor and his council at the head of the column, reached the Hornwork gate. As the troops and officials filed into the city, a few citizens (many had earlier fled to the safety of outlying plantations) cheered them to the effect of "God bless you, gentlemen!" and "Welcome home!" And the Americans, as Greene recalled later, thereafter went about the city, dispersing to see friends or the sights and basking almost anticlimactically in the glow of an achievement long in coming.[30]

It had been two years and twelve days since Greene had succeeded Gates at Charlotte, North Carolina, in command of the Americans' Southern Department in December 1780. In that time he had not beaten the British in a single battle. Cornwallis had taken the measure of Greene tactically, as had Rawdon and Stewart, two opponents younger than he and considerably junior in rank. But Greene's sense of strategy—of how to apply limited resources in order to attain a specific end, of how to reach a final goal or outcome that would yield what the Americans needed in the South—had been unfailing. He had built and then kept together an American army in the South, had brought the operations of the irregulars into concert with his own, and had rolled up the British outposts across South Carolina one by one.

Finally, he had closed and held a ring around Charleston, Britain's last base in the South, and its last after New York in the Thirteen Colonies, permitting thereby the return of civil government to the state. Cornwallis was Greene's superior on the battlefield. Yet the strategy he sought to apply—crushing the Americans in drawn battle as Cumberland had crushed the Scots at Culloden—could only have worked if the British had brought overwhelming and totally decisive forces of regulars to bear. But they could not; nor could they effectively rally the loyalist population.[31]

Indeed, many of the loyalists now simply disappeared, quietly slipping into the general population and saying little about the past. Cornwallis's approach, with far greater resources, would work in Ireland nearly twenty years later. It did not work in South Carolina because, lacking such resources, it did not fit the situation. But Greene's did. Every time he lost a battle, he was winning the war. And now Greene, the commander of the Southern Department and always defeated in battle, stood victorious where a previous American general had, two and a half years before, surrendered a city and an army.

Fourteen days before, on the other side of the Atlantic, Henry Laurens of South Carolina—father of the Lieutenant Colonel John Laurens killed that summer on the Combahee—along with Benjamin Franklin, John Adams, and John Jay, signed the agreement that eventually, as the Treaty of Paris, 1783, ended the war.

CONCLUSION

SOUTH CAROLINA—that rich, fertile land where winter was gentler than summer and that commenced at barrier-island beaches, which rose after marshes to a coastal flat that became sandhills, foothills, and finally the slope of the Blue Ridge—was a battleground that, between 1775 and 1782, brought ruin to imperial Britain's hopes for winning back America.

The battles fought in South Carolina were integral and vital to the goals and means by which the Americans waged the war. Washington, the commander in chief, would not himself personally come to South Carolina until after being elected president and his famous tour of 1791. He understood from the start, however, during the years of strife and fighting, that South Carolina's role must be the crucial one of anchoring the southern flank of the American colonies. It would as well be a zone in which the manpower of Georgia, North Carolina, and Virginia, as well as South Carolina's own sons, could be arrayed in order to fight. He gave his trusted subordinate, Greene, full charter to carry out a program intended to work harm, dislocation, and frustration to British plans for regaining the South.[1]

He was by that point sadder but wiser from his own frustrations and setbacks earlier in the war. He believed that the best chance of winning was for the Americans to stay generally on the defensive and wait the British out. He also placed faith in limited offensives. These, mounted here and there on the periphery of British power, might seize the moment to score useful gains. He continued steadfastly to await the arrival of a French fleet.

Washington had not arrived at this approach easily. Personally inclined towards the offensive, bitter defeats early in the war had led him to the strategic defensive–limited offensive approach as a way of achieving the larger goal of victory. Even on the defensive, however, he held two elements of the American approach paramount: to keep a government in existence—to include government in the states—and an army in the field. The government was the mechanism of decision making and marshaling resistance in support of the cause. The army—especially Washington's—was both a symbol of that cause and the means of fighting for it. It was not necessary for the army to win all the battles in order to win the war.[2]

From mid-1776 onward the British resort, on the other hand, was to the offensive. Whitehall had shifted to the defensive only in the wake of French entry into the war. Following Clinton's consolidation of forces in New York and the ineffectual showing of the first French fleet sent to America, the British had then embarked on the strategy that brought the war to the South. Once the decision was made to use force, the British had before them several approaches or combinations of approaches by which to use that force. All were offensive in nature, the application of force—and in more definitive fashion than the mere conduct of a naval blockade to hurt the Americans economically—being judged the only way they could impose their will.

One approach that appealed was to capture the Americans' capital, the place where the Continental Congress carried out the processes of government. A second approach was to seek to destroy American forces in the field, most chiefly Washington's army. A third was to occupy substantial areas of American territory. By establishing enclaves and bases, the king's forces could keep the rebels restricted to the hinterland. The enclaves would also help in the task of mobilizing loyalists. So cut off from population centers and presumably demoralized by the apparent restoration of royal authority, the ranks of the Americans still in organized resistance would diminish into mere handfuls. That was the theory. Meanwhile, British faith—even after Saratoga—in the capacity of the redcoats to beat Americans in battle remained unshaken. This faith could only strengthen the arguments made in favor of the territories-enclaves-bases approach.[3]

South Carolina played no role in dealing with the first of these approaches, the conquest of the American capital at Philadelphia. Yet British conquest of that point, as seen, yielded little real advantage; the Americans continued to fight. Nor did South Carolina play any direct role in British efforts in 1776–1777 to destroy Washington's army, located some hundreds of miles to the north. Those efforts, of course, failed. Nor as well could South Carolina play any role in the first British attempt to gain territory—the effort to isolate New England by a junction of forces in the Hudson valley, and which resulted in defeat at Saratoga. But South Carolina did play a crucial role in defeating other British efforts in this territorial approach—twice. This role contributed directly to American victory in the war.

The first occasion came in the first year of the conflict. Those elements of South Carolina's population inclined to resist British authority had already defeated or intimidated into inactivity their neighbors who desired to remain loyal to the Crown. But the British mounted a strong counterattack from two directions in summer 1776. The Cherokee offensive on the frontier was defeated in a fashion which saw the destruction of their towns east of the mountains.

But the other component of the counterattack—the seaborne thrust at Sullivan's Island—was a vastly more lethal threat. It threatened not just South Carolina but the overall American struggle. British success at this early stage would have imperiled the Revolutionary cause in the South. Moreover, key leaders of South Carolina's war effort—Moultrie and Marion in the fort itself, Sumter close at hand at Haddrell's Point and Rutledge in Charleston—were present. Their potential loss to wounds, death or capture at this stage would have done material harm to the state's Revolutionary fortunes. It is worth noting as well that the victory at Sullivan's Island proved to be the only occasion of the war where a British force of this size and composition was deflected from its amphibious purpose by the actions of American defenders ashore.

The second occasion came three years later. With the commencement of Britain's offensive efforts to regain the colonies in the South, South Carolina became the key—the point that Washington and Greene both so clearly grasped—to whether those efforts would succeed or fail. At first they were successes, the conquest of Georgia and South Carolina constituting Britain's single largest achievement of the war. But the partisan leaders Sumter, Marion, and Pickens initiated a guerrilla campaign that vexed and dislocated British plans. This became even more the case with the arrival of the army under Greene. The combining of regular and irregular forces in an overall campaign led to King's Mountain, Cowpens, and Guilford Courthouse. This last was a battle fought in North Carolina that was in reality the last attempt by Cornwallis to defeat American forces and so win by decisive military victory in South Carolina. After it he gave up and decided to move instead against Virginia. These battles in their sequence proved turning-point events that frustrated the British at the highest levels. They helped to divide a command already in disagreement about what to do next.

British plans for holding a large territory, the South, were in deep peril well before Cornwallis reached his new base at Yorktown—and before the combination of American land and French sea and land power was sent against it. The reason they were in this state of peril was the war waged by the Americans in South Carolina, a war that continued in full fury. Even had Washington and Rochambeau and de Grasse not prevailed at Yorktown in that late summer and fall of 1781, the war in South Carolina had already gained its inexorable momentum: British and loyalist forces were being driven back and into an enclave around Charleston. It was a continental approach—as opposed to a sea power-based naval strategy—that was steadily wearing down Britain's ability to put forces in the field. It was a contest of endurance, one in which the Americans held the advantage in time and numbers.[4]

The combat and actions that achieved this result came in four main categories: conventional, eighteenth-century European-style battles between armies of regulars that happened to be fought not in Europe but in South Carolina; guerrilla attacks against the lines of communication that sustained a conventional army; civil war-type actions fought between groups of Americans drawn from the same region and state—and in some cases the same neighborhood—and in which partisan warfare techniques proved a mainstay; and frontier fights between groups of Indians and groups of whites. And yet it was not, especially with regard to the first category, the conventional European style of the day, that simple. The war in America was different. Camden, Hobkirk's Hill, Stono Ferry, and the sieges of Charleston and the Star Fort at Ninety Six, for example, all appear versions of this first type of warfare. They were set-piece engagements fought at close range by opposing lines of musket-armed infantry backed up by artillery and cavalry or, in the case of the sieges, were fought using the same saps-and-parallels techniques as employed in Europe. Yet each of these battles had, in addition to their battalions of regulars, a significant presence of citizen-soldier militiamen. That fact alone made them different. The Americans used the militia—and the guerrillas against the lines of communication—because they had to. The regulars might place little faith in the militiamen's steadiness or capacity in maneuver, but it was clear that these men were there because they had chosen to be there. They were fighting for a cause. And there were more of them choosing the rebel cause than the British one. This war was a departure from the European model of the day.

Both sides deviated from that model whenever it suited or the opportunity arose to experiment with new techniques. In the French and Indian War, British troops had cut the tails off their red coats for freer movement and British officers had left their swords and sashes behind to participate in deep-woods operations with American rangers. In this war, especially in South Carolina, they developed forces of loyalist American riflemen or issued rifles to picked men in their line regiments. In their line infantry they as well dropped a third rank from formations in order to put more men on the firing line. They were particularly successful with a cavalry-infantry force, the Legion. This force, under Tarleton, repeatedly got the best of the Americans. And both sides were willing to employ African Americans as soldiers in a way that would not be seen in America again until the North's decision in 1863 to employ black regiments in the Civil War. Some ideas for mobilizing blacks—those especially of the younger Laurens, for example—were judged too radical and were rejected. But black soldiers fought in Marion's band, at Cowpens, in the ranks of the Continentals and probably in each of the engagements that helped defeat British plans for restoring South Carolina to royal authority.[5]

The fact of the clashes between opposing groups of Americans—an internal civil war played out most viciously in the South—was a central feature of the war in South Carolina. It helped to brutalize the war there, and the numbers, scope, and degree of reliance the British placed upon loyalist forces helped to make it different from fighting in other theaters. Loyalist participation on the side of the Indians helped to ensure that the rebel side would employ the harshest possible measures against the Cherokees in reprisal for their raids of 1776.

These battles—with their blending of European and American practices and styles, techniques and weapons, of regular and irregular approaches, of frontier warfare and Indian-white struggles admixed in a revolutionary conflict—were what decided the outcome in South Carolina. Defeat there led to Britain's defeat in the South and in the war. But the battles also had their effect upon South Carolina. The war engendered in the white South Carolinians who had endured it a deep hunger for order and stability. The war also proved a crucible in which forces and processes already at work continued and had their effect. One of these was the process of political and social unification whereby the slave-holding planter class consolidated its hold over the entire state. This fusion of interests and coming together of lowcountry and backcountry groups had been a factor in determining that the Whig side, not the loyalist one, would prevail. A characteristic of the older planter elite of the lowcountry had been a willingness to serve in leadership roles in militia and provincial ranks in a series of colonial wars and expeditions against French, Spanish, or Indian enemies. The Revolutionary experience helped transfer this planter-soldier ethic as a right and as a duty that could now be taken up and embraced by the new planters of the backcountry.[6]

In the decades ahead, South Carolina found much in that experience to honor and cherish: Pickens's steady riflemen at Cowpens; the gunners trading roundshot with British warships on the edge of the Atlantic; the frontiersmen holding the fort or driving the Indians back. The role of the women was an especially heroic one: Jane Thomas and Emily Geiger and others risking their lives to carry messages—in Emily Geiger's case, through British territory to go between Sumter and Greene. The image of Rebecca Motte—an image conveying grace and refinement even under great stress—was especially appealing as the model of the lady of a plantation.[7]

But most of all, it was the partisan image that appealed to South Carolinians, and particularly those of the planter class, who saw themselves as the functional descendants of the men who had ridden with Sumter, Marion, and Pickens. In the bitterest days of the struggle, when help from sisters-in-arms had seemed far away, South Carolina's partisan leaders had carried on the fight. The example of Sumter, Marion, and Pickens and their followers served to provide for South Carolina a citizen-soldier tradition in a cavalier version. The socialization of the planters around this model took hold early and held on. When the contributions of blacks who had fought in the war were remembered, it was in the image of faithful servants who, riding with their planter masters, were willing to pay the ultimate price.[8]

The gamecock image also appealed. Indeed the original Carolina Gamecock, Thomas Sumter, was elected by his fellow citizens to terms in the House of Representatives and the United States Senate. When he

NOTES

Introduction

1. For a study of casualties, 1775–1782, the standard work is Howard H. Peckham, ed., *The Toll of Independence: Engagements and Battle Casualties of the American Revolution* (Chicago: University of Chicago Press, 1974). According to one estimate, the thirteen colonies together lost on the order of 25,550 men and women from war-related deaths. As a percentage of the overall population, this makes the Revolution the nation's costliest war save for the Civil War of 1861–1865. See Edward McCrady, *The History of South Carolina in the Revolution, 1775–1780* (1901; reprint, New York: Paladin Press, 1969), 850–51 for an accounting of casualties, battle by battle, in critical periods of the war in South Carolina.

2. Larry H. Addington, *The Patterns of War since the Eighteenth Century*, 2d ed. (Bloomington and Indianapolis: Indiana University Press, 1994), esp. 1–42; Jeremy Black, *Western Warfare, 1775–1882* (Bloomington and Indianapolis: Indiana University Press, 2001) esp. 1–36; and Hew Strachan, *European Armies and the Conduct of War* (London: George Allen & Unwin, 1983), 8–59.

3. For the black experience, see in particular Benjamin Quarles, *The Negro in the American Revolution*, published for the Omohundro Institute of Early American History and Culture at Williamsburg, Va. (Chapel Hill: University of North Carolina Press, 1961), and David B. Davis, *The Problem of Slavery in the Age of the Revolution, 1770–1823* (Ithaca, N.Y.: Cornell University Press, 1975) 68–133; Mary L. Clifford, *From Slavery to Freedom: Black Loyalists after the American Revolution* (Jefferson, N.C., and London: McFarland, 1999), esp. 23–25; and Alexia J. Helsley, *South Carolinians in the War for American Independence* (Columbia: South Carolina Department of Archives and History, 2000), 25. Regarding the loyalists and the divided backcountry, see Wallace Brown, *The King's Friends: The Composition and Motives of the American Loyalist Claimants* (Providence, R.I.: Brown University Press, 1965), 213–30; Claude H. Van Tyne, *The Loyalists in the American Revolution* (New York and London: Macmillan, 1902), esp. 184–86; George L.

Jr., *The Frontier in the Colonial South: South Carolina Backcountry, –1800* (Westport, Conn., and London: Greenwood Press, 1997), esp. 65–70; Robert S. Lambert, *South Carolina Loyalists in the American Revolution* (Columbia: University of South Carolina Press, 1987); and Robert M. Calhoon, *The Loyalists in Revolutionary America, 1760–1781* (New York: Harcourt Brace Jovanovich, 1973). For the Cherokees see David H. Corkran, *The Carolina Indian Frontier* (Columbia: University of South Carolina Press, 1970), 62–69; Armstrong Starkey, *European and Native American Warfare, 1675–1815* (Norman: University of Oklahoma Press, 1998), 111–36; and Andrew R. L. Cayton and Fredrika J. Teute, eds., *Contact Points: American Frontiers from the Mohawk Valley to the Mississippi, 1750–1830*, published for the Omohundro Institute of Early American History and Culture, Williamsburg, Va. (Chapel Hill and London: University of North Carolina Press, 1998), esp. 1–15.

4. Regarding military terminology and concepts, useful works are Patrick O'Sullivan and Jesse W. Miller Jr., *The Geography of Warfare* (New York: St. Martin's Press, 1983); John I. Alger, *Definitions and Doctrine of the Military Art: Past and Present* (West Point, N.Y.: Department of History, U.S. Military Academy, 1981); John Quick, ed., *Dictionary of Weapons and Military Terms* (New York: McGraw-Hill, 1973); and John Lynn, ed., *Tools of War: Instruments, Ideas, and Institutions of Warfare, 1445–1871* (Urbana and Chicago: University of Illinois Press, 1990). Regarding present-day definitions and applications of terms and concepts, readers may wish to consult U.S. Joint Chiefs of Staff, *Department of Defense Dictionary of Military and Associated Terms: Joint Terminology Master Database as of 10 June 1998*, Joint Publication 1–02 (Washington: U.S. Department of Defense, 1998); or U.S. Department of the Navy, *Campaigning*, MCDP 1–2 (Washington: U.S. Marine Corps, 1997).

5. Ian V. Hogg, *Artillery* (New York: Ballantine Books, 1972); E. M. E. Lloyd, *A Review of the History of Infantry* (Westport, Conn., and London: Greenwood Press, 1976); and Addington, *Patterns of War*, esp. 1–7.

6. See Anthony Farrar-Hockley, *Infantry Tactics* (London: Altmark, 1976). The proper name for the Brown Bess was "Short, Land, New Pattern Musket." See Lawrence E. Babits, *A Devil of a Whipping: The Battle of Cowpens* (Chapel Hill and London: University of North Carolina Press, 1998), 10–13; and Thomas E. Griess, ed., *The Dawn of Modern Warfare* (Wayne, N.J.: Avery Publishing Group for Department of History, U.S. Military Academy, 1984), esp. 102–6. Two classics are A. F. Becke, *An Introduction to the History of Tactics, 1740–1905* (London: Hugh Rees, 1909); and F. N. Maude, *Notes on the Evolution of Infantry Tactics* (London: William Clowes, 1905).

7. John Moncure, *The Cowpens Staff Ride and Battlefield Tour* (Fort Leavenworth, Kans.: Combat Studies Institute, U.S. Army Command and General Staff College, 1996), 17, 28–29; and John W. Fortescue, *A History of the British Army*, vol. 3, part 2, *From the Close of the Seven Years' War to the Second Peace of Paris, 1763–1793* (1911; reprint, New York: AMS Press, 1976), 3:315.

8. The standard works are Edward E. Curtis, *The Organization of the British Army in the American Revolution* (New Haven and London: Yale University Press, 1926) 1–4; and J. A. Houlding, *Fit for Service: The Training of the British Army, 1715–1795* (Oxford: Oxford University Press, 1981).

9. Strachan, *European Armies*, 28–30; Jeremy Black, *Warfare in the Eighteenth Century* (London: Cassell, 1999), 112: and Russell F. Weigley, *History of the United States Army* (New York and London: Macmillan, 1967), 27, 66–67. See also Edward Hutton, ed., *A Brief History of the King's Royal Rifle Corps, 1755 to 1915* (Winchester: Warren and Son, 1917), esp. 2–7; and J. F. C. Fuller, *British Light Infantry in the Eighteenth Century* (London: Hutchinson, 1925).

10. For muskets and rifles of the American Revolutionary period, see Harold L. Peterson, *Arms and Armor in Colonial America* (Harrisburg, Pa.: Stackpole, 1956); and W. H. B. Smith and Joseph E. Smith, *The Book of Rifles* (New York: Castle, 1948). Ian V. Hogg and John Batchelor, *Armies of the American Revolution* (Englewood Cliffs, N.J.: Prentice-Hall, 1975) covers loading and firing of these weapons (43–67). See also Curtis, *Organization of the British Army*, 16–22.

11. Addington, *Patterns of War*, 1–7; and Peter Young and J. P. Lawford, eds., *History of the British Army* (New York: A. P. Putnam's Sons, 1970), 44–72, 80–92.

12. A short summary of Age of Sail ship types and tactics is found in E. B. Potter and Chester W. Nimitz, eds., *Sea Power: A Naval History* (Englewood Cliffs, N.J.: Prentice-Hall, 1960), 34–45.

13. Addington, *Patterns of War*, 7–12; Geoffrey Parker, *The Military Revolution: Military Innovation and the Rise of the West, 1500–1800* (Cambridge: Cambridge University Press, 1996), 153; and Antony Preston, David Lyon, and John Batchelor, *The Navies of the American Revolution* (Englewood Cliffs, N.J.: Prentice-Hall, 1975). Surveys of the evolution of the British and other navies are found in John Keegan, *The Price of Admiralty: The Evolution of Naval Warfare* (New York: Viking Penguin, 1989); and Clark G. Reynolds, *Command of the Sea: The History and Strategy of Maritime Empires* (New York: William Morrow, 1974).

14. For the factors relating to sea power as he saw them, see A. T. Mahan, *The Influence of Sea Power upon History, 1660–1783* (Boston: Little, Brown,

1890), 29–89. See also Black, *Warfare in the Eighteenth Century*, 128–53; and Brian Lavery, ed., *Shipboard Life and Organisation, 1731–1815* (Aldershot, Hants.: Ashgate for the Council of the Navy Records Society, 1998), esp. 13, 57–84, 98, 122–23, 129, 135.

15. William Laird Clowes et al., *The Royal Navy: A History from the Earliest Times to the Present*, vol. 3 (Boston: Little, Brown and Co.; London: S. Law, Marston and Co., 1898), covers the period of the American Revolution in terms of major and minor operations and other categories. Useful studies are Richard Buel, Jr., *In Irons: Britain's Naval Supremacy and the American Revolutionary Economy* (New Haven and London: Yale University Press, 1998); Neil R. Stout, *The Royal Navy in America, 1760–1775: A Study of Enforcement of British Colonial Policy in the Era of the American Revolution* (Annapolis: Naval Institute Press, 1973); and David Syrett, *The Royal Navy in European Waters during the American Revolutionary War* (Columbia: University of South Carolina Press, 1998). For the South Carolina State Navy, see P. C. Coker, *Charleston's Maritime Heritage, 1660–1863: An Illustrated History* (Charleston, S.C.: Coker Craft Press, 1987), esp. 75–80, 86–125. An account of American naval efforts against Britain is found in Potter and Nimitz, *Sea Power*, 66–107. The best survey is Nathan Miller, *Sea of Glory: A Naval History of the American Revolution* (Annapolis, Md.: Naval Institute Press, 1974).

16. See Allan R. Millett and Peter Maslowski, *For the Common Defense: A Military History of the United States of America* (New York and London: Free Press, 1984), esp. 1–46, for the militia system in use in the American colonies. Robert Mills, *Statistics of South Carolina: Including a View of Its Natural, Civil, and Military History, General and Particular* (1826; reprint, Spartanburg, S.C.: The Reprint Company, 1972), 292–93, describes the militia system of South Carolina as it existed by the early nineteenth century. For the militia on the eve of the Revolution, see McCrady, *History of South Carolina in the Revolution*, 10–16.

17. Robert M. Weir, *Colonial South Carolina: A History* (Columbia: University of South Carolina, 1997), 110, 197, 268–69.

18. The fears of slave revolt were commented upon by Hessian officers serving with Clinton's army. See Bernhard A. Uhlendorf, trans. and ed., *The Siege of Charleston: With an Account of the Province of South Carolina: Diaries and Letters of Hessian Officers from the von Jungkenn Papers in the William L. Clements Library* (Ann Arbor: University of Michigan Press, 1938), 323.

19. Weir, *Colonial South Carolina: A History*, 195–96.

20. The importance of ensuring that officers with the correct political outlook were appointed to key positions was clearly in the minds of those who favored the Whig cause. See Rachel N. Klein, *Unification of a Slave State:*

The Rise of the Planter Class in the South Carolina Backcountry, 1760–1808, published for the Institute of Early American History and Culture, Williamsburg, Va. (Chapel Hill: University of North Carolina Press, 1990), 40–41, 84–88, 162–63.

Chapter 1. South Carolina Makes a Revolution, 1775

1. Important interpretations of the American Revolution are John R. Alden, *A History of the American Revolution* (New York: Alfred A. Knopf, 1969); Alden, *The South in the Revolution, 1763–1789* (Baton Rouge: Louisiana State University Press, 1957); Don Higginbotham, *The War of American Independence: Military Attitudes, Policies, and Practice, 1763–1789* (Bloomington and London: Indiana University Press, 1971); Piers Mackesy, *The War for America, 1775–1783* (Cambridge: Harvard University Press, 1964); Robert Middlekauff, *The Glorious Cause: The American Revolution, 1763–1789* (New York and Oxford: Oxford University Press, 1986); Howard H. Peckham, *The War for Independence: A Military History* (Chicago: University of Chicago Press, 1958); Charles Royster, *A Revolutionary People at War: The Continental Army and American Character, 1775–1783*, published for the Institute of Early American History and Culture, Williamsburg, Va. (Chapel Hill: University of North Carolina Press, 1986); John Shy, *A People Numerous and Armed: Reflections on the Military Struggle for American Independence* (New York: Oxford University Press, 1976); and Gordon S. Wood, *The Creation of the American Republic 1776–1787*, published for the Omohundro Institute of Early American History and Culture at Williamsburg, Va. (Chapel Hill and London: University of North Carolina Press, 1998). On the coming of the war to South Carolina, see Walter Edgar, *South Carolina: A History* (Columbia: University of South Carolina Press, 1998), esp. 204–25; Lewis P. Jones, *South Carolina: A Synoptic History for Laymen* (Orangeburg, S.C.: Sandlapper Publishing, 1971), esp. 90–115; Terry W. Lipscomb, *South Carolina Becomes a State: The Road from Colony to Independence, 1765–1776* (Columbia: South Carolina Department of Archives and History, 1988); Lipscomb, *South Carolina Revolutionary War Battles*, vol. 1, *The Carolina Lowcountry, April 1775–June 1776* (Columbia: South Carolina Department of Archives and History, 1991); and Robert M. Weir, *"A Most Significant Epoch": The Coming of the Revolution in South Carolina* (Columbia: University of South Carolina Press, 1970).

2. Jack P. Greene, *The Quest for Power: The Lower Houses of Assembly in the Southern Royal Colonies, 1689–1776* (New York: W. W. Norton, 1963), esp. 438–53; and Fred Anderson, *Crucible of War: The Seven Years' War and the Fate of Empire in British North America, 1754–1766* (New York: Alfred A. Knopf, 2000), 597–99.

3. Regarding population, see comments in Dave R. Palmer, *The Way of the Fox: American Strategy in the War for America, 1775–1783* (Westport, Conn., and London: Greenwood Press, 1975), 25–28; 207–8. Edgar, *South Carolina: A History*, 78, table 5.2. Useful in terms of the events leading to the war and of the war itself is George C. Rogers, Jr., *A South Carolina Chronology, 1497–1970* (Columbia: University of South Carolina Press, 1973), esp. 30–44.

4. George L. Johnson, Jr., *The Frontier in the Colonial South: South Carolina Backcountry, 1730–1800* (Westport, Conn., and London: Greenwood Press, 1997), 65–91; Weir, *Colonial South Carolina: A History*, 265–89; and Robert L. Meriwether, *The Expansion of South Carolina, 1729–1765* (Kingsport, Tenn.: Southern Publishers, 1940), 160–211.

5. For Charleston in this period see George C. Rogers, Jr., *Charleston in the Age of the Pinckneys* (Columbia: University of South Carolina Press, 1984). On the Regulator movement and political issues, see Weir, *Colonial South Carolina: A History*, 265–315, and Alden, *The South in the Revolution*, 146–52. Useful perspectives on frontier defense are in Larry E. Ivers, *British Drums on the Southern Frontier: The Military Colonization of Georgia, 1733–1749* (Chapel Hill: University of North Carolina Press, 1974), esp. 6–7, 27–30.

6. See accounts in Edgar, *South Carolina: A History*, 219–24; Lipscomb, *South Carolina Revolutionary War Battles*, 1:3–7; David Lee Russell, *The American Revolution in the Southern Colonies* (Jefferson, N.C., and London: McFarland, 2000), 55; and Rogers, *A South Carolina Chronology, 1497–1970*, 36.

7. William Moultrie, *Memoirs of the American Revolution* (1802; reprint, New York: Arno Press, 1968), 1:57–58; Edgar, *South Carolina: A History*, 222; and Russell, *American Revolution in the Southern Colonies*, 55.

8. Weir, *Colonial South Carolina: A History*, 200–201, and Russell, *American Revolution in the Southern Colonies*, 56.

9. See Greene, *The Quest for Power*, 37, 413, and 458. Campbell held the rank of post-captain in the Royal Navy and had earlier proved an able governor in Nova Scotia. Edgar uses the term "colonial administrator" (*South Carolina: A History*, 224) as does this work, and Mark M. Boatner, *Encyclopedia of the American Revolution* (New York: David McKay Company, 1966), describes Campbell as a "capable governor" (172).

10. Regarding the fort's site, see Judith M. Andrews, ed., *South Carolina Highway Historical Marker Guide*, 2d ed., rev. (Columbia: South Carolina Department of Archives and History, 1998), 153; and Larry E. Ivers, *Colonial Forts of South Carolina, 1670–1775* (Columbia: University of South Carolina Press, 1970), 42.

11. See accounts in Robert D. Bass, *Ninety Six: The Struggle for the South Carolina Back Country* (Lexington, S.C.: The Sandlapper Store, 1978), 84–85; Jones, *Synoptic History*, 99–101; Lipscomb, *South Carolina Becomes a State*, 15; and Warren Ripley, *Battleground: South Carolina in the Revolution* (Charleston, S.C.: The News & Courier and The Evening Post, 1983), 2–3. On ranger service see Ivers, *British Drums on the Southern Frontier*, 7, 9, 12–15, 23, 28, 118, 209.

12. Palmer, *Way of the Fox*, 53–61; Weigley, *History of the United States Army*, 29–34; and Alden, *The South in the Revolution*, 190.

13. John William Gerard De Brahm, *Report of the General Survey in the Southern District of North America*, ed. with an introd. by Louis De Vorsey, Jr. (Columbia: University of South Carolina Press, 1971), 11, 52, 91; Mills, *Statistics of South Carolina*, 230; Ivers, *Colonial Forts of South Carolina*, 24–28, 51–52; and Lipscomb, *South Carolina Revolutionary War Battles*, 1:12–15; Russell, *American Revolution in the Southern Colonies*, 60.

14. On the origins of the flag, see Lipscomb, *South Carolina Revolutionary War Battles*, 1:51–58n; Lipscomb, *South Carolina Becomes a State*, 18; McCrady, *History of South Carolina in the Revolution*, 137–42; and J. Percival Petit, ed., *South Carolina and the Sea: Day by Day toward Five Centuries*, vol. 1, *1492–1800* (Charleston: Maritime and Ports Activities Committee of the State Ports Authority of South Carolina, 1976), 91.

15. For the loyalists see Wallace Brown, *The King's Friends: The Composition and Motives of the American Loyalist Claimants* (Providence: Brown University Press, 1965), 212–28; and Calhoon, *Loyalists in Revolutionary America*, 1:448–57.

16. See accounts in Coker, *Charleston's Maritime Heritage*, 75–76; Lipscomb, *South Carolina Revolutionary War Battles*, 1:11–16–18; Ripley, *Battleground: South Carolina in the Revolution*, 7–9; and Mills, *Statistics of South Carolina*, 230.

17. For a chronological listing of actions, see Terry W. Lipscomb, *Battles, Skirmishes, and Actions of the American Revolution in South Carolina* (Columbia: South Carolina Department of Archives and History, 1991), 3–24; and McCrady, *History of South Carolina in the Revolution*, vol. 2, app. B, 744–50.

18. For Stuart's career, see John R. Alden, *John Stuart and the Southern Colonial Frontier* (Ann Arbor: University of Michigan Press, 1944); and Corkran, *Carolina Indian Frontier*, 64–65.

19. Weir, *"A Most Significant Epoch,"* 64–66.

20. Ivers, *Colonial Forts of South Carolina*, 64–65, Bass, *Ninety Six*, 20–87; Andrews, *South Carolina Highway Historical Marker Guide*, 121; and John Mack Faragher, *Daniel Boone: The Life and Legend of an American Pioneer* (New York: Henry Holt, 1992), 64.

21. See accounts in Faragher, 104–16; Henry Lumpkin, *From Savannah to Yorktown: The American Revolution in the South* (Columbia: University of South Carolina Press, 1981), 1; and Russell, *American Revolution in the Southern Colonies*, 60.

22. Bass indicates that the first rifles reached the South Carolina backcountry by 1750, brought south by the stream of hunters, traders, and settlers arriving from Pennsylvania and Virginia (*Ninety Six*, 34). There is a wealth of material on rifles and muskets in the colonial period, including John G. W. Dillin, *The Kentucky Rifle* (New York: Ludlum and Beebe, 1946), Carl P. Russell, *Guns on the Early Frontier: A History of Firearms from Colonial Times through the Years of the Western Fur Trade* (Berkeley: University of California Press, 1957); and Norman B. Wilkinson, "The Pennsylvania Rifle," *American Heritage* 1 (summer 1950), 3–5, 64–66.

23. Jones, *Synoptic History*, 100–102; Edgar, *South Carolina: A History*, 226–27; and Alden, *The South in the Revolution*, 200–201.

24. For the Cherokees in the Seven Years' War, see Corkran, *Carolina Indian Frontier*, 47–61; Cayton and Teute, *Contact Points*, 114–50; Anderson, *Crucible of War*, 457–71.

25. On slavery in South Carolina, see Philip D. Morgan, *Slave Counterpoint: Black Culture in the Eighteenth-Century Chesapeake and Lowcountry* (Chapel Hill: University of North Carolina Press, 1998); Peter H. Wood, *Black Majority: Negroes in Colonial South Carolina from 1670 through the Stono Rebellion* (New York: Alfred A. Knopf, 1974); and Daniel C. Littlefield, *Rice and Slaves: Ethnicity and the Slave Trade in Colonial South Carolina* (Urbana: University of Illinois Press, 1991).

26. Coker, *Charleston's Maritime Heritage, 1670–1865*, 77; Lipscomb, *South Carolina Revolutionary War Battles*, 1:19–20; Alden, *The South in the Revolution*, 200–201; Russell, *American Revolution in the Southern Colonies*, 59–61; and De Brahm, *Report*, map facing p. 90.

Chapter 2. Counterattack, 1776–1777

1. Palmer, *Way of the Fox*, esp. 95–114; Don Higginbotham, *George Washington and the American Military Tradition*, Mercer University Lamar Memorial Lectures no. 27 (Athens and London: University of Georgia Press, 1985), 64–105; and Charles Royster, *A Revolutionary People at War: The Continental Army and American Character, 1775–1783*, published for the Institute of Early American History and Culture, Williamsburg, Va. (Chapel Hill: University of North Carolina Press, 1979), 3–24.

2. For British strategy and policy in the war as to background, determinants, and key players, see Mackesy, *The War for America*, 36–72; Higginbotham, *War of American Independence*, 122–47; Alden, *History of the*

American Revolution, 158–93; and Ira D. Gruber, *The Howe Brothers and the American Revolution,* published for the Institute of Early American History and Culture, Williamsburg, Va. (New York: Atheneum, 1972), esp. 72–88.

3. Peckham, *The War for Independence,* 38–42.

4. Russell, *American Revolution in the Southern Colonies,* 78–86; William B. Willcox, ed., *The American Rebellion: Sir Henry Clinton's Narrative of His Campaigns, 1775–1782, with an Appendix of Original Documents* (1954; reprint, Hamden, Conn.: Archon Books/Shoe String Press, 1971), xvi–xx, 18–38; and Higginbotham, *War of American Independence,* 135–37.

5. Sir Peter Parker to Admiralty, July 9, 1776, in Willcox, *The American Rebellion,* 376–78; Coker, *Charleston's Maritime Heritage,* 83–84; and "A N. W. b. N. View of Charles Town . . . July 29th, 1776," in *Divers Accounts of the Battle of Sullivan's Island in His Majesty's Province of South Carolina, the 28th June 1776: From the Collections and Publications of the South Carolina Historical Society* (Charleston: The South Carolina Historical Society, 1976), plate, pp. 8–9. See also "Sir Peter Parker," *Dictionary of National Biography* (London: Oxford University Press, 1973) 15:265–66.

6. See Potter and Nimitz, *Sea Power,* 46–65 for operations in the Seven Years' War. See also "Sir Henry Clinton" in *Dictionary of National Biography* (London: Oxford University Press, 1973), 4:550–51; and George A. Billias, ed., *George Washington's Generals and Opponents: Their Exploits and Leadership* (1964; reprint, New York: Da Capo Press, 1994), 73–102. For Cornwallis see *Dictionary of National Biography* (London: Oxford University Press, 1973) 4:1159–66; and Billias, *George Washington's Generals and Opponents,* 193–232.

7. For descriptions of the fort, see Coker, *Charleston's Maritime Heritage,* 79–81; and Jim Stokely, *Constant Defender: The Story of Fort Moultrie* (Washington, D.C.: National Park Service, U.S. Department of the Interior, 1978), 18–23. On Lee's role see Higginbotham, *War of American Independence,* 135–37; and Stokely, *Constant Defender,* 20.

8. Willcox, *The American Rebellion,* 28–37; and Willcox, *Portrait of a General: Sir Henry Clinton in the War of Independence* (New York: Alfred A. Knopf, 1964), 68–89.

9. Stokely, *Constant Defender,* 20–28; and Ripley, *Battleground: South Carolina in the Revolution,* 17; and Russell, *American Revolution in the Southern Colonies,* 87–95. McCrady indicates that the American engineer, Captain De Brahm, had laid out breastworks of palmetto logs, but he makes no mention of any bricks being used in this fortification (*History of South Carolina in the Revolution,* 145).

10. Most—but not all—harbor pilots were white. The example of the freedman-black Thomas Jeremiah has already been noted. Sir Peter Parker blamed the pilots he used for running the frigates aground and for not getting

the fifty-gun ships close enough to the fort to do maximum damage. See Sir Peter Parker to Admiralty, July 9, 1776, in Willcox, *The American Rebellion,* 377; and Lipscomb, *South Carolina Revolutionary War Battles,* 1:26–27.

11. For accounts of the battle, see Coker, *Charleston's Maritime Heritage,* 79–85; *Divers Accounts of the Battle of Sullivan's Island;* Higginbotham, *The War of American Independence,* 136–37; Lipscomb, *South Carolina Revolutionary War Battles,* 1:22–41; Lumpkin, *From Savannah to Yorktown,* 10–18; Stokely, *Constant Defender,* 22–30; Willcox, *The American Rebellion,* 26–38; Willcox, *Portrait of a General,* 82–93; and McCrady, *History of South Carolina in the Revolution,* 135–62.

12. Quoted in Stokely, *Constant Defender,* 27, from William Moultrie, *Memoirs of the American Revolution* (1802; reprint, New York: Arno Press, 1968).

13. McCrady says that Jasper gave "three cheers[, and then] returned to his gun" (*History of South Carolina in the Revolution,* 157).

14. Stokely, *Constant Defender,* 27–28.

15. See Clowes et al., *The Royal Navy,* 3:372–79. For Midshipmen Saumarez's subsequent naval career, see *Dictionary of National Biography* (London: Oxford University Press, 1973), 17:803–6.

16. On frontier warfare, see Howard Peckham, *The Colonial Wars, 1689–1762* (Chicago and London: University of Chicago Press, 1964), 1–4; Ian K. Steele, *Warpaths: Invasions of North America* (New York, Oxford: Oxford University Press, 1994), 226–47; and Cayton and Teute, *Contact Points,* 1–15. See also Patrick M. Malone, *The Skulking Way of War: Technology and Tactics among the New England Indians* (Baltimore and London: Johns Hopkins University Press, 1991).

17. The standard accounts are in McCrady, *History of South Carolina in the Revolution,* 186–91; and Corkran, *Carolina Indian Frontier,* 66–67.

18. Andrews, *South Carolina Historical Marker Guide,* 143. Steve Rajtar, *Indian War Sites: A Guide to Battlefields, Monuments, and Memorials, State by State with Canada and Mexico* (Jefferson, N.C., and London: McFarland, 1995), identifies it as the "Attack at Ludley's Fort . . . near Robbin's Creek" (228).

19. John Mack Faragher, *Daniel Boone: The Life and Legend of an American Pioneer* (New York: Henry Holt and Company, 1992), 19–23.

20. Armstrong Starkey, *European and Native American Warfare, 1675–1815* (Norman: University of Oklahoma Press, 1998), 115–17.

21. McCrady, *History of South Carolina in the Revolution,* 195–96; Jones, *Synoptic History,* 106; and Andrews, *South Carolina Historical Marker Guide,* 1–2.

22. See John H. Logan, *A History of The Upper Country of South Carolina: From the Earliest Periods to the Close of the War of Independence* (1859;

reprint, Spartanburg: The Reprint Company, 1960), 221–40; and Rajtar, *Indian War Sites,* 228.

23. Corkran, *Carolina Indian Frontier,* 66–67; Bass, *Ninety Six,* 136–37; and McCrady, *History of South Carolina in the Revolution,* 196.

24. Mills, *Statistics of South Carolina,* 237–38.

25. For accounts of the "Ring Fight," see Corkran, *Carolina Indian Frontier,* 67; Bass, *Ninety Six,* 137; McCrady, *History of South Carolina in the Revolution,* 197; and Lumpkin, *From Savannah to Yorktown,* 23–24.

26. See Logan, *A History of The Upper Country of South Carolina: From the Earliest Periods to the Close of the War of Independence,* vol. 2 (Easley, S.C.: Southern Historical Press, 1980), 50–51, 104–5; and Margaret Mills Seaborn, ed., *Benjamin Hawkins's Journeys through Oconee Country, South Carolina in 1796 and 1797* (Columbia: R. L. Bryan Company, 1973), 18–22, also describing Pickens's later home and its proximity to the site of the August 1776 fight. Mark M. Boatner, *Landmarks of the American Revolution: A Guide to Locating and Knowing What Happened at the Sites of Independence* (New York: Hawthorne Books, 1975), places the fight in 1779 and repeats the story that Pickens set fire to a canebrake, the noise of which burning supposedly sounded like gunfire and set the Indians to flight (503). For an additional perspective on Indian warfare, see Jared Diamont, *Guns, Germs, and Steel: The Fates of the Human Societies* (New York and London: W. W. Norton & Company, 1997), esp. 85–92, 131–56.

27. McCrady, *History of South Carolina in the Revolution,* 198–99; Rajtar, *Indian War Sites,* 228–29; Alden, *The South in the Revolution,* 272–73; and Corkran, *Carolina Indian Frontier,* 67–68.

28. Edgar, *South Carolina: A History,* 229–30.

29. On the seal, see David C. R. Heisser, *The Seal of the State of South Carolina: A Short History* (Columbia: South Carolina Department of Archives and History, 1992), esp. 7–11.

30. Royster, *Revolutionary People at War,* 54–126; and Potter and Nimitz, *Sea Power,* 67–69.

31. Gruber, *Howe Brothers,* 189–223; and John S. Pancake, *1777: The Year of the Hangman* (University: University of Alabama Press, 1977), 82–101.

32. Pancake, *1777,* 146–91.

33. For Britain's new situation, see Mackesy, *The War for America,* esp. 180–211.

Chapter 3. The War Comes South, 1778–1779

1. Mackesy, *The War for America,* 148–73; Black, *Warfare in the Eighteenth Century,* 120–22; and Syrett, *The Royal Navy in European Waters,* 17–19.

2. Gruber, *Howe Brothers*, 351–65; Mackesy, *The War for America*, 152–61; and Willcox, *Portrait of a General*, 207–26.

3. For Pitt's role in the Seven Years' War see Anderson, *Crucible of War*, esp. 176–79, 181, 211–16, 297–311; Steele, *Warpaths*, 207–9, 222–25; and Potter and Nimitz, *Sea Power*, 51–65.

4. Russell F. Weigley, *The American Way of Warfare: A History of United States Military Strategy and Policy* (New York and London: Macmillan, 1973), 3–17; and Willcox, *Portrait of a General*, 211–59.

5. Royster, *Revolutionary People at War*, 255; Higginbotham, *War of American Independence*, 245–48; and Willcox, *The American Rebellion*, 90–98.

6. Potter and Nimitz, *Sea Power*, 77–80; and Clowes et al., *The Royal Navy*, 3:396–412.

7. See essay by Ira D. Gruber, "Britain's Southern Strategy," in W. Robert Higgins, ed., *The Revolutionary War in the South: Power, Conflict, and Leadership* (Durham, N.C.: Duke University Press, 1979); Mackesy, *The War for America*, 249–62; and Alden, *The South in the Revolution*, 230–35.

8. Lieutenant Colonel Archibald Campbell quoted in Mackesy, *The War for America*, 234.

9. Fortescue, *History of the British Army*, 3:276–79.

10. Russell, *American Revolution in the Southern Colonies*, 104–5; McCrady, *History of South Carolina in the Revolution*, 337–39; and Boatner, *Landmarks of the American Revolution*, 82–85. For Lincoln see Billias, *George Washington's Generals and Opponents*, 193–211.

11. Accounts are in McCrady, *History of South Carolina in the Revolution*, 399–401; Ripley, *Battleground: South Carolina in the Revolution*, 20–23; and Russell, *American Revolution in the Southern Colonies*, 104–5.

12. Fortescue, *History of the British Army*, 3:275–82; and Mills, *Statistics of South Carolina*, 240–41.

13. See Russell, *American Revolution in the Southern Colonies*, 106; and McCrady, *History of South Carolina in the Revolution*, 352–53.

14. On Laurens, see Gregory D. Massey, *John Laurens and the American Revolution* (Columbia: University of South Carolina Press, 2000), esp. 135–36.

15. Accounts of Prevost's move against Charleston are in McCrady, *History of South Carolina in the Revolution*, 352–81; Fortescue, *History of the British Army*, 3:282–83; Ripley, *Battleground: South Carolina in the Revolution*, 29–33; Mills, *Statistics of South Carolina*, 240–42; and Massey, *John Laurens*, 136–39.

16. Ripley, *Battleground: South Carolina in the Revolution*, 35.

17. Fortescue, *History of the British Army*, 3:282–83; McCrady, *History of South Carolina in the Revolution*, 384–91; and Russell, *American Revolution*

in the Southern Colonies, 110–11. See also Curtis, *Organization of the British Army*, esp. 1–32 and 150–52.

18. Mackesy, *The War for America*, 267–69, 339.

19. For the siege of Savannah, see Lumpkin, *From Savannah to Yorktown*, 32–40; Fortescue, *History of the British Army*, 3:282–86; and Mahan, *The Influence of Sea Power*, 375–76.

20. Fortescue, *History of the British Army*, 3:299–302; and Syrett, *The Royal Navy in European Waters*, 61–94.

21. See Willcox, *The American Rebellion*, 137–56.

Chapter 4. In the Path of Invasion, 1780

1. Willcox, *The American Rebellion*, 149–53, 160–61, 188. For the career of George Keith Elphinstone, see *Dictionary of National Biography* (London: Oxford University Press, 1973), 6:734–38; and Tom Wareham, *The Star Captains: Frigate Command in the Napoleonic Wars* (Annapolis, Md.: Naval Institute Press, 2001), 38, 81, 121, 124, 146, 195–98 for his influence within the Royal Navy's officer corps. The papers of Lord Keith are in the Public Record Office (Admiralty 6/65) and in the National Maritime Museum at Greenwich.

2. Willcox, *Portrait of a General*, 294, 300–304.

3. For details of the plans for organizing and deploying row galleys, see various files, covering especially the period February–March 1780, in Keith Papers, National Maritime Museum, Greenwich. For a representation of a row galley, see Coker, *Charleston's Maritime Heritage*, which shows one such vessel in use by the South Carolina State Navy (101).

4. Willcox, *The American Rebellion*, 158–59; Willcox, *Portrait of a General*, 301–2; Ira D. Gruber, ed., *John Peebles' American War: The Diary of a Scottish Grenadier, 1776–1782*, Publications of the Army Records Society, vol. 13 (Mechanicsburg, Pa.: Stackpole Books, 1998), 306–34; Uhlendorf, *Siege of Charleston*, 105–39, 367–71; and Clowes et al., *The Royal Navy*, 3:470–74.

5. See George F. Jones, "The 1780 Siege of Charleston as Experienced by a Hessian Officer," part 1, *South Carolina Historical Magazine* 88:1 (January 1987), 26–27; and Coker, *Charleston's Maritime Heritage*, 35–45, for pilots and commercial issues; as well as Weir, *Colonial South Carolina: A History*, 181, 188.

6. Willcox, *The American Rebellion*, 161, and Uhlendorf, *Siege of Charleston*, 181–85.

7. McCrady, *History of South Carolina in the Revolution*, 431; and Uhlendorf, *Siege of Charleston*, 183, 189.

8. The pace seemed slow to the British troops deployed ashore as well. See Gruber, *John Peebles' American War*, 335–73. Willcox, *The American Rebellion*, 161; and Willcox, *Portrait of a General*, 304–12.

9. Uhlendorf, *Siege of Charleston*, 189–203.

10. See Willcox, *Portrait of a General*, 303; and McCrady, *History of South Carolina in the Revolution*, 432–44, dealing with Lincoln's reasons for defending Charleston. Regarding Washington's decision to defend New York in 1776, See Higginbotham, *War of American Independence*, 150–62.

11. Willcox, *The American Rebellion*, 163. Descriptions of the defenses are in Uhlendorf, *Siege of Charleston*, 27, 39, 55, 91–95, 201, 211, 415; and Fortescue, *History of the British Army*, 3:314.

12. Regarding Whipple, his squadron, and the state navy, see Coker, *Charleston's Maritime Heritage*, 77, 86–88, 103–6. Regarding blacks and militia service and service as sailors, see Edgar, *South Carolina: A History*, 231. In 1826, Robert Mills noted that "free people of color . . . [could be] enrolled as pioneers" in South Carolina's militia system (*Statistics of South Carolina*, 292).

13. For Lincoln's numbers and units, see McCrady, *History of South Carolina in the Revolution*, 427–31, 507–10.

14. Uhlendorf, *Siege of Charleston*, 217–19; and Willcox, *The American Rebellion*, 163.

15. See Lumpkin, *From Savannah to Yorktown*, 31, 49; McCrady, *History of South Carolina in the Revolution*, 357–81; and Edgar, *South Carolina: A History*, 233. On the issue of slavery and freeing blacks to serve on the American side, see Alden, *The South in the Revolution*, 225–26; Massey, *John Laurens*, 154–56.

16. Russell F. Weigley, *The Partisan War: The South Carolina Campaign of 1780–1782* (Columbia: University of South Carolina Press, 1970), 6–7; and McCrady, *History of South Carolina in the Revolution*, 453–54.

17. For Elphinstone's role see files in Keith Papers, National Maritime Museum, Greenwich, February–March 1780; Uhlendorf, *Siege of Charleston*, 31–33, 223–24; and McCrady, *History of South Carolina in the Revolution*, 453.

18. Massey, *John Laurens*, 158; Willcox, *The American Rebellion*, 163; and Willcox, *Portrait of a General*, 306.

19. Fortescue, *History of the British Army*, 3:314–15; McCrady, *History of South Carolina in the Revolution*, 451–58; and Uhlendorf, *Siege of Charleston*, 229–41.

20. Coker, *Charleston's Maritime Heritage*, 110; and McCrady, *History of South Carolina in the Revolution*, 456.

21. Clowes et al., *The Royal Navy*, 3:471–72; and Willcox, *The American Rebellion*, 162–63.

22. Uhlendorf, *Siege of Charleston*, 241–45; Coker, *Charleston's Maritime Heritage*, 110–14; Willcox, *The American Rebellion*, 163–64; and "Intelligence From Charleston," May 3, 1780, in Franklin B. Hough, ed., *The Siege of Charleston: By the British Fleet and Army Under the Command of Admiral*

Arbuthnot and Sir Henry Clinton (1887; reprint, Spartanburg: The Reprint Company, 1975), 70–73. For the career and admiralship of Marriott Arbuthnot, see Willcox, "Arbuthnot, Gambier, and Graves: 'Old Women of the Navy,'" in Billias, *George Washington's Generals and Opponents*, 260–90.

23. Higginbotham, *War of American Independence*, 356–57; and McCrady, *History of South Carolina in the Revolution*, 432; and Fortescue, *History of the British Army*, 3:314–15.

24. Willcox, *The American Rebellion*, 165–67; Mills, *Statistics of South Carolina*, 249; and Fortescue, *History of the British Army*, 3:315–16. For Tarleton's life and career, see Robert D. Bass, *The Green Dragoon: The Lives of Banastre Tarleton and Mary Robinson* (New York: Henry Holt, 1957).

25. Uhlendorf, *Siege of Charleston*, 83, 285–87, 393; and Lumpkin, *From Savannah to Yorktown*, 48; and Andrews, *South Carolina Highway Historical Marker Guide*, 31.

26. Uhlendorf, *Siege of Charleston*, 69, 75, 271, 274–75.

27. See McCrady, *History of South Carolina in the Revolution*, 463–78.

28. Willcox, *The American Rebellion*, 169; Massey, *John Laurens*, 159–62; and Hough, *Siege of Charleston*, 134.

29. Uhlendorf, *Siege of Charleston*, 281–89.

30. See accounts in Gruber, *John Peebles' American War*, 372–73; Willcox, *The American Rebellion*, 170–71; Uhlendorf, *Siege of Charleston*, 87, 289–93; and Hough, *Siege of Charleston*, 78–80, 203–6.

31. Willcox, *The American Rebellion*, 172; and Uhlendorf, *Siege of Charleston*, 295; but see also Clowes et al., *The Royal Navy*, 3:441–42, 471–72.

32. Mackesy, *The War for America*, 342; Fortescue, *History of the British Army*, 3:316–18; and Lumpkin, *From Savannah to Yorktown*, 50.

33. Uhlendorf, *Siege of Charleston*, 327; Willcox, *Portrait of a General*, 308; Mackesy, *The War for America*, 342; and Fortescue, *History of the British Army*, 3:316.

34. Mackesy, *The War for America*, 342.

35. Rogers, *A South Carolina Chronology*, 41.

36. Higginbotham, *War of American Independence*, 360; Edgar, *South Carolina: A History*, 233; and Royster, *Revolutionary People at War*, 34.

37. McCrady, *History of South Carolina in the Revolution*, 588.

38. See accounts in Ripley, *Battleground: South Carolina in the Revolution*, 72–74; and Lumpkin, *From Savannah to Yorktown*, 83; and McCrady, *History of South Carolina in the Revolution*, 589–99, 616.

39. Lumpkin, *From Savannah to Yorktown*, 83; and Ripley, *Battleground: South Carolina in the Revolution*, 75–76.

40. Mackesy, *The War for America*, 343; and Anne King Gregorie, *Thomas Sumter* (1964; reprint, Sumter, S.C.: Gamecock City Printing, 2000), 73–75.

41. McCrady, *History of South Carolina in the Revolution,* 562–68; and Lumpkin, *From Savannah to Yorktown,* 83–84.

42. Gregorie, *Thomas Sumter,* 91–96, 98.

43. For Gates's generalship, see Billias, *George Washington's Generals and Opponents,* 79–108. Alden, *History of the American Revolution,* 418; Weigley, *Partisan War,* 17–18; and Higginbotham, *War of American Independence,* 357–59.

44. Mackesy, *The War for America,* 343.

45. In the eighteenth-century form in Curtis, *Organization of the British Army,* the 23rd Foot is styled variously "Welch Fuzileers" and "Welsh Fusileers" (150). Lumpkin, *From Savannah to Yorktown,* 57–67; and Weigley, *Partisan War,* 19.

46. Higginbotham, *War of American Independence,* 359–60.

47. Gregorie, *Thomas Sumter,* 101–5; and McCrady, *History of South Carolina in the Revolution,* 680–83.

48. Fortescue, *History of the British Army,* 3:326.

Chapter 5. The War in the Backcountry, 1780

1. Fortescue, *History of the British Army,* 3:318–27; and Black, *Western Warfare, 1775–1882,* 20–21. Moultrie at first had harbored hopes for Ninety Six and its potential for joining the Whig side. When the new regiment of mounted rangers was raised in 1775, he argued that judicious appointment of officers from among key backcountry candidates would help bind that region to the revolutionary camp. Other observers believed that, at best, the proportion of Whigs to loyalists in the Ninety Six region was about even. See in particular Klein, *Unification of a Slave State,* 88.

2. Brown, *The King's Friends,* 213–28: and analysis in Klein, *Unification of a Slave State,* esp. 81.

3. See Weigley, *Partisan War,* 8–9. Some pre-Napoleonic European professionals—Charles Lee, for example—were interested in a strategy and tactics of "the little war." See Black, *Western Warfare,* 14–15; Strachan, *European Armies,* 28–29; and John W. Shy, "Charles Lee: The Soldier as Radical," in Billias, *George Washington's Generals and Opponents,* 22–53.

4. Weigley, *Partisan War,* 16–17; Samuel B. Griffith, trans., *Mao Tse-tung on Guerrilla Warfare* (New York: Frederick A. Praeger, 1961), esp. 41–65; and Mark Kwasny, *Washington's Partisan War, 1775–1783* (Kent, Ohio, and London: Kent State Press, 1996), 329–39.

5. See Moncure, *Cowpens Staff Ride and Battlefield Tour,* 19; Corkran, *Carolina Indian Frontier,* esp. 47–65, for the Cherokee War; Weir, *Colonial South Carolina: A History,* 269–75; and Meriwether, *The Expansion of South Carolina,* 213–40.

6. Klein, *Unification of a Slave State*, 47–77; and Edgar, *South Carolina: A History*, 204–25.

7. Claude H. Van Tyne, *The Loyalists in the American Revolution* (New York and London: Macmillan, 1902), 184; and Weigley, *Partisan War*, 11.

8. See McCrady, *History of South Carolina in the Revolution*, 186–88, 193; and Klein, *Unification of a Slave State*, 37–38.

9. Edgar, *South Carolina: A History*, 229–30.

10. Assessments and interpretations in Klein, *Unification of a Slave State*, 82–92, 107–8.

11. McCrady, *History of South Carolina in the Revolution*, 531–33.

12. Klein, *Unification of a Slave State*, 85–86; and McCrady, *History of South Carolina in the Revolution*, 203.

13. The point made in Edgar, *South Carolina: A History*, 240.

14. A Georgetown planter quoted in Klein, *Unification of a Slave State*, 101; McCrady, *History of South Carolina in the Revolution*, 533, 721; and Willcox, *The American Rebellion*, 175.

15. For Cornwallis's life and career, see *Dictionary of National Biography* 4:1159–66; Hugh F. Rankin, "Charles Lord Cornwallis: Study in Frustration," in Billias, *George Washington's Generals and Opponents*, 193–232; and Franklin B. and Mary Wickwire, *Cornwallis: The American Adventure* (Boston: Houghton Mifflin, 1970), 7–78.

16. Major James Wemyss quoted in McCrady, *History of South Carolina in the Revolution*, 747–48; Klein, *Unification of a Slave State*, 95–107; and Edgar, *South Carolina: A History*, 234.

17. For Tarleton's British Legion, see Moncure, *Cowpens Staff Ride and Battlefield Tour*, 28–29; Weigley, *Partisan War*, 21–22; and quotation in Klein, *Unification of a Slave State*, 101.

18. McCrady, *History of South Carolina in the Revolution*, 517.

19. See Robert D. Bass, *Swamp Fox: The Life and Campaigns of General Francis Marion* (New York: Henry Holt and Company, 1959), 5–6; Gregorie, *Thomas Sumter*, 1–2; and McCrady, *History of South Carolina in the Revolution*, 564–68; and John M. Logan, *A History of the Upper Country of South Carolina* (1960; reprint. Easley, S.C.: Southern Historical Press, 1980), 50–51.

20. Gregorie, *Thomas Sumter*, 5–69.

21. Bass, *Swamp Fox*, 18–31, and Weigley, *Partisan War*, 22–23.

22. Klein, *Unification of a Slave State*, 34–35, 243, 270.

23. McCrady, *History of South Carolina in the Revolution*, 649–50.

24. Lumpkin, *From Savannah to Yorktown*, 87–88; and Dan L. Morrill, *Southern Campaigns of the American Revolution* (Baltimore: Nautical & Aviation Publishing Company of America, 1993), 98.

25. Weigley, *Partisan War*, 23; and Fortescue, *History of the British Army*, 3:327.

26. McCrady, *History of South Carolina in the Revolution*, 699–700; Tarleton quoted in Edgar, *South Carolina: A History*, 235; and in McCrady, *History of South Carolina in the Revolution*, 818–19.

27. See Lumpkin, *From Savannah to Yorktown*, 72; Fortescue, *History of the British Army*, 3:362.

28. McCrady, *History of South Carolina in the Revolution*, 749–50; Morrill, *Southern Campaigns of the American Revolution*, 121; Lumpkin, *From Savannah to Yorktown*, 72; and Russell, *American Revolution the Southern Colonies*, 204.

29. Mackesy, *The War for America*, 342–43.

Chapter 6. Pegasus Galloped, 1780–1781

1. Strachan, *European Armies*, 29; Fortescue, *History of the British Army*, 3:259; Morrill, *Southern Campaigns of the American Revolution*, 101–2; Pancake, *1777*, 168–70; Wickwire and Wickwire, *Cornwallis: The American Adventure*, 201.

2. Weigley, *Partisan War*, 24–25; Mackesy, *The War for America*, 344–45; and Fortescue, *History of the British Army*, 3:328.

3. Weigley, *Partisan War*, 24; McCrady, *History of South Carolina in the Revolution*, 755–56.

4. Morrill, *Southern Campaigns of the American Revolution*, pp. 106–7.

5. Higginbotham, *War of American Independence*, 364.

6. Wickwire and Wickwire, *Cornwallis*, 194–216; Fortescue, *History of the British Army*, 3:328–30; Lumpkin, *From Savannah To Yorktown*, 91–104; and McCrady, *History of South Carolina in the Revolution*, 773–805.

7. Russell, *American Revolution the Southern Colonies*, 194–95.

8. Fortescue, *History of the British Army*, 3:330.

9. Bass, *Swamp Fox*, 76–78; Ripley, *Battleground: South Carolina in the Revolution*, 105; and McCrady, *History of South Carolina in the Revolution*, 751.

10. Quarles, *The Negro in the American Revolution*, 103.

11. According to another account, Marion's nephew was shot at point-blank range but without having first been tied to a tree (Bass, *Swamp Fox*, 89–90).

12. Fortescue, *History of the British Army*, 3:330.

13. McCrady, *History of South Carolina in the Revolution*, 820–23; Lumpkin, *From Savannah To Yorktown*, 107–10.

14. Gregorie, *Thomas Sumter*, 115–18.

15. Accounts in Fortescue, *History of the British Army*, 3:363; Lumpkin, *From Savannah to Yorktown*, 105–15; Morrill, *Southern Campaigns of the*

American Revolution, 122; and McCrady, *History of South Carolina in the Revolution*, 827–30.

16. Edgar, *South Carolina: A History*, 242.

17. Gregorie, *Thomas Sumter*, 120–24.

18. McCrady, *History of South Carolina in the Revolution*, 830–32.

19. Lumpkin, *From Savannah to Yorktown*, 89.

20. The listing of the 7th Foot as "Royal Fusileers" follows the style in Curtis, *Organization of the British Army*, 150.

21. See accounts in Bass, *Swamp Fox*, 100–112; Lumpkin, *From Savannah to Yorktown*, 74–75; and Ripley, *Battleground: South Carolina in the Revolution*, 142–44.

22. See Weigley, *American Way of War*, 18–39, and Theodore Thayer, "Nathanael Greene: Revolutionary War Strategist," in Billias, *George Washington's Generals and Opponents*, 109–38.

23. Higginbotham, *War of American Independence*, 364–66.

24. Fortescue, *History of the British Army*, 3:365.

25. Lawrence E. Babits, *A Devil of a Whipping: The Battle of Cowpens* (Chapel Hill and London: University of North Carolina Press, 1998), 9, 23, 28, 33.

26. Don Higginbotham, "Daniel Morgan: Guerrilla Fighter," in Billias, *George Washington's Generals and Opponents*, 291–316; and Higginbotham, *Daniel Morgan: Revolutionary Rifleman*, published for the Institute of Early American History and Culture at Williamsburg, Va. (Chapel Hill: University of North Carolina Press, 1961), esp. 20–77.

27. See Lumpkin, *From Savannah to Yorktown*, 72; Morrill, *Southern Campaigns of the American Revolution*, 124; and Ripley, *Battleground: South Carolina in the Revolution*, 126–28.

28. See Moncure, *Cowpens Staff Ride and Battlefield Tour*, 26–27; and Babits, *A Devil of a Whipping*, 8–9; and Fortescue, *History of the British Army*, 3:363–66.

29. Weigley, *Partisan War*, 29–30; Higginbotham, *Daniel Morgan*, 131–32; and Moncure, *Cowpens Staff Ride and Battlefield Tour*, 45–46.

30. For Morgan's plan, see Babits, *A Devil of a Whipping*, esp. 61–80.

31. See observations of Major Thomas Young, South Carolina militia, quoted in Moncure, *Cowpens Staff Ride and Battlefield Tour*, 135–36.

32. Fortescue, *History of the British Army*, 3:366–67.

33. For rates of fire, compare Higginbotham, *Daniel Morgan*, 20; Babits, *A Devil of a Whipping*, 11–15; and, for functioning of the flintlock mechanism, see Arcadi Gluckman, *United States Muskets, Rifles and Carbines* (Buffalo, N.Y.: Otto Ulbrich, 1948), 23–38.

34. Weigley, *Partisan War*, 30–31.

35. See the orders of battle for both sides in Lumpkin, *From Savannah to Yorktown*, appendix, 294–95.

36. Fortescue, *History of the British Army*, 3:366–67.

37. Accounts in Babits, *A Devil of a Whipping*, 81–149; Lumpkin, *From Savannah to Yorktown*, 116–34; Moncure, *Cowpens Staff Ride and Battlefield Tour*, 46–63; Higginbotham, *Daniel Morgan*, 135–55; and Morrill, *Southern Campaigns of the American Revolution*, 123–33.

38. Gregorie, *Thomas Sumter*, 148–49, for "Sumter's law." Klein, *Unification of a Slave State*, 84, 104.

39. Cornwallis quoted in Lumpkin, *From Savannah to Yorktown*, 134.

Chapter 7. Against the Outposts, 1781

1. Black, *Warfare in the Eighteenth Century*, 183–85.

2. For British strategic assessments and plans for the South, see Mackesy, *The War for America*, 43–44, 156–59, 252–57.

3. For a discussion of naval strategy, 1778–1781, see Mahan, *The Influence of Sea Power*, 268–71, 505–41.

4. Sir Henry Clinton remained guardedly optimistic regarding mobilization of the loyalists. See Willcox, *The American Rebellion*, 8, 113, 192, 399–400. Lord Cornwallis, on the other hand, increasingly saw a different picture. See Wickwire and Wickwire, *Cornwallis: The American Adventure*, 171–73.

5. Morrill, *Southern Campaigns of the American Revolution*, 132–50; and Weigley, *Partisan War*, 36–43.

6. For a sober assessment of British hopes for the campaign, see Mackesy, *The War for America*, 385–405.

7. See accounts in Lumpkin, *From Savannah to Yorktown*, 75–76; and Henry Lee, *The American Revolution in the South*, ed., with a biography of his father by Robert E. Lee (1869; reprint, New York: Arno Press, 1969), 224–25. For Lee see also John W. Hartmann, *The American Partisan: Henry Lee and the Struggle for Independence, 1776–1780* (Shippensburg, Pa.: Burd Street Press, 2000).

8. Accounts in Lumpkin, *From Savannah to Yorktown*, 76; Russell, *American Revolution in the Southern Colonies*, 233–37, for overall situation; and Ripley, *Battleground: South Carolina in the Revolution*, 148–52.

9. Mills, *Statistics of South Carolina*, 272–73.

10. See Weigley, *Partisan War*, 34–38; and Fortescue, *History of the British Army*, 3:372–73.

11. Weigley, *Partisan War*, 39–43; and Fortescue, *History of the British Army*, 3:373.

12. Russell, *American Revolution in the Southern Colonies*, 225–32.

13. Accounts in Lumpkin, *From Savannah to Yorktown*, 169–75; Weigley, *Partisan War*, 43–45; Thayer, "Nathanael Greene: Revolutionary War Strategist," 124–30; and Fortescue, *History of the British Army*, 3:373–80.

14. Mackesy, *The War for America*, 406; and Theodore Thayer, *Nathanael Greene: Strategist of the American Revolution* (New York: Twayne, 1960), 328–31.

15. Thayer, "Nathanael Greene: Revolutionary War Strategist," 130.

16. Fortescue, *History of the British Army*, 3:382–85.

17. Accounts in Lumpkin, *From Savannah to Yorktown*, 76–77; Russell, *American Revolution in the Southern Colonies*, 236–37; Lee, *American Revolution in the South*, 330–33; Ripley, *Battleground: South Carolina in the Revolution*, 158–60; and Weigley, *Partisan War*, 48–49.

18. Fortescue, *History of the British Army*, 3:385.

19. Accounts in Lumpkin, *From Savannah to Yorktown*, 176–85; Russell, *American Revolution in the Southern Colonies*, 237–38; Fortescue, *History of the British Army*, 3:385–87; and Weigley, *Partisan War*, 49–52.

20. Accounts in Lumpkin, *From Savannah to Yorktown*, 77–78; Russell, *American Revolution in the Southern Colonies*, 242; Lee, *American Revolution in the South*, 345–49; and Bass, *Swamp Fox*, 182–95.

21. Accounts in Lumpkin, *From Savannah to Yorktown*, 184–85; Russell, *American Revolution in the Southern Colonies*, 242; Lee, *American Revolution in the South*, 349–53; and Weigley, *Partisan War*, 53–54.

22. Accounts in Lumpkin, *From Savannah to Yorktown*, 187–89; Russell, *American Revolution in the Southern Colonies*, 243; Lee, *American Revolution in the South*, 353–55; and Weigley, *Partisan War*, 56.

23. Thayer, *Nathanael Greene*, 354–56.

24. Accounts in Lumpkin, *From Savannah to Yorktown*, 187–92; Russell, *American Revolution in the Southern Colonies*, 242–44; Lee, *American Revolution in the South*, 355–58; and Weigley, *Partisan War*, 56–57.

25. For Browne, see Edward J. Cashin, *The King's Ranger: Thomas Brown and the American Revolution on the Southern Frontier* (New York: Fordham University Press, 1999), esp. 130–38.

26. Bass, *Ninety Six*, 386–407.

27. For Kosciuszko, see Francis C. Kajencki, *Thaddeus Kosciuszko: Military Engineer of the American Revolution* (El Paso, Tex.: Southwest Polonia Press, 1998). Accounts in Lumpkin, *From Savannah to Yorktown*, 192–205; Russell, *American Revolution in the Southern Colonies*, 245–48; Lee, *American Revolution in the South*, 358–60, 371–381; and Weigley, *Partisan War*, 57–63.

28. Fortescue, *History of the British Army*, 3:388–89.

29. Weigley, *Partisan War*, 62; and Thayer, *Nathanael Greene*, 356–63.

30. As described by Greene and quoted in Klein, *Unification of a Slave State*, 103.

31. Accounts in Lumpkin, *From Savannah to Yorktown*, 186–87; Russell, *American Revolution in the Southern Colonies*, 242; Robert D. Bass, *Gamecock: The Life and Campaigns of General Thomas Sumter* (New York: Holt, Rinehart and Winston, 1961), 199–200; Ripley, *Battleground: South Carolina in the Revolution*, 180–81; and Weigley, *Partisan War*, 55.

Chapter 8. The Struggle Fought Out, 1781–1782

1. For Biggin Church, see Andrews, *South Carolina Highway Historical Marker Guide*, 32, which states that the church was burned in a forest fire that occurred in 1755. Accounts in Lumpkin, *From Savannah to Yorktown*, 206–11; Russell, *The American Revolution in the Southern Colonies*, 247–48; Weigley, *Partisan War*, 64–65; Bass, *Swamp Fox*, 206–8; Lee, *The American Revolution in the South*, 387–94; and Ripley, *Battleground: South Carolina in the Revolution*, 186–89.

2. Gregorie, *Thomas Sumter*, 173–81.

3. Regarding the overall situation of the British garrisons in South Carolina in this period, see Fortescue, *History of the British Army*, 3:388–89.

4. Bass, *Swamp Fox*, 206–10; Gregorie, *Thomas Sumter*, 173–80; Weigley, *Partisan War*, 65; Ripley, *Battleground: South Carolina in the Revolution*, 190–91; and Lee, *American Revolution in the South*, 387–93.

5. Gregorie, *Thomas Sumter*, 179–89.

6. Hayne's raid against the outskirts of Charleston had resulted in the capture of Andrew Williamson, Whig defender of Ninety Six in 1775 and leader of the punitive expedition against the Cherokees. Williamson had switched sides after Lincoln's surrender, becoming an aggressive and active loyalist; the Americans now despised him as a turncoat. But Williamson was only briefly Hayne's prisoner, Fraser's troops rescuing Williamson in the same action in which they captured Hayne. See Lee, *American Revolution in the South*, 449–58; and Lumpkin, *From Savannah to Yorktown*, 212–13.

7. Fortescue, *History of the British Army*, 3:389–90; Gregorie, *Thomas Sumter*, 186; and Thayer, *Nathanael Greene*, 366–75.

8. Accounts in Bass, *Swamp Fox*, 214–15; and Ripley, *Battleground: South Carolina in the Revolution*, 197–98.

9. Accounts in Fortescue, *History of the British Army*, 3:389–92 (which uses "Stuart" rather than "Stewart"); Lumpkin, *From Savannah to Yorktown*, 212–21; Russell, *American Revolution in the Southern Colonies*, 248–50; Lee, *American Revolution in the South*, 462–77; Bass, *Swamp Fox*, 215–19; and Weigley, *Partisan War*, 65–68.

10. Greene quoted in Anthony J. Joes, *America and Guerrilla Warfare* (Lexington: University Press of Kentucky, 2000), 30. Regarding Nelson's Ferry

see Weigley, *Partisan War*, 34–38; and Andrews, *South Carolina Highway Historical Marker Guide*, 33, 178–79.

11. For an assessment of the import of the battle, see Mackesy, *The War for America*, 490.

12. Fortescue, *History of the British Army*, 3:392.

13. Weigley, *Partisan War*, 70.

14. See Fortescue, *History of the British Army*, 3:392–98; Willcox, *The American Rebellion*, 282–312; Willcox, *Portrait of a General*, 392–444; Wickwire and Wickwire, *Cornwallis: The American Adventure*, 311–53; Palmer, *Way of the Fox*, 171–78; Weigley, *American Way of War*, 38–39; and Mackesy, *The War for America*, 406–30.

15. Black, *Warfare in the Eighteenth Century*, 123–24; Germain to Clinton, July 7, 1781, in Willcox, *The American Rebellion*, 540; and Alden, *History of the American Revolution*, 468–71.

16. Mahan, *The Influence of Sea Power*, 364–96.

17. Alden, *History of the American Revolution*, 472–73; and Lumpkin, *From Savannah to Yorktown*, 222–36.

18. Clowes et al., *The Royal Navy*, 3:496–502.

19. Lumpkin, *From Savannah to Yorktown*, 236–45; Fortescue, *History of the British Army*, 3:399–403; and Mackesy, *The War for America*, 433–35.

20. Washington quoted in Fortescue, *History of the British Army*, 3:404; and Alden, *History of the American Revolution*, 406–7.

21. Accounts in Lumpkin, *From Savannah to Yorktown*, 52–53; Ripley, *Battleground: South Carolina in the Revolution*, 193–94; and Andrews, *South Carolina Highway Historical Marker Guide*, 147.

22. See Weigley, *Partisan War*, 69–70, for overall situation regarding loyalist raids; Lumpkin, *From Savannah to Yorktown*, 52; Ripley, *Battleground: South Carolina in the Revolution*, 194–95; and Andrews, *South Carolina Highway Historical Marker Guide*, 141–43.

23. Accounts in Bass, *Swamp Fox*, 227–31; Lumpkin, *From Savannah to Yorktown*, 56; Ripley, *Battleground: South Carolina in the Revolution*, 217–23; and Thayer, *Nathanael Greene*, 403.

24. Accounts in Bass, *Swamp Fox*, 230–33; Lumpkin, *From Savannah to Yorktown*, 78; and Ripley, *Battleground: South Carolina in the Revolution*, 220–22.

25. Edgar, *South Carolina: A History*, 239; and Thayer, *Nathanael Greene*, 392–93.

26. For Laurens's life and contributions, see Massey, *John Laurens*, and, particularly for an account of his death in the skirmish on the Combahee, 219–27. Other accounts are in Weigley, *Partisan War*, 71–72; Thayer, *Nathanael Greene*, 405; Andrews, *South Carolina Highway Historical Marker Guide*, 63; and Ripley, *Battleground: South Carolina in the Revolution*, 224–29.

27. A later clash, supposedly on November 4, 1782, on Johns Island near Charleston, may have been the last action of the war. See Weigley, *Partisan War*, 72; see Fortescue, *History of the British Army*, 3:413–15, 500–504; and Mackesy, *The War for America*, 434–36.

28. The standard work is Robert S. Lambert, *South Carolina Loyalists in the American Revolution* (Columbia: University of South Carolina Press, 1987). See also Calhoon, *The Loyalists in America*, esp. 500–506; Brown, *The King's Friends*, 249–83; Fortescue, *History of the British Army*, 3:504; and Weigley, *Partisan War*, 72.

29. Two key works are Sylvia R. Frey, *Water from the Rock: Black Resistance in a Revolutionary Age* (Princeton: Princeton University Press, 1991); and Clifford, *From Slavery to Freedom*; Quarles, *The Negro in the American Revolution*, 158–81; and Weigley, *Partisan War*, 72.

30. Accounts in Thayer, *Nathanael Greene*, 408–9; Edgar, *South Carolina: A History*, 240; Russell, *American Revolution in the Southern Colonies*, 317; Ripley, *Battleground: South Carolina in the Revolution*, 229–32; and Mills, *Statistics of South Carolina*, 283–86.

31. See Fortescue, *History of the British Army*, 3:409–10: and Mackesy, *The War for America*, 510–22, for British assessments of how the war was concluded. Other perspectives are available in Marion Balderston and David Syrett, eds., *The Lost War: Letters from British Officers during the American Revolution*, with introduction by Henry Steele Commager (New York: Horizon Press, 1975), esp. 224–25, discussing aspects of the evacuation of Charleston, December 1782.

Conclusion

1. See Terry W. Lipscomb, *South Carolina in 1791: George Washington's Southern Tour* (Columbia: South Carolina Department of Archives and History, 1993), for Washington's post–American Revolutionary War visit to the state. Regarding Greene as practitioner of a strategy agreeable to Washington, see Palmer, *Way of the Fox*, 144–78. Analysis based on ideas in Joes, *America and Guerrilla Warfare*, 5–50. The standard work is Weigley, *American Way of War*, 3–39.

2. Ideas in Theodore Ropp, *War in the Modern World*, rev. ed. (London: Collier-Macmillan, 1962), 84–97. Regarding the existence of a particular American "center of gravity," the British believed that there was not one— rather, there were many, and such existed in the "atomized political and social structure of the colonies." See Mackesy, *The War for America*, 252.

3. Important assessments are in Joes, *America and Guerrilla Warfare*, 5–49; Barbara W. Tuchman, *The March of Folly: From Troy to Vietnam* (New York: Ballantine Books, 1984), 208–31; Robert A. Doughty and Ira D. Gruber, et al., *Warfare in the Western World: Military Operations from 1600 to*

1871 (Lexington, Ky.: D. C. Heath and Company, 1996), vol. 1, 131–70; and Mackesy, *The War for America,* 510–16.

4. Fortescue, *History of the British Army,* 3:405–11.

5. For Laurens's ideas for using black troops to be raised from the slave population, see in particular Massey, *John Laurens,* esp. 2–4, 93–97, 130–33, 137–55, 202–9 and, regarding British employment of black troops, 75–77, 209, 223. Clifford details the cases of four black men from Charleston who served with the British (*From Slavery to Freedom,* 23–25). See also the standard study, Quarles, *The Negro in the American Revolution,* 134–57, which likewise details blacks in British service.

6. On the evolution of tactics, see Strachan, *European Armies,* 28–37. For the political consolidation of South Carolina, standard interpretations are Klein, *Unification of a Slave State;* Rogers, *Charleston in the Age of the Pinckneys;* James Haw, *John and Edward Rutledge of South Carolina* (Athens and London: University of Georgia Press, 1997); and Meriwether, *The Expansion of South Carolina.*

7. Two key sources for women's roles are Charles Claghorn, *Women Patriots of the American Revolution: A Biographical Dictionary* (Metuchen, N.J., and London: Scarecrow Press, 1991) and Cynthia A. Kierner, *Southern Women in Revolution, 1776–1800: Personal and Political Narratives* (Columbia: University of South Carolina Press, 1998). Edgar, *South Carolina: A History,* 242; and Lee, *American Revolution in the South,* 224–355.

8. Regarding the post–Revolutionary War image of blacks and military service, see Quarles, *The Negro in the American Revolution,* 182–200. Key works on the American military ethos are Jack D. Foner, *Blacks and the Military in American History: A New Perspective* (New York: Praeger, 1974); and Marcus Cunliffe, *Soldiers and Civilians: The Martial Spirit in America, 1775–1865* (Boston: Little, Brown and Company, 1968).

BIBLIOGRAPHY

Manuscripts, Memoirs and Printed Documents

Balderston, Marion, and David Syrett, eds. *The Lost War: Letters from British Officers during the American Revolution.* Introduction by Henry Steele Commager. New York: Horizon Press, 1975.

Clinton, Henry. *The American Rebellion: Sir Henry Clinton's Narrative of His Campaigns, 1775–1782, with an Appendix of Original Documents.* Edited by William B. Willcox. Hamden, Conn.: Archon/Shoe String Press, 1971.

Clinton Papers (Sir Henry Clinton's letters, dispatches, reports, etc., dealing with the war in America) in the William L. Clements Library, Ann Arbor, Mich.

Clinton Papers (Sir Henry Clinton's manuscript notebooks, in particular those kept during the operations against Charleston, February–May 1780) in the John Rylands University Library of Manchester, Manchester, England.

Cornwallis Papers (correspondence, dispatches, reports and career information) in the Public Record Office, Kew, London, England.

De Brahm, John William Gerard. *Report of the General Survey in the Southern District of North America.* Ed., with an introduction by Louis De Vorsey, Jr. Columbia: University of South Carolina Press, 1971.

Divers Accounts of the Battle of Sullivan's Island: In His Majesty's Province of South Carolina, the 28th June 1776. From Collections and Publications of the South Carolina Historical Society. Charleston, S.C.: South Carolina Historical Society, 1976.

Gruber, Ira D., ed. *John Peebles' American War: The Diary of a Scottish Grenadier, 1776–1782.* Mechanicsburg, Pa.: Stackpole Books, 1998.

Hough, Franklin B., ed. *The Siege of Charleston: By the British Fleet and Army under the Command of Admiral Arbuthnot and Sir Henry Clinton: Which Terminated with the Summer of That Place on the 12th of May, 1780.* 1867. Reprint, Spartanburg, S.C.: Reprint Company, 1975.

Hunter, Robert, Jr. *Quebec to Carolina in 1785–1786: Being the Travel Diary and Observations of Robert Hunter, Jr., a Young Merchant of London.* Edited by Lewis B. Wright, et al. San Marino, Calif.: Huntington Library, 1943.

Johnson, William. *Sketches of the Life and Correspondence of Nathanael Greene.* New York: Da Capo Press, 1973.

Jones, George F. "The 1780 Siege of Charleston as Experienced by a Hessian Officer." Parts 1 and 2. *South Carolina Historical Magazine* 88 (January 1987): 23–33; (April 1987): 63–75.

Keith Papers (Admiral Lord Keith of Elphinstone logbooks, ships papers, and other records and correspondence) in the National Maritime Museum, Greenwich, London, England.

Lavery, Brian, ed. *Shipboard Life and Organisation, 1731–1815.* Aldershot, Hants.: Ashgate for the Council of the Navy Records Society, 1998.

Lee, Henry. *The American Revolution in the South.* Originally published as *Memoirs of the War in the Southern Department* by Henry Lee. Edited, with a biography of his father, by Robert E. Lee. 1869. Reprint, New York: Arno Press, 1969.

Logan, John H. *A History of the Upper Country of South Carolina: From the Earliest Periods to the Close of the War of Independence.* Vol. 1. 1859. Reprint, Spartanburg, S.C.: Reprint Company, 1960.

———. *A History of the Upper Country of South Carolina: From the Earliest Periods to the Close of the War of Independence.* Vol. II, *A Journal of Personalities, Reminiscences, Traditions and History of the Revolution in South Carolina.* 1910. Reprint, Easley, S.C.: Southern Historical Press, 1980.

Marshall, Douglas W., and Howard H. Peckham. *Campaigns of the American Revolution: An Atlas of Manuscript Maps.* Ann Arbor: University of Michigan Press, 1976.

Moultrie, William. *Memoirs of the American Revolution.* 2 vols. 1802. Reprint, New York: Arno Press, 1968.

Ramsay, David. *The History of the Revolution of South Carolina.* 1785. Reprint, Spartanburg, S.C.: Reprint Company, 1960.

Tarleton, Banastre. *A History of the Campaigns of 1780 and 1781, in the Southern Provinces of South Carolina.* 1787. Reprint, Spartanburg: Reprint Company, 1967.

Uhlendorf, Bernhard A., trans and ed. *The Siege of Charleston: With an Account of the Province of South Carolina: Diaries and Letters of Hessian Officers from the von Jungken Papers in the William L. Clements Library.* Ann Arbor: University of Michigan Press, 1938.

War Office Papers (regimental strengths and other data relating to the British Army) in the Public Record Office, Kew, London, England.

General Works

Addington, Larry H. *The Patterns of War since the Eighteenth Century.* 2d ed. Bloomington and Indianapolis: Indiana University Press, 1994.

Alden, John R. *General Charles Lee: Traitor or Patriot?* Baton Rouge: Louisiana State University Press, 1951.

———. *A History of the American Revolution.* New York: Alfred A. Knopf, 1969.

———. *John Stuart and the Southern Colonial Frontier.* Ann Arbor: University of Michigan Press, 1944.

———. *The South in the Revolution, 1763–1789.* Baton Rouge: Louisiana State University Press, 1957.

Alger, John I. *Definitions and Doctrine of the Military Art: Past and Present.* West Point, N.Y.: Department of History, U.S. Military Academy, 1981.

Anderson, Fred. *Crucible of War: The Seven Years' War and the Fate of Empire in British North America, 1754–1766.* New York: Alfred A. Knopf, 2000.

———. *A People's Army: Massachusetts Soldiers and Security in the Seven Years' War.* New York: W. W. Norton and Company, 1985.

Andrews, Judith M., ed. *South Carolina Highway Historical Marker Guide.* 2d ed. Columbia: South Carolina Department of Archives and History, 1998.

Babits, Lawrence E. *A Devil of a Whipping: The Battle of Cowpens.* Chapel Hill: University of North Carolina Press, 1998.

Bailey, Louise, Elizabeth Ivey Cooper, and Alexander Moore, eds. *Biographical Dictionary of the South Carolina House of Representatives.* 5 vols. Columbia: University of South Carolina Press, 1974–2001.

Bailyn, Bernard. *The Ideological Origins of the American Revolution.* Cambridge: Harvard University Press, 1967.

Barker, A. J. *Redcoats.* London: Gordon & Cremonesi, 1976.

Barnett, Correlli. *Britain and Her Army, 1509–1970: A Military, Political and Social Survey.* New York: William Morrow, 1970.

Bass, Robert D. *Gamecock: The Life and Campaigns of General Thomas Sumter.* New York: Holt, Rinehart and Winston, 1961.

———, ed. *George Washington's Generals and Opponents: Their Exploits and Leadership.* 1964. Reprint, New York: Da Capo Press, 1994.

———. *The Green Dragoon: The Lives of Banastre Tarleton and Mary Robinson.* New York: Henry Holt, 1957.

———. *Ninety Six: The Struggle for the South Carolina Back Century.* Lexington, S.C.: The Sandlapper Store, 1978.

———. *Swamp Fox: The Life and Campaigns of General Francis Marion.* New York: Henry Holt, 1959.

Baugh, Daniel A. "Why Did Britain Lose Command of the Sea during the War for America?" In *The British Navy and the Use of Naval Power in the Eighteenth Century,* ed. Jeremy Black and Philip Woodfine. Leicester: Leicester University Press, 1988.

Bearss, Edwin C. *The Battle of the Cowpens.* Washington, D.C.: U.S. Department of the Interior, 1967.

Becke, A. F. *An Introduction to the History of Tactics, 1740–1905.* London: Hugh Rees, 1909.

Bidwell, Shelford. "Irregular Warfare: Partisans, Raiders and Guerrillas." *Journal of the Royal United Services Institute for Defense Studies* 122 (September 1977): 80.

Billias, George A., ed. *George Washington's Opponents: British Generals and Admirals in the American Revolution.* New York: Morrow, 1969.

Black, Jeremy. *Warfare in the Eighteenth Century.* London: Cassell, 1999.

———. *Western Warfare, 1775–1882.* Bloomington and Indianapolis: Indiana University Press, 2001.

Boatner, Mark M. *Encyclopedia of the American Revolution.* New York: David McKay Company, 1966.

———. *Landmarks of the American Revolution: A Guide to Locating and Knowing What Happened at the Sites of Independence.* New York: Hawthorn Books, 1975.

Bolton, S. Charles. *Southern Anglicanism: The Church of England in Colonial South Carolina.* Contributions to the Study of Religion, no. 5. Westport, Conn.: Greenwood Press, 1982.

Brodie, Bernard. *A Guide to Naval Strategy.* Rev. ed. New York, Washington, and London: Frederick A. Praeger, 1965.

Brown, Gerald S. *The American Secretary: The Colonial Policy of Lord George Germain, 1776–1778.* Ann Arbor: University of Michigan Press, 1963.

Brown, Wallace. *The King's Friends: The Composition and Motives of the American Loyalist Claimants.* Providence, R.I.: Brown University Press, 1965.

Buchanan, John. *The Road to Guilford Courthouse: The American Revolution in the Carolinas.* New York: Wiley, 1997.

Buel, Richard, Jr. *In Irons: Britain's Naval Supremacy and the American Revolutionary Economy.* New Haven, Conn.: Yale University Press, 1998.

Calhoon, Robert M. *The Loyalists in America, 1760–1781.* New York: Harcourt Brace Jovanovich, 1973.

Cappon, Lester J., ed. *Atlas of Early American History: The Revolutionary Era, 1760–1790.* Princeton, N.J.: Princeton University Press, 1976.

Cashin, Edward J. *William Bartram and the American Revolution.* Columbia: University of South Carolina Press, 2000.

Cayton, Andrew R. L., and Fredrika J. Teute. *Contact Points: American Frontiers from the Mohawk Valley to the Mississippi, 1750–1830.* Chapel Hill and London: University of North Carolina Press, 1998.

Claghorn, Charles. *Women Patriots of the American Revolution: A Biographical Dictionary.* Metuchen, N.J. and London: Scarecrow Press, 1991.

Clifford, Mary L. *From Slavery to Freetown: Black Loyalists after the American Revolution.* Jefferson, N.C. and London: McFarland & Company, 1999.

Clowes, William Laird, et al. *The Royal Navy: A History from the Earliest Times to the Present.* 7 vols. Boston: Little, Brown and Co.; London: S. Law, Marston and Co., 1897–1903.

Coker, P. C., III. *Charleston's Maritime Heritage, 1670–1865: An Illustrated History.* Charleston, S.C.: Coker Craft Press, 1987.

Coleman, Kenneth. *The American Revolution in Georgia, 1763–1789.* Athens: University of Georgia Press, 1958.

Corkran, David H., *The Carolina Indian Frontier.* Columbia: University of South Carolina Press, 1970.

Cowley, Robert, ed. *What If? Essays by Stephen E. Ambrose, John Keegan, David McCullough, James M. McPherson and Others.* New York: G. P. Putnam's Sons, 1998.

Cunliffe, Marcus. *Soldiers and Civilians: The Martial Spirit in America, 1775–1865.* Boston: Little, Brown and Company, 1968.

Curtis, Edward E. *The Organization of the British Army in the American Revolution.* New Haven, Conn.: Yale University Press, 1926.

Darling, Anthony D. *Red Coat and Brown Bess.* Alexandria Bay, N.Y.: Museum Restoration Service, 1987.

Davis, David B. *The Problem of Slavery in the Age of Revolution, 1770–1823.* Ithaca: Cornell University Press, 1975.

Dederer, John M. *Making Bricks without Straw: Nathanael Greene's Southern Campaign and Mao Tse-Tung's Mobile War.* Manhattan, Kans.: Sunflower University Press, 1983.

Diamond, Jared. *Guns, Germs, and Steel: The Fates of Human Societies.* New York and London: W. W. Norton and Company, 1997.

Diamont, Lincoln, ed. and annot. *Revolutionary Women in the War for American Independence.* Westport, Conn. and London: Praeger, 1998.

Dictionary of National Biography. 21 vols. London: Oxford University Press, 1921–1922.

Dillin, John G. W. *The Kentucky Rifle.* New York: Ludlum and Beebe, 1946.

Doughty, Robert A., and Ira D. Gruber et al. *Warfare in the Western World.* 2 vols., *Military Operations from 1600–1871* and *Military Operations since 1871.* Lexington, Mass.: D. C. Heath and Company, 1996.

Draper, Lyman C. *King's Mountain and Its Heroes.* 1881. Reprint, Spartanburg, S.C.: Reprint Company, 1967.

Dupuy, T. N. *The Evolution of Weapons and Warfare.* Indianapolis and New York: Bobbs-Merrill, 1980.

———. *Understanding War: History and Theory of Combat.* New York: Paragon House, 1987.

Edgar, Walter. *South Carolina: A History.* Columbia: University of South Carolina Press, 1998.

English, John A. *On Infantry.* New York: Praeger Publishing, 1984.

Esposito, Vincent J., ed. *The West Point Atlas of American Wars.* Vol. 1, *1689–1900.* New York: Frederick A. Praeger Publishers, 1959.

Faragher, John Mack. *Daniel Boone: The Life and Legend of an American Pioneer.* New York: Henry Holt and Company, 1992.

Farrar-Hockley, Anthony. *Infantry Tactics.* London: Altmark, 1976.

Flexner, James T. *George Washington and the American Revolution (1775–1783).* Boston: Little, Brown, 1967.

Foner, Jack D. *Blacks and the Military in American History: A New Perspective.* New York: Praeger, 1974.

Fortescue, John W. *A History of the British Army.* Vol. 3, pt. 2. *From the Close of the Seven Years' War to the Second Peace of Paris, 1763–1793.* 1911. Reprint, New York: AMS Press, 1976.

Frey, Sylvia R. *Water from the Rock: Black Resistance in a Revolutionary Age.* Princeton, N.J.: Princeton University Press, 1991.

Fuller, J. F. C. *British Light Infantry in the Eighteenth Century.* London: Hutchinson, 1925.

———. *The Conduct of War, 1789–1961.* New Brunswick, N.J.: Rutgers University Press, 1961.

Gelbert, Doug. *American Revolutionary War Sites, Memorials, Museums and Library Collections: A State-by-State Guidebook.* Jefferson, N.C.: McFarland & Company, 1998.

Gerson, Noel B. *Light-Horse Harry: A Biography of Washington's Great Cavalryman, General Henry Lee.* Garden City, N.Y.: Doubleday, 1966.

Gluckman, Arcadi. *United States Muskets, Rifles and Carbines.* Buffalo, N.Y.: Otto Ulbrich, 1948.

Greene, Jack P. *The Quest for Power: The Lower Houses of Assembly in the Southern Royal Colonies, 1689–1776.* Chapel Hill: University of North Carolina Press, 1963.

Gregorie, Anne K. *Thomas Sumter.* 1931. Reprint, Sumter, S.C.: Gamecock City Printing, 2000.

Griess, Thomas E., ed. *Early American Wars and Military Institutions.* West Point, N.Y.: Department of History, U.S. Military Academy, 1979.

———. *The Dawn of Modern Warfare.* Wayne, N.J.: Avery Publishing Group for Department of History, U.S. Military Academy, 1984.

Griffith, Samuel B., trans. *Mao Tse-Tung on Guerrilla Warfare.* New York: Praeger, 1961.

Gruber, Ira D. *The Howe Brothers and the American Revolution.* New York: Atheneum, 1972.

———. "Britain's Southern Strategy." In *The Revolutionary War in the South—Power, Conflict, and Leadership: Essays in Honor of John Richard Alden*, edited by W. Robert Higgins. Durham, N.C.: Duke University Press, 1979.

Hackett, John W. *The Profession of Arms.* London: Times Publishing, 1963.

Hall, Walter Phelps, Robert G. Albion, and Jennie B. Pepe. *A History of England and the Empire-Commonwealth.* 4th ed. Boston: Ginn and Company, 1961.

Hartmann, John W. *The American Partisan: Henry Lee and the Struggle for Independence, 1776–1780.* Shippensburg, Pa.: Burd Street Press, 2000.

Haw, James. *John and Edward Rutledge of South Carolina.* Athens and London: University of Georgia Press, 1997.

Heisser, David C. R. *The Seal of the State of South Carolina: A Short History.* Columbia: South Carolina Department of Archives and History, 1992.

Helsley, Alexia J. *South Carolinians in the War for American Independence.* Columbia: South Carolina Department of Archives and History, 2000.

Hibbert, Christopher. *Redcoats and Rebels: The American Revolution through British Eyes.* New York: Avon Books, 1991.

Higginbotham, Don. *Daniel Morgan: Revolutionary Rifleman.* Chapel Hill: University of North Carolina Press, 1961.

———. *George Washington and the American Military Tradition.* Mercer University Lamar Memorial Lectures, no. 27. Athens: University of Georgia Press, 1985.

———. *The War of American Independence: Military Attitudes, Policies and Practice, 1763–1789.* New York: Macmillan, 1971.

Higham, Robin. *A Guide to the Sources of British Military History.* Berkeley: University of California Press, 1971.

———. *A Guide to the Sources of United States Military History.* New York: Archon, 1975.

Hoffman, Ronald, and Peter J. Albert, eds. *Arms and Independence: The Military Character of the American Revolution.* Charlottesville: University Press of Virginia, 1984.

Hoffman, Ronald, et al. *An Uncivil War: The Southern Backcountry during the American Revolution.* Charlottesville: University Press of Virginia, 1985.

Hogg, Ian V. *Artillery.* New York: Ballantine Books, 1972.

Hogg, Ian V., and John Batchelor. *Armies of the American Revolution.* Englewood Cliffs, N.J.: Prentice-Hall, 1975.

Houlding, J. A. *Fit for Service: The Training of the British Army, 1715–1795.* Oxford: Oxford University Press, 1981.

Howard, Michael, ed. *The Theory and Practice of War.* London: Cassell, 1965.

Huntington, Samuel P. *The Soldier and the State: The Theory and Politics of Civil-Military Relations.* New York: Vintage Books, 1957.

Hutton, Edward, ed. *A Brief History of the King's Royal Rifle Corps, 1755 to 1915.* Winchester: Warren and Son, 1917.

Ivers, Larry E. *British Drums on the Southern Frontier: The Military Colonization of Georgia, 1733–1749.* Chapel Hill: University of North Carolina Press, 1974.

———. *Colonial Forts of South Carolina, 1670–1775.* Columbia: University of South Carolina Press, 1970.

James, W. M. *The British Navy in Adversity: A Study of the War of American Independence.* London: Longmans, Green, and Co., 1926.

Janowitz, Morris. *The Professional Soldier: A Social and Political Study.* New York: Free Press, 1960.

Jensen, Merrill. *The Founding of a Nation: A History of the American Revolution, 1763–1776.* New York: Oxford University Press, 1968.

Joes, Anthony J. *America and Guerrilla Warfare.* Lexington: University Press of Kentucky, 2000.

Johnson, George Lloyd, Jr. *The Frontier in the Colonial South: South Carolina Backcountry, 1736–1800.* Westport, Conn.: Greenwood Press, 1997.

Jones, Lewis P. *Books and Articles on South Carolina History.* Columbia: University of South Carolina Press, 1970.

———. *South Carolina: A Synoptic History for Laymen.* Orangeburg, S.C.: Sandlapper Press, 1978.

Jordan, Winthrop D. *White over Black: American Attitudes towards the Negro, 1550–1812.* Chapel Hill: University of North Carolina Press, 1968.

Kajencki, Francis C. *Thaddeus Kosciuszko: Military Engineer of the American Revolution.* El Paso, Tex.: Southwest Polonia Press, 1998.

Keegan, John. *The Face of Battle.* New York: Viking, 1976.

———. *Fields of Battle: The Wars for North America.* New York: Alfred A. Knopf, 1996.

———. *The Mask of Command.* New York: Viking Penguin, 1987.

———. *The Price of Admiralty: The Evolution of Naval Warfare.* New York: Viking Penguin, 1989.

Kemp, Peter. *History of the Royal Navy.* New York: G. P. Putnam's Sons, 1969.

———. *The Oxford Companion to Ships and the Sea.* London: Oxford University Press, 1976.

Kiernan, V. G. *The Duel in European History: Honour and the Reign of Aristocracy.* Oxford: Oxford University Press, 1988.

Klein, Rachel N. *Unification of a Slave State: The Rise of the Planter Class in the South Carolina Backcountry, 1760–1808.* Chapel Hill: University of North Carolina, 1990.

Kwasny, Mark V. *Washington's Partisan War, 1775–1783*. Kent, Ohio: Kent State University Press, 1996.

Liddell Hart, B. H. *The British Way in Warfare*. London: Faber and Faber, 1932.

Lippy, Charles H., ed. *Religion in South Carolina*. Columbia: University of South Carolina Press, 1993.

Lipscomb, Terry W. *Battles, Skirmishes, and Actions of the American Revolution in South Carolina*. Columbia: South Carolina Department of Archives and History, 1991.

———. *The Carolina Lowcountry, April 1775–June 1776*. Vol. 1 of *South Carolina Revolutionary Battles*. Columbia: South Carolina Department of Archives and History, 1991.

———. *South Carolina Becomes a State: The Road from Colony to Independence 1765–1776*. Columbia: South Carolina Department of Archives and History, 1988.

———. *South Carolina in 1791: George Washington's Southern Tour*. Columbia: South Carolina Department of Archives and History.

Littlefield, Daniel C. *Rice and Slaves: Ethnicity and the Slave Trade in Colonial South Carolina*. Urbana: University of Illinois Press, 1991.

Lloyd, E. M. E. *A Review of the History of Infantry*. Westport, Conn. and London: Greenwood Press, 1976.

Lumpkin, Henry. *From Savannah to Yorktown: The American Revolution in the South*. Columbia: University of South Carolina Press, 1981.

Luttwak, Edward N. *Strategy: The Logic of War and Peace*. Cambridge, Mass.: The Belknap Press of Harvard University Press, 1987.

Lynn, John A., ed. *Tools of War: Instruments, Ideas, and Institutions of Warfare, 1445–1871*. Urbana and Chicago: University of Illinois Press, 1984.

Mackesy, Piers. *The War for America, 1775–1783*. 1964. Reprint, Lincoln: University of Nebraska Press, 1992.

MacLeod, Duncan. *Slavery, Race and the American Revolution*. London: Cambridge University Press, 1974.

Mahan, Alfred Thayer. *The Influence of Sea Power upon History, 1660–1783*. Boston: Little, Brown and Company, 1890.

Malone, Patrick M. *The Skulking Way of War: Technology and Tactics among the New England Indians*. Baltimore and London: Johns Hopkins University Press, 1993.

Massey, Gregory D. *John Laurens and the American Revolution*. Columbia: University of South Carolina Press, 2000.

Mattern, David B. *Benjamin Lincoln and the American Revolution*. Columbia: University of South Carolina Press, 1995.

Maude, F. N. *Notes on the Evolution of Infantry Tactics*. London: William Clowes, 1905.

Mayer, Holly B. *Belonging to the Army: Camp Followers and Community during the American Revolution.* Columbia: University of South Carolina Press, 1999.

McCrady, Edward. *The History of South Carolina in the Revolution, 1775–1780.* 1901. Reprint, New York: Paladin Press, 1969.

———. *The History of South Carolina in the Revolution, 1780–1783.* New York: Macmillan, 1902.

McGowan, George S., Jr. *The British Occupation of Charleston, 1780–1782.* Columbia: University of South Carolina Press, 1972.

Meriwether, Robert L. *The Expansion of South Carolina, 1729–1765.* Kingsport, Tenn.: Southern Publishers, 1940.

Miller, Nathan. *Sea of Glory: A Naval History of the American Revolution.* Annapolis, Md.: Naval Institute Press, 1974.

Millett, Allan R. *The American Political System and Civilian Control of the Military: A Historical Perspective.* Columbus, Ohio: Mershon Center, Ohio State University, 1979.

———, and Peter Maslowski. *For the Common Defense: A Military History of the United States of America.* New York and London: The Free Press/Collier Macmillan, 1984.

Mills, Robert. *Statistics of South Carolina.* 1826. Reprint, Spartanburg, S.C.: Reprint Company, 1972.

Moncure, John. *The Cowpens Staff Ride and Battlefield Tour.* Fort Leavenworth, Kans.: Combat Studies Institute, U.S. Army Command and General Staff College, 1996.

Morgan, Philip D. *Slave Counterpoint: Black Culture in the Eighteenth Century Chesapeake and Lowcountry.* Chapel Hill: University of North Carolina Press, 1998.

Morrill, Dan L. *Southern Campaigns of the American Revolution.* Baltimore, Md.: Nautical & Aviation Publishing Company, 1993.

Nadelhaft, Jerome J. *The Disorders of War: The Revolution of South Carolina.* Orono: University of Maine at Orono Press, 1981.

Norton, Mary B. *Liberty's Daughters: The Revolutionary Experience of American Women, 1750–1800.* Boston: Little, Brown, 1980.

O'Sullivan, Patrick, and Jesse W. Miller, Jr. *The Geography of Warfare.* New York: St. Martins Press, 1983.

Palmer, Dave R. *The Way of the Fox: American Strategy in the War for America, 1775–1783.* Westport, Conn. and London: Greenwood Press, 1975.

Pancake, John S. *1777, The Year of the Hangman.* University: University of Alabama Press, 1977.

———. *This Destructive War: The British Campaign in the Carolinas, 1780–1781.* University: University of Alabama Press, 1985.

Paret, Peter, ed. *Makers of Modern Strategy: From Machiavelli to the Nuclear Age.* Princeton: Princeton University Press, 1986.

Parker, Geoffrey. *The Military Revolution: Military Innovation and the Rise of the West, 1500–1800.* Cambridge: Cambridge University Press, 1996.

Peckham, Howard H. *The Colonial Wars, 1659–1782.* Chicago: University of Chicago Press, 1964.

———. *The Toll of Independence: Engagements and Battle Casualties of the American Revolution.* Chicago: University of Chicago Press, 1974.

———. *The War of Independence: A Military History.* Chicago: University of Chicago Press, 1958.

Peterson, Harold L. *Arms and Armor in Colonial America, 1526–1783.* Harrisburg, Pa.: Stackpole Co., 1956.

Petit, J. Percival, ed. *South Carolina and the Sea: Day by Day toward Five Centuries, 1496–1976 A.D.* Vol. 1, *1496–1800 A.D.* Charleston, S.C.: Published under the auspices of the Maritime and Ports Activities Committee of the State Ports Authority as a Bicentennial project, 1976.

Preston, Antony, David Lyon, and John Batchelor. *Navies of the American Revolution.* Englewood Cliffs, N.J.: Prentice-Hall, 1975.

Quarles, Benjamin. *The Negro in the American Revolution.* Chapel Hill: University of North Carolina Press, 1961.

Quick, John, ed. *Dictionary of Weapons and Military Terms.* New York: McGraw-Hill, 1973.

Rajtar, Steve. *Indian War Sites: A Guidebook to Battlefields, Monuments, and Memorials, State by State with Canada and Mexico.* Jefferson, N.C. and London: McFarland & Company, 1999.

Reiss, Oscar. *Medicine and the American Revolution.* Jefferson, N.C. and London: McFarland & Company, 1998.

Reynolds, Clark G. *Command of the Sea: The History and Strategy of Maritime Empires.* New York: William Morrow, 1974.

Ripley, Warren. *Battleground: South Carolina in the Revolution.* Charleston: News & Courier, 1983.

Rodger, N. A. M. *The Insatiable Earl: The Life of John Montagu, Fourth Earl of Sandwich.* London: Harper Collins, 1993.

Rogers, George C., Jr. *Charleston in the Age of the Pinckneys.* Columbia: University of South Carolina Press, 1984.

———. *A South Carolina Chronology, 1497–1970.* Columbia: University of South Carolina Press, 1973.

Ropp, Theodore. *War in the Modern World.* New York: Collier, 1962.

Roskill, Stephen W. *The Strategy of Sea Power: Its Development and Application.* London: Collins, 1962.

Rowland, Lawrence S., Alexander Moore, and George C. Rogers, Jr. *The History of Beaufort County, South Carolina, Vol. 1: 1514–1861.* Columbia: University of South Carolina Press, 1996.

Royster, Charles. *A Revolutionary People at War: The Continental Army and the American Character, 1775–1783.* Chapel Hill: University of North Carolina Press, 1979.

Russell, Carl P. *Guns on the Early Frontier: A History of Firearms from Colonial Times through the Years of the Western Fur Trade.* Berkeley: University of California Press, 1957.

Russell, David Lee. *The American Revolution in the Southern Colonies.* Jefferson, N.C. and London: McFarland & Company, 2000.

Scheer, George F., and Hugh F. Rankin. *Rebels and Redcoats.* Cleveland and New York: World Publishing Company, 1957.

Seaborn, Margaret M., ed. *Benjamin Hawkins's Journeys through Oconee County, South Carolina, in 1796 and 1797.* Columbia, S.C.: R. L. Bryan Company, 1973.

Shaffer, Arthur. *To Be an American: David Ramsay and the Making of the American Consciousness.* Columbia: University of South Carolina Press, 1991.

Shy, John. *A People Numerous and Armed: Reflections on the Military Struggle for American Independence.* New York: Oxford University Press, 1976.

Silver, Timothy. *New Face on the Countryside: Indians, Colonials and Slaves in South Atlantic Forests, 1500–1800.* New York: Cambridge University Press, 1990.

Smith, W. H. B., and Joseph E. Smith. *The Book of Rifles.* New York: Castle, 1948.

Starkey, Armstrong. *European and Native American Warfare, 1675–1815.* Norman: University of Oklahoma Press, 1998.

Steele, Ian K. *Warpaths: Invasions of North America.* New York: Oxford University Press, 1994.

Stokeley, Jim. *Constant Defender: The Story of Fort Moultrie.* Washington, D.C.: National Park Service, U.S. Department of the Interior, 1978.

Stout, Neil R. *The Royal Navy in America, 1760–1775: A Study of Enforcement of British Colonial Policy in the Era of the American Revolution.* Annapolis, Md.: Naval Institute Press, 1973.

Strachan, Hew. *European Armies and the Conduct of War.* London: George Allen & Unwin, 1983.

Symonds, Craig L., and cartography by William J. Clipson. *A Battlefield Atlas of The American Revolution.* Annapolis, Md.: Nautical & Aviation Publishing Company of America, 1986.

Syrett, David. *The Royal Navy in American Waters, 1775–1783.* London: Scolar Press, 1989.

————. *The Royal Navy in European Waters during the American Revolutionary War.* Columbia: University of South Carolina Press, 1998.

Thayer, Theodore. *Nathanael Greene: Strategist of the American Revolution.* New York: Twayne Publishers, 1960.

Thomas, Peter D. G. *Lord North.* New York: St. Martin's Press, 1976.

Townsend, Leah. *South Carolina Baptists, 1670–1805.* Florence, S.C.: Florence Printing, 1935.

Tuchman, Barbara W. *The March of Folly: From Troy to Vietnam.* New York: Alfred Knopf, 1984.

Turner, E. S. *Gallant Gentlemen: A Portrait of the British Officer, 1600–1956.* London: Michael Joseph, 1956.

U.S. Department of Defense. *Department of Defense Dictionary of Military and Associated Terms: Joint Terminology Master Database as of 10 June 1998.* Joint Publication 1-02. Washington, D.C.: Joint Chiefs of Staff, 1998.

U.S. Department of the Navy. *Campaigning.* MCDP 1–2. Washington, D.C.: U.S. Marine Corps, 1997.

van Creveld, Martin. *Fighting Power.* Westport: Greenwood Press, 1982.

van Tyne, Claude H. *The Loyalists in the American Revolution.* New York: Macmillan Company, 1902.

von Clausewitz, Carl. *On War.* Ed. and trans. Michael Howard and Peter Paret. Princeton, N.J.: Princeton University Press, 1984.

Wallace, David Duncan. *The History of South Carolina.* 4 vols. New York: American Historical Society, Inc., 1934.

Walsh, Richard. *Charleston's Sons of Liberty: A Study of the Artisans, 1763–1789.* Columbia: University of South Carolina Press, 1968.

Ward, Christopher. *The War of the American Revolution.* Ed. John R. Alden. 2 vols. New York: Macmillan, 1952.

Wareham, Thomas. *The Star Captains: Frigate Command in the Napoleonic Wars.* Annapolis, Md.: Naval Institute Press, 2001.

Waring, Alice N. *Fighting Elder: Andrew Pickens, 1739–1817.* Columbia: University of South Carolina Press, 1962.

Wavell, Archibald P. *Generals and Generalship: The Lees-Knowles Lectures at Trinity College, Cambridge University.* 2d ed. New York: Macmillan, 1943.

————. *Soldiers and Soldiering: or Epithets of War.* London: Jonathan Cape, 1953.

Weigley, Russell F. *History of the United States Army.* The Wars of the United States, Louis Morton, general ed. New York: Macmillan, 1967.

————. *The American Way of Warfare: A History of United States Military Strategy And Policy.* New York: Macmillan, 1973.

———. *The Partisan War: The South Carolina Campaign of 1780–1782.* Columbia: University of South Carolina Press, 1970.

Weir, Robert M. *"A Most Significant Epoch": The Coming of the Revolution in South Carolina.* Columbia: University of South Carolina Press, 1970.

———. *Colonial South Carolina: A History.* Columbia: University of South Carolina Press, 1983.

White, A. S. *A Bibliography of Regimental Histories of the British Army.* London: Stockwell, 1965.

Wickwire, Franklin B. and Mary. *Cornwallis: The American Adventure.* Boston: Houghton Mifflin Company, 1970.

Wilkinson, Norman B. "The Pennsylvania Rifle." *American Heritage* 1 (summer 1950): 3–5, 64–66.

Willcox, William B. "British Strategy in America, 1778." *The Journal of Modern History* 19 (1947): 84–106.

———. *Portrait of a General: Sir Henry Clinton in the War of Independence.* New York: Alfred A. Knopf, 1964.

———, ed. *The American Rebellion: Sir Henry Clinton's Narrative of His Campaigns, 1775–1782, with an Appendix of Original Documents.* 1954. Reprint, Hamden, Conn.: Archon Books/Shoe String Press, 1971.

Wood, Peter H. *Black Majority: Negroes in Colonial South Carolina from 1670 through the Stono Rebellion.* New York: Alfred A. Knopf, 1974.

Wood, W. J. *Battles of the Revolutionary War, 1775–1781.* Chapel Hill, N.C.: Algonquin Books, 1990.

Writers' Program of the Works Projects Administration. *South Carolina: The WPA Guide to the Palmetto State.* 1941. Reprint, with a new introduction and two new appendices by Walter Edgar. Columbia: University of South Carolina Press, 1988.

Young, Peter, and J. P. Lawford, eds. *History of the British Army.* New York: G. P. Putnam's Sons, 1970.

INDEX

Island, assault by, 37; surrenders at
Yorktown, 170
Corps of Continental Marines, 11
Council of Safety: backcountry forays,
31; created, 20; drives away Major
Stuart, 28; efforts to win Cherokee
support, 29–30; efforts to win loyal-
ist support, 28–29; Hog Island
Channel Fight (battle), 27, 28
Cowpens (battle), 129–36; aftermath,
135; American battle plan, 129,
131; American forces, 131–32;
Andrew Pickens, 131; battle of,
133–36; blacks as soldiers at, 2;
British battleplan for, 132; British
forces, 133, 134; Cornwallis' com-
mentary on, 136; field artillery, 134;
John Howard, 131; Joseph McDow-
ell, 131; Marion quoted on, 112;
McCall, 131; Morgan, 129, 132, 133;
Tarleton, 129, 132, 134; Tarleton's
quarter, 134; terrain of, 129; Triplett,
132; William Washington, 131;
Young, 112
Creeks, 45, 46, 53
Cruger, Lieutenant Colonel John Har-
ris, 155–56, 164
Culloden, 137, 141, 146, 177
Cumberland, Duke of (William
Augustus), 137, 140, 177
Cunningham, Brigadier General
Robert, 156
Cunningham, Patrick, 29–33
Cunningham, William (Bloody Bill),
171–72

Davidson, William, 143
Davie, William, 91, 92, 113
de Kalb, Major General Baron Johann,
91, 92, 94, 107–8
deaths. See casualties
Declaration of Independence, 54
Defence (armed schooner), 27
Delaware Continentals, 91, 94, 156, 164
Delawares, 46
d'Estaing, Admiral the Count, 60–61,
69–70

Dillard, Mary, 121
disestablishment, 54, 100
Downs, Major Jonathan, 48
Doyle, Lieutenant Colonel Welbore,
142, 143
dragoons, 5
Drayton, William Henry, 27
duel, 124
dynastic warfare, 1–2, 7

Edgar, Walter, 198n. 12
Elphinstone, Captain George Keith,
71, 73–75, 79
engineers, 4, 86, 156. See also siege
operations
Esseneca Ambush (battle), 49–51
European warfare, 35, 46
Eutaw Springs (battle), 164–67
Experiment (50-gun fourth rate), 37, 43

Fairlawn plantation (battle), 173
Ferguson, Major Patrick: background
of, 112–13; Biggin Church and
Quinby Bridge (battle), 159; Big-
gin's Bridge/Moncks Corner (bat-
tle), 112; inspector of militia, 113;
killed at Kings Mountain, 116;
King's Mountain, 115; led loyalist
rangers, 112–13; Washington,
George, 112
Few, Benjamin, 123
field artillery: Biggin Church and
Quinby Bridge (battle), 161;
Cowpens (battle), 134; Guilford
Courthouse (battle), 145; Hobkirk's
Hill (battle), 149; smoothbore, 4;
types of shot, 4
First South Carolina Regiment, 26
Fish Dam Ford (battle), 119–20
Fishing Creek (battle), 94–96
flank companies, 5
fleet-in-being, 9
Fletchall, Thomas, 31
Florida, 21
Flying Army, 127
Fort Charlotte (battle), 22–23
Fort Cornwallis (battle), 154